A NIGHT MARCH ON THE ARABIAN DESERT.

TRAVELS IN ARABIA

COMPILED AND ARRANGED BY
BAYARD TAYLOR

REVISED BY
THOMAS STEVENS

DARF PUBLISHERS LIMITED
LONDON
1986

FIRST PUBLISHED 1892
NEW IMPRESSION 1986

ISBN 978 1 85077 084 8

REVISER'S NOTE

THE continuance of Bayard Taylor's Library of Travel in the popular favor is one of the accepted facts of the literary world. So much so, indeed, that a revision of his works on the part of another is to be permitted only on certain conditions of reserve, and by reason of events that have transpired since the death of the distinguished traveller.

Travellers and authors die; but the tribes, nations, and races visited by them continue on, making war or peace, changing frontiers, setting up or pulling down dynasties.

The whole political complexion of a country may be changed in a decade. Though the people of Arabia, the genuine Bedouins, are believed to have changed little or nothing in their mode of life since the days of the Shepherd Kings of Abraham's time, waves of political and religious agitation have occasionally rippled over one part or another of the ancient peninsula. Seemingly they make as little permanent impression on the undercurrent of Bedouin life, as do the waves of the sea on its immutable whole, so that the accounts of the earlier chroniclers of Arabian life and manners agree in a singular manner with the descriptions of contemporary visitors. For this reason, no less than for the respect and admiration entertained by the reviser for Mr. Taylor's conscientiousness and judgment as a traveller and compiler, and his literary excellence as an author, this volume remains, practically, as fully the work of its original editor as before.

By way of bringing it up to date, however, Chapter XVII. has been added, and such slight revision of preceding chapters has been made as was found necessary, consistent with the scope and intention of the new edition.

THOMAS STEVENS.

CONTENTS

CHAPTER I.
SKETCH OF ARABIA: ITS GEOGRAPHICAL POSITION, AND ANCIENT HISTORY, ... 1

CHAPTER II.
EARLY EXPLORERS OF ARABIA, ... 8

CHAPTER III.
NIEBUHR'S TRAVELS IN YEMEN, ... 14

CHAPTER IV.
BURCKHARDT'S JOURNEY TO MECCA AND MEDINA, . . 29

CHAPTER V.
WELLSTED'S EXPLORATIONS IN OMAN, ... 40

CHAPTER VI.
WELLSTED'S DISCOVERY OF AN ANCIENT CITY IN HADRAMAUT, ... 55

CHAPTER VII.
BURTON'S PILGRIMAGE, ... 62

CHAPTER VIII.
PALGRAVE'S TRAVELS IN CENTRAL ARABIA: FROM PALESTINE TO THE DJOWF, ... 83

CHAPTER IX.

PALGRAVE'S TRAVELS—RESIDENCE IN THE DJOWF, . 107

CHAPTER X.

PALGRAVE'S TRAVELS—CROSSING THE NEFOOD, . . 127

CHAPTER XI.

PALGRAVE'S TRAVELS—LIFE IN HA'YEL, ... 138

CHAPTER XII.

PALGRAVE'S TRAVELS—JOURNEY TO BEREYDAH, . . 176

CHAPTER XIII.

PALGRAVE'S TRAVELS—JOURNEY TO RI'AD THE CAPITAL OF NEDJED, ... 201

CHAPTER XIV.

PALGRAVE'S TRAVELS—ADVENTURES IN RI'AD, . . 217

CHAPTER XV.

PALGRAVE'S TRAVELS — HIS ESCAPE TO THE EASTERN COAST, ... 240

CHAPTER XVI.

PALGRAVE'S TRAVELS—EASTERN ARABIA, . . . 259

CHAPTER XVII.

LADY BLUNT'S PILGRIMAGE TO NEJD, ... 279

LIST OF ILLUSTRATIONS

A Night March on the Arabian Desert,	*Frontispiece*
	FACING PAGE
Coffee Hills of Yemen,	19
View of El-Medina,	39
A Valley in Oman,	51
Ruins of Nakab-El-Hadjar, in Hadramaut,	59
View of Medina from the West,	69
Camp at Mount Arafat,	77
Costume of Pilgrims to Mecca,	81
William Gifford Palgrave,	84
An Arab Chief,	105
Captain Burton as a Pilgrim,	129
The Village of El-Suwayrkiyah,	184
An Arab Encampment,	190
Death on the Desert,	208

TRAVELS IN ARABIA

CHAPTER I.

SKETCH OF ARABIA: ITS GEOGRAPHICAL POSITION, AND ANCIENT HISTORY

THE Peninsula of Arabia, forming the extreme southwestern corner of Asia, is partly detached, both in a geographical and historical sense, from the remainder of the continent. Although parts of it are mentioned in the oldest historical records, and its shores were probably familiar to the earliest navigators, the greater portion of its territory has always remained almost inaccessible and unknown.

The desert lying between Syria and the Euphrates is sometimes included by geographers as belonging to Arabia, but a line drawn from the Dead Sea to the mouth of the Euphrates (almost coinciding with the parallel of 30° N.) would more nearly represent the northern boundary of the peninsula. As the most southern point of the Arabian coast reaches the latitude of 12° 40′, the greater part of the entire territory, of more than one million square miles, lies within the tropics. In shape it is an irregular rhomboid, the longest diameter, from Suez to the Cape

El-Had, in Oman, being 1,660, and from the Euphrates to the Straits of Bab-el-Mandeb, 1,400 miles.

The entire coast region of Arabia, on the Red Sea, the Indian Ocean, and the Gulfs of Oman and Persia, is, for the most part, a belt of fertile country, inhabited by a settled, semi-civilized population. Back of this belt, which varies in width from a few miles to upward of a hundred, commences a desert table-land, occasionally intersected by mountain chains, and containing in the interior many fertile valleys of considerable extent, which are inhabited. Very little has been known of this great interior region until the present century.

The ancient geographers divided Arabia into three parts—*Arabia Petræa*, or the Rocky, comprising the northwestern portion, including the Sinaitic peninsula, between the Gulfs of Suez and Akaba; *Arabia Deserta*, the great central desert; and *Arabia Felix*, the Happy, by which they appear to have designated the southwestern part, now known as Yemen. The modern Arabic geography, which has been partly adopted on our maps, is based, to some extent, on the political divisions of the country. The coast region along the Red Sea, down to a point nearly half way between Jedda and the Straits of Bab-el-Mandeb, and including the holy cities of Medina and Mecca, is called the Hedjaz. Yemen, the capital of which is Sana, and the chief seaports Mocha, Hodeida, and Loheia, embraces all the southwestern portion of the peninsula. The southern coast, although divided into various little chiefdoms, is known under the general name of Hadramaut. The kingdom of Oman has extended itself along the eastern shore, nearly to the head of the Persian Gulf. The northern oases, the seat of the powerful sect of the Wahabees, are called Nedjed; and the unknown southern interior, which is believed to be almost wholly desert, inhabited only by a few wandering Bedouins, is known as the Dahna or Akhaf.

Arabia has been inhabited by the same race since the earliest times, and has changed less, in the course of thousands of years, than any other country of the globe, not excepting China. According to Biblical genealogy, the natives are descended from Ham, through Cush; but the Bedouins have always claimed that they are the posterity of Ishmael. Some portions of the country, such as Edom, or Idumæa, Teman, and Sheba (the modern Yemen), are mentioned in the Old Testament; but neither the Babylonian, Assyrian, Persian, nor Egyptian monarchies succeeded in gaining possession of the peninsula. Alexander the Great made preparations for a journey of conquest, which was prevented by his death, and Trajan was the only Roman emperor who penetrated into the interior.

The inhabitants were idolaters, whose religion had probably some resemblance to that of the Phœnicians. After the destruction of Jerusalem, both Jews and Christians found their way thither, and made proselytes. There were Jews in Medina, Mecca, and Yemen; and even the last Hymyaritic king of the latter country became a convert to Mosaic faith. Thus the strength of the ancient religion was already weakened when Mohammed was born (A.D. 570); and there are strong evidences for the conjecture that the demoralization of both Jews and Christians, resulting from their long enmity, was the chief cause which prevented Mohammed from adopting the belief of the latter. At the time of his birth, the civilization of the dominant Arab tribes was little inferior to that of Europe or the Eastern Empire. There was already an Arabic literature; and the arts and sciences of the ancient world had found their way even to the oases of Nedjed.

The union of the best and strongest elements in the race which followed the establishment of the new religion, gave to men of Arabian blood a part to play in the history of the world. For six hundred years after Mohammed's death Islam and Christendom were nearly equal powers, and it is difficult, even now, to decide which contributed the more to the arts from which modern civilization has sprung. Arabia flourished, as never before, under the Caliphs; yet it does not appear that the life of the inhabitants was materially changed, or that any growth, acquired during the new importance of the country, became permanent. Its commerce was restricted to the products of its narrow belt of fertile shore; an arid desert separated it from Bagdad and Syria; none of the lines of traffic between Europe and the East Indies traversed its territory, and thus it remained comparatively unknown to the Christian world.

After the downfall of the Caliphate the tribes relapsed into their former condition of independent chiefdoms, and the old hostilities, which had been partially suppressed for some centuries, again revived. In the sixteenth century the Turks obtained possession of Hedjaz and Yemen; the Portuguese held Muscat for a hundred and fifty years, and the Persians made some temporary conquests, but the vast interior region easily maintained its independence. The deserts, which everywhere intervene between its large and fertile valleys and the seacoast, are the home of wandering Bedouin tribes, whose only occupation is plunder—whose hand is against every man's and every man's hand against them. Thus they serve as a body-guard even to their own enemies.

The long repose and seclusion of Central Arabia was first broken during the present century. It may be well to state, very briefly, the circumstances which led to it, since they will explain the great difficulty and danger which all modern explorers must encounter. Early in the last century, an Arabian named Abd el-Wahab, scandalized at what he believed to be the corruption of the Moslem faith, began preaching a Reformation. He advocated the slaughter or forcible conversion of heretics, the most rigid forms of fasting and prayer, the disuse of tobacco, and various other changes in the Oriental habits of life. Having succeeded in converting the chief of Nedjed, Mohammed Ibu-Saoud, he took up his residence in Derreyeh, the capital, which thenceforth became the rendezvous for all his followers, who were named *Wahabees*. They increased to such an extent that their authority became supreme throughout Central Arabia, and the successor of Ibu-Saoud was able to call an army of 100,000 men into the field, and defy the Ottoman power.

In the year 1803 the Wahabees took and plundered Mecca, and slew great numbers of the pilgrims who had gathered there. A second expedition against Medina failed, but the annual caravan of pilgrims was robbed and dispersed. Finally, in 1809, the Sultan transferred to Mohammed Ali, of Egypt, the duty of suppressing this menacing religious and political rebellion. The first campaign in Arabia was a failure; the second, under Ibrahim Pasha, was successful. He overcame the Wahabees in 1818, captured Derreyeh, and razed it to the ground. In 1828 they began a second war against Turkey, but were again defeated. Since then they have refrained from any further aggressive movement, but their hostility and bigotry are as active as ever. The Wahabee doctrine flatters the clannish and exclusive spirit of the race, and will probably prevent, for a long time, any easy communication between Arabia and the rest of the world.

The greater part of our present knowledge of Arabia has been obtained since the opening of this century. The chief seaports and the route from Suez to Mt. Sinai were known during the Middle Ages, but all else was little better than a blank. Within the last fifty or sixty years the mountains of Edom have been explored, the rock-hewn city of Petra discovered, the holy cities of Medina and Mecca visited by intelligent Europeans; Yemen, Hadramaut, and Oman partly traversed; and, last of all we have a very clear and satisfactory account of Nedjed and the other central regions of Arabia, by the intrepid English traveller, Mr. Palgrave.

Thus, only the southern interior of the peninsula remains to be visited. The name given to it by the Arabs, *Roba el-Khaly*, "the abode of emptiness," no doubt describes its character. It is an immense, undulating, sandy waste, dotted with scarce and small oases, which give water and shelter to the Bedouins, but without any large tract of habitable land, and consequently without cities, or other than the rudest forms of political organization.

CHAPTER II.

EARLY EXPLORERS OF ARABIA

WHEN the habit of travel began to revive in the Middle Ages, its character was either religious or commercial, either in the form of pilgrimages to Rome, Palestine (whenever possible), and the shrines of popular saints, or of journeys to the Levant, Persia, and the Indies, with the object of acquiring wealth by traffic, the profits of which increased in the same proportion as its hazards. From the time of Trajan's expedition to Arabia (in A.D. 117) down to the sixteenth century, we have no report of the history or condition of the country except such as can be drawn from the earlier Jewish and Christian traditions and the later Mohammedan records.

The first account of a visit to Arabia which appears to be worthy of credence, is that given by Ludovico Bartema, of Rome. After visiting Egypt, he joined the caravan of pilgrims at Damascus, in 1503, in the company of a Mameluke captain, himself disguised as a Mameluke renegade. After several attacks from the Bedouins of the desert, the caravan reached Medina, which he describes as containing three hundred houses. Bartema gives a very correct description of the tomb of the Prophet, and scoffs at the then prevalent belief that the latter's coffin is suspended in the air between four lodestones.

He thus describes an adventure which befell his company the same evening after their visit to the mosque. "At almost three of the night, ten or twelve of the elders of the sect of Mohammed entered into our caravan, which remained not past a stone's cast from the gate of the city. These ran hither and thither, crying like madmen with these words: 'Mohammed, the messenger and apostle of God, shall rise again! O Prophet, O God, Mohammed shall rise again! Have mercy on us, God!' Our captain and we, all raised with this cry, took weapon with all expedition, suspecting that the Arabs were come to rob our caravan. We asked what was the cause of that exclamation, and what they cried? For they cried as do the Christians when suddenly any marvellous thing chanceth. The elders answered: 'Saw you not the lightning which shone out of the sepulchre of the Prophet Mohammed?' Our captain answered that he saw nothing, and we also being demanded, answered in like manner. Then said one of the old men: 'Are you slaves?' This to say bought men, meaning thereby, Mamelukes. Then said our captain: 'We are indeed Mamelukes.' Then again the old man said: 'You, my lords, cannot see heavenly things, as being *neophiti*, that is, newly come to the faith, and not yet confirmed in our religion.' It is therefore to be understood that none other shining came out of the sepulchre than a certain flame, which the priests caused to come out of the open place of the tower, whereby they would have deceived us."

Leaving Medina, the caravan travelled for three days over a "broad plain," all covered with white sand, in manner as small as flour. Then they passed a mountain, where they heard "a certain horrible noise and cry," and after journeying for ten days longer, during which time they twice fought with "fifty thousand Arabians," they reached Mecca, of which Bartema says: "The city is very fair, and well inhabited, and containeth in round form six thousand houses as well builded as ours, and some that cost three or four thousand pieces of gold: it hath no walls."

Bartema describes the ceremonies performed by the pilgrims with tolerable correctness. His fellowship with the Mamelukes seems to have been a complete protection up to the time when the caravan was ready to set out on its return to Damascus, and the members of the troop were ordered to accompany it, on pain of death. Then he managed to escape by persuading a Mohammedan that he understood the art of casting cannon, and wished to reach India, in order to assist the native monarchs in defending themselves against the Portuguese. Reaching Jedda in safety, Bartema sailed for Persia, visiting Yemen on the way; made his way to India, and after various adventures, returned to Europe by way of the Cape of Good Hope.

The second European who made his way to the holy cities was Joseph Pitts, an Englishman, who was captured by an Algerine pirate, as a sailor-boy of sixteen, and forced by his master to become a Mussulman. After some years, when he had acquired the Arabic and Turkish languages, he accompanied his master for a pilgrimage to Mecca by way of Cairo, Suez, and the Red Sea. Here he received his freedom; but continued with the pilgrims to Medina, and returned to Egypt by land, through Arabia Petræa. After fifteen years of exile he succeeded in escaping to Italy, and thence made his way back to England.

Pitts gives a minute and generally correct account of the ceremonies at Mecca. He was not, of course, learned in Moslem theology, and his narrative, like that of all former visitors to Mecca, has been superseded by the more intelligent description of Burckhardt; yet it coincides with the latter in all essential particulars. His description of the city and surrounding scenery is worth quoting, from the quaint simplicity of its style.

"First, as to Mecca. It is a town situated in a barren place (about one day's journey from the Red Sea), in a valley, or rather in the midst of many little hills. It is a place of no force, wanting both walls and gates. Its buildings are, as I said before, very ordinary, insomuch that it would be a place of no tolerable entertainment, were it not for the anniversary resort of so many thousand Hagges (Hadjis), or pilgrims, on whose coming the whole dependence of the town (in a manner) is; for many shops are scarcely open all the year besides.

"The people here, I observed, are a poor sort of people, very thin, lean and swarthy. The town is surrounded for several miles with many thousands of little hills, which are very near one to the other. I have been on the top of some of them near Mecca, where I could see some miles about, yet was not able to see the farthest of the hills. They are all stony-rock and blackish, and pretty near of a bigness, appearing at a distance like cocks of hay, but all pointing toward Mecca. Some of them are half a mile in circumference, but all near of one height. The people here have an odd and foolish sort of tradition concerning them, viz., that when Abraham went about building the Beat-Allah (Beit-Allah, or 'House of God'), God by his wonderful providence did so order it, that every mountain in the world should contribute something to the building thereof; and accordingly every one did send its proportion, though there is a mountain near Algier which is called Corradog, *i.e.*, Black Mountain, and the reason of its blackness, they say, is because it did not send any part of itself toward building the temple at Mecca. Between these hills is good and plain travelling, though they stand one to another.

"There is upon the top of one of them a cave, which they term Hira, *i.e.*, Blessing, into which, they say, Mohamet did usually retire for his solitary devotions, meditations, and fastings; and here they believe he had a great part of the Alcoran brought him by the angel Gabriel. I have been in this cave, and observed that it is not at all beautified, at which I admired.

"About half a mile out of Mecca is a very steep hill, and there are stairs made to go to the top of it, where is a cupola, under which is a cloven rock; into this, they say, Mahomet when very young, viz., about four years of age, was carried by the angel Gabriel, who opened his breast and took out his heart, from which he picked some black blood specks, which was his original corruption; then put it into its place again, and afterward closed up the part; and that during this operation Mahomet felt no pain."

The next account of the same pilgrimage is given by Giovanni Tinati, an Italian, who deserted from the French service on the coast of Dalmatia, and became an Albanian soldier. Making his way to Egypt, after various adventures, he became at last a corporal in Mohammed Ali's body-guard, and shared in several campaigns against the Wahabees. He did not, however, penetrate very far inland from the coast, and his visit to Mecca was the result of his desertion from the Egyptian army after a defeat. His narrative contains nothing which has not been more fully and satisfactorily stated by later travellers.

By this time, however, the era of careful scientific exploration had already commenced, and the descriptions which have since then been furnished to us are positive contributions to our knowledge of Arabia. With the exception of the journey of Carsten Niebuhr, which embraces only the Sinaitic Peninsula and Yemen, the important explorations—all of which are equally difficult and daring—have been made since the commencement of this century.

CHAPTER III.

NIEBUHR'S TRAVELS IN YEMEN

IN 1760 the Danish government decided to send an expedition to Arabia and India, for the purpose of geographical exploration. The command was given to Carsten Niebuhr, a native of Hanover, and a civil engineer. Four other gentlemen, an artist, a botanist, a physician, and an astronomer, were associated with him in the undertaking; yet, by a singular fatality, all died during the journey, and Niebuhr returned alone, after an absence of nearly seven years, to publish the first narrative of travel based on scientific observation.

The party sailed from Copenhagen for Smyrna in January, 1761, visited Constantinople, and then proceeded to Egypt, where they remained nearly a year. After a journey to Sinai, they finally succeeded in engaging passage on board a vessel carrying pilgrims from Suez to Jedda, and sailed from the former port in October, 1762. They took the precaution of adopting the Oriental dress, and conformed, as far as possible, to the customs of the Mussulman passengers; thus the voyage, although very tedious and uncomfortable, was not accompanied with any other danger than that from the coral reefs along the Arabian shore. The vessel touched at Yambo, the port of Medina, and finally reached Jedda, after a voyage of nineteen days.

The travellers entered Jedda under strong apprehensions of ill-treatment from the inhabitants, but were favorably disappointed. The people, it seemed, were already accustomed to the sight of Christian merchants in their town, and took no particular notice of the strangers, who went freely to the coffee-houses and markets, and felt themselves safe so long as they did not attempt to pass through the gate leading to Mecca. The Turkish Pasha of the city received them kindly, and they were allowed to hire a house for their temporary residence.

After waiting six weeks for the chance of a passage to Mocha, they learned that an Arabian vessel was about to sail for Hodeida, one of the ports of Yemen. The craft, when they visited it, proved to be more like a hogshead than a ship; it was only seven fathoms long, by three in breadth. It had no deck; its planks were extremely thin, and seemed to be only nailed together, but not pitched. The captain wore nothing but a linen cloth upon his loins, and his sailors, nine in number, were black slaves from Africa or Malabar. Nevertheless, they engaged passage, taking the entire vessel for themselves alone; but when they came to embark, it was filled with the merchandise of others. The voyage proved to be safe and pleasant, and in sixteen days they landed at Loheia, in Yemen.

The governor of this place was a negro, who had formerly been a slave. He received the travellers with the greatest kindness, persuaded them to leave the vessel, and gave them a residence, promising camels for the further journey by land. Although they were somewhat annoyed by the great curiosity of the inhabitants, their residence was so agreeable, and offered the naturalists so many facilities for making collections, that they remained nearly four months. "We had one opportunity," says Niebuhr, "of learning their ideas of the benefits to be derived from medicine. Mr. Cramer had given a scribe an emetic which operated with extreme violence. The Arabs, being struck at its wonderful effects, resolved all to take the same excellent remedy, and the reputation of our friend's skill thus became very high among them. The Emir of the port sent one day for him; and, as he did not go immediately, the Emir soon after sent a saddled horse to our gate. Mr. Cramer, supposing that this horse was intended to bear him to the Emir, was going to mount him, when he was told that this was the patient he was to cure. We luckily found another physician in our party; our Swedish servant had been with the hussars in his native country, and had acquired some knowledge of the diseases of horses. He offered to cure the Emir's horse, and succeeded. The cure rendered him famous, and he was afterward sent for to human patients."

Having satisfied themselves by this time that there was no danger in travelling in Yemen, they did not wait for the departure of any large caravan, but, on February 20, 1763, set out from Loheia, mounted on asses, and made their way across the *Tehama*, or low country, toward the large town of

Beit el-Fakih, which stands near the base of the coffee-bearing hills. They wore dresses somewhat similar to those of the natives, a long shirt, reaching nearly to the feet, a girdle, and a mantle over the shoulders. The country was barren, but there were many villages, and at intervals of every few miles they found coffee-houses, or, rather, huts, for the refreshment of travellers. After having suffered no further inconvenience than from the brackish water, which is drawn from wells more than a hundred feet deep, they reached Beit el-Fakih in five days.

Here they were kindly received by one of the native merchants, who hired a stone house for them. The town is seated upon a well-cultivated plain; it is comparatively modern, but populous, and the travellers, now entirely accustomed to the Arabian mode of life, felt themselves safe. The Emir took no particular notice of them, a neglect with which they were fully satisfied, since it left them free to range the country in all directions. Niebuhr, therefore, determined to make the place the temporary headquarters of the expedition, and to give some time to excursions in that part of Yemen. "I hired an ass," says he, "and its owner agreed to follow me as my servant on foot. A turban, a great coat wanting the sleeves, a shirt, linen drawers, and a pair of slippers, were all the dress that I wore. It being the fashion of the country to carry arms in travelling, I had a sabre and two pistols hung by my girdle. A piece of old carpet was my saddle, and served me likewise for a seat, a table, and various other purposes. To cover me at night, I had the linen cloak which the

Arabs wrap about their shoulders, to shelter them from the sun and rain. A bucket of water, an article of indispensable necessity to a traveller in these arid regions, hung by my saddle."

After a trip to the seaport of Hodeida, Niebuhr visited the old town of Zebid, built on the ruins of an older city, which is said to have once been the capital of all the low country. Zebid is situated in a large and fertile valley, traversed during the rainy season by a considerable stream, by which a large tract of country is irrigated. There are the remains of an aqueduct built by the Turks, but the modern town does not cover half the space of the ancient capital. Zebid, however, is still distinguished for its academy, in which the youth of all that part of Yemen study such sciences as are now cultivated by the Mussulmans.

Niebuhr's next trip was to the plantations of the famous Mocha coffee, whither the other members of the party had already gone, during his visit to Zebid. After riding about twenty miles eastward from Beit el-Fakih, he reached the foot of the mountains. He thus describes the region: "Neither asses nor mules can be used here. The hills are to be climbed by steep and narrow paths; yet, in comparison with the parched plains of the Tehama, the scenery seemed to me charming, as it was covered with gardens and plantations of coffee-trees.

"Up to this time I had seen only one small basaltic hill; but here whole mountains were composed chiefly of those columns. Such detached rocks formed grand objects in the landscape, especially

COFFEE HILLS OF YEMEN.

where cascades of water were seen to rush from their summits. The cascades, in such instances, had the appearance of being supported by rows of artificial pillars. These basalts are of great utility to the inhabitants; the columns, which are easily separated, serve as steps where the ascent is most difficult, and as materials for walls to support the plantations of coffee-trees upon the steep declivities of the mountains.

"The tree which affords the coffee is well known in Europe; so that I need not here describe it particularly. The coffee-trees were all in flower at Bulgosa, and exhaled an exquisitely agreeable perfume. They are planted upon terraces, in the form of an amphitheatre. Most of them are only watered by the rains that fall, but some, indeed, from large reservoirs upon the heights, in which spring-water is collected, in order to be sprinkled upon the terraces, where the trees grow so thick together that the rays of the sun can hardly enter among their branches. We were told that those trees, thus artificially watered, yielded ripe fruit twice in the year; but the fruit becomes not fully ripe the second time, and the coffee of this crop is always inferior to that of the first.

"Stones being more common in this part of the country than in the Tehama, the houses—as well of the villages as those which are scattered solitarily over the hills—are built of this material. Although not to be compared to the houses of Europe for commodiousness and elegance, yet they have a good appearance; especially such of them as stand upon the heights, with amphitheatres of beautiful gardens and trees around them.

"Even at this village of Bulgosa we were greatly above the level of the plain from which we had ascended; yet we had scarcely climbed half the ascent to Kusma, where the Emir of this district dwells, upon the loftiest peak of the range of mountains. Enchanting landscapes there meet the eye on all sides.

"We passed the night at Bulgosa. Several of the men of the village came to see us, and after they retired we had a visit from our hostess, with some young women accompanying her, who were all very desirous to see the Europeans. They seemed less shy than the women in the cities; their faces were unveiled, and they talked freely with us. As the air is fresher and cooler upon these hills, the women have a finer and fairer complexion than in the plain. Our artist drew a portrait of a young girl who was going to draw water, and was dressed in a shirt of linen, checkered blue and white. The top and middle of the shirt, as well as the lower part of the drawers, were embroidered with needlework of different colors."

Having met with no molestation so far, Niebuhr determined to make a longer excursion into the southern interior of Yemen, among the mountains, to the important towns of Udden and Taas. The preparations were easily made. The travellers hired asses, the owners accompanying them on foot as guides and servants. As a further disguise they assumed Arabic names, and their real character was so well concealed that even the guides supposed them to be Oriental Christians—not Europeans. Entering the mountains by an unfrequented road, they found a barren region at first, but soon reached valleys where coffee was cultivated. The inhabitants, on account of the cooler nights, sleep in linen bags, which they draw over the head, and thus keep themselves warm by their own breathing.

After reaching Udden, which Niebuhr found to be a town of only three hundred houses, the hill-country became more thickly settled. Beside the roads, which had formerly been paved with stones, there were frequent tanks of water for the use of travellers, and, in exposed places, houses for their shelter in case of storms. The next important place was Djobla, a place of some importance in the annals of Yemen, but with no antiquities, except some ruined mosques. A further march of two days brought the party to the fortified city of Taas, but they did not venture within its walls, not having applied to the Emir for permission. They returned to their quarters at Beit el-Fakih, by way of Haas, another large town at the base of the mountains, having made themselves acquainted with a large portion of the hill-country of Arabia Felix.

The journey to Mocha lasted three days, over a hot, barren plain, with no inhabitants except in the wadys or valleys, which are well watered during the rainy season. Their arrival at Mocha was followed by a series of annoyances, first from the custom-house officials, and then from the Emir, who conceived a sudden prejudice against the travellers, so that they were in danger of being driven out of the city. An English merchant, however, came to their assistance, a present of fifty ducats mollified the Emir, and at the end of a very disagreeable week they received permission to stay in the city. From heat and privation they had all become ill, and in a short time one of the party died.

Niebuhr now requested permission to proceed to Sana, the capital of Yemen. This the Emir refused, until he could send word to the Imâm; but, after a delay of a month, he allowed the party to go as far as Taas, which they reached in four days, and where they were well received. The refreshing rains every evening purified the air, and all gradually recovered their health, except the botanist, who died before reaching Sana.

Taas stands at the foot of the fertile mountain of Sabber, upon which, the Arabs say, grow all varieties of plants and trees to be found in the world. Nevertheless they did not allow the travellers to ascend or even approach it. The city is surrounded with a wall, between sixteen and thirty feet high, and flanked with towers. The patron saint of the place is a former king, Ismael Melek, who is buried in a mosque bearing his name. No person is allowed to visit the tomb since the occurrence of a miracle, which Niebuhr thus relates: "Two beggars had asked charity of the Emir of Taas, but only one of them had tasted of his bounty. Upon this the other went to the tomb of Ismael Melek to implore his aid. The saint, who, when alive, had been very charitable, stretched his hand out of the tomb and gave the beggar a letter containing an order on the Emir to pay him a hundred crowns. Upon examining this order with the greatest care it was found that Ismael Melek had written it with his own hand and sealed it with his own seal. The governor could not refuse payment; but to avoid all subsequent trouble from such bills of exchange, he had a wall built, inclosing the tomb."

The Emir of Taas so changed in his behavior toward the travellers, after a few days, that he ordered them to return to Mocha. Finding all their arguments and protests in vain, they were about to comply, when a messenger arrived from Mocha, bringing the permission of the Imâm of Yemen for them to continue their journey to Sana. They set out on June 28th, and, after crossing the mountain ranges of Mharras and Samara, by well-paved and graded roads, reached, in a week, the town of Jerim, near the ruins of the ancient Himyaritic city of Taphar, which, however, they were unable to visit on account of the illness of Mr. Forskal, the botanist of the expedition. This gentleman died in a few days; and they were obliged to bury him by night, with the greatest precaution.

From Jerim it is a day's journey to Damar, the capital of a province. The city, which is seated in the midst of a fertile plain, and is without walls, contains five thousand well-built houses. It has a famous university, which is usually attended by five hundred students. The travellers were here very much annoyed by the curiosity of the people, who threw stones at their windows in order to force them to show themselves. There is a mine of native sulphur near the place, and a mountain where cornelians are found, which are highly esteemed throughout the East.

Beyond Damar the country is hilly, but every village is surrounded with gardens, orchards, and vineyards, which are irrigated from large artificial reservoirs built at the foot of the hills. On reaching Sana the travellers were not allowed to enter the city, but conducted to an unfurnished house without the walls, where they were ordered to wait two days in entire seclusion, until they could be received by the Imâm. During this time they were not allowed to be visited by anyone. Niebuhr thus describes their interview, which took place on the third day:

"The hall of audience was a spacious square chamber, having an arched roof. In the middle was a large basin, with some *jets d'eau*, rising fourteen feet in height. Behind the basin, and near the throne, were two large benches, each a foot and a half high; upon the throne was a space covered with silken stuff, on which, as well as on both sides of it, lay large cushions. The Imâm sat between the cushions, with his legs crossed in the Eastern fashion; his gown was of a bright green color, and had large sleeves. Upon each side of his breast was a rich filleting of gold lace, and on his head he wore a great white turban. His sons sat on his right hand, and his brothers on the left. Opposite to them, on the highest of the two benches, sat the Vizier, and our place was on the lower bench.

"We were first led up to the Imâm, and were permitted to kiss both the back and the palm of his hand, as well as the hem of his robe. It is an extraordinary favor when the Mohammedan princes permit any person to kiss the palm of the hand. There was a solemn silence through the whole hall. As each of us touched the Imâm's hand a herald still proclaimed, 'God preserve the Imâm!' and all who were present repeated these words after him. I was thinking at the time how I should pay my compliments in Arabic, and was not a little disturbed by this noisy ceremony.

"We did not think it proper to mention the true reason of our expedition through Arabia; but told the Imâm that, wishing to travel by the shortest ways to the Danish colonies, in the East Indies, we had heard so much of the plenty and security which prevailed through his dominions, that we had resolved to see them with our own eyes, so that we might describe them to our countrymen. The Imâm told us we were welcome to his dominions, and might stay as long as we pleased. After our return home he sent to each of us a small purse containing ninety-nine *komassis*, two and thirty of which make a crown. This piece of civility might, perhaps, appear no compliment to a traveller's delicacy. But, when it is considered that a stranger, unacquainted with the value of the money of the country, obliged to pay every day for his provisions, is in danger of being imposed upon by the money-changers, this care of providing us with small money will appear to have been sufficiently obliging."

"The city of Sana," says Niebuhr, "is situated at

the foot of Mount Nikkum, on which are still to be seen the ruins of a castle, which the Arabs suppose to have been built by Shem. Near this mountain stands the citadel; a rivulet rises upon the other side, and near it is the Bostan el-Metwokkel, a spacious garden, which was laid out by the Imâm of that name, and has been greatly embellished by the reigning Imâm. The walls of the city, which are built of bricks, exclude this garden, which is inclosed within a wall of its own. The city, properly so called, is not very extensive; one may walk around it in an hour. There are a number of mosques, some of which have been built by Turkish Pashas. In Sana are only twelve public baths, but many noble palaces, three of the most splendid of which have been built by the reigning Imâm. The materials of these palaces are burnt bricks, and sometimes even hewn stones; but the houses of the common people are of bricks which have been dried in the sun.

"The suburb of Bir el-Arsab is nearly adjoining the city on the east side. The houses of this village are scattered through the gardens, along the banks of a small river. Fruits are very plenteous; there are more than twenty kinds of grapes, which, as they do not all ripen at the same time, continue to afford a delicious refreshment for several months. The Arabs likewise preserve grapes by hanging them up in their cellars, and eat them almost through the whole year. Two leagues northward from Sana is a plain named Rodda, which is overspread with gardens and watered by a number of rivulets. This place bears a great resemblance to the neighborhood of Damascus. But

Sana, which some ancient authors compare to Damascus, stands on a rising ground, with nothing like florid vegetation about it. After long rains, indeed, a small rivulet runs through the city ; but all the ground is dry through the rest of the year. However, by aqueducts from Mount Nikkum the town and castle of Sana are, at all times, supplied with abundance of excellent fresh water."

After a stay of a week the travellers obtained an audience of leave, fearing that a longer delay might subject them to suspicions and embarrassments. Two days afterward the Imâm sent each of them a complete suit of clothes, with a letter to the Emir of Mocha, ordering him to pay them two hundred crowns as a farewell present. He also furnished them with camels for the journey. Instead of returning by the same road they determined to descend from the hill-country to their old headquarters at Beit el-Fakih, and thence cross the lowland to Mocha.

For two days they travelled over high, rocky mountains, by the worst roads they found in Yemen. The country was poor and thinly inhabited, and the declivities only began to be clothed with trees and terraced into coffee plantations as they approached the plains. The poorer regions are not considered entirely safe by the Arabs, as the people frequently plunder defenceless travellers; but the party passed safely through this region, and reached Beit el-Fakih after a week's journey from Sana.

Niebuhr and his companions reached Mocha early in August, and toward the end of that month sailed in an English vessel for Bombay, after a stay of ten months in Yemen. The artist of the expedition and the Swedish servant died on the Indian Ocean, and the physician in India, a few months afterward, leaving Niebuhr the sole survivor of the six persons who left Copenhagen three years before. After having sent home the journals and collections of the expedition he continued his travels through the Persian Gulf, Bagdad, Armenia, and Asia Minor, finally reaching Denmark in 1767. The era of intelligent, scientific exploration, which is now rapidly opening all parts of the world to our knowledge, may be said to have been inaugurated by his travels.

CHAPTER IV.

BURCKHARDT'S JOURNEY TO MECCA AND MEDINA

BURCKHARDT, to whom we are indebted for the first careful and complete description of the holy cities of Arabia, was a native of Lausanne, in Switzerland. After having been educated in Germany, he went to London with the intention of entering the English military service, but was persuaded by Sir Joseph Banks to apply to the African Association for an appointment to explore the Sahara, and the then unknown negro kingdoms of Central Africa. His offer was accepted, and after some preparation he went to Aleppo, in Syria, where he remained for a year or two, engaged in studying Arabic and familiarizing himself with Oriental habits of life.

His first journeys in Syria and Palestine, which were only meant as preparations for the African exploration, led to the most important results. He was the first to visit the country of Hauran—the Bashan of Scripture—lying southeast of Damascus. After this he passed through Moab, east of the Dead Sea, and under the pretence of making a pilgrimage to the tomb of Aaron on Mount Hor, discovered the rock-hewn palaces and temples of Petra, which had been for many centuries lost to the world.

Burckhardt reached Cairo in safety, and after vainly waiting some months for an opportunity of joining a caravan to Fezzan, determined to employ his time in making a visit to Upper Egypt and Nubia. Travelling alone, with a single guide, he succeeded in reaching the frontiers of Dongola, beyond which it was then impossible to proceed. He therefore returned to Assouan, and joined a small caravan, which crossed the Nubian Desert to Ethiopia, by very nearly the same route which Bruce had taken in returning from Abyssinia. He remained some time at Shendy, the capital of Ethiopia, and then, after a journey of three months across the country of Takka, which had never before been visited by a European, reached the port of Suakin, on the Red Sea. Here he embarked for Jedda, in Arabia, where he arrived in July, 1814.

By this time his Moslem character had been so completely acquired that he felt himself free from suspicion. Accordingly he decided to remain and take part in the pilgrimage to Mecca and Medina, which was to take place that year, in November. His funds, however, were nearly exhausted, and the Jedda merchants refused to honor an old letter of credit upon Cairo, which he still carried with him. In this emergency he wrote to the Armenian physician of Mohammed Ali, who was at that time with the Pasha at the city of Tayf (or Tayef), about seventy miles southeast of Mecca. Mohammed Ali happening to hear of this application, immediately sent a messenger with two dromedaries, to summon Burckhardt to visit him. It seems most probable that the Pasha suspected the traveller of being an English spy, and wished to examine him personally. The guide had orders to conduct the latter to Tayf by a circuitous route, instead of by the direct road through Mecca.

Burckhardt set out without the least hesitation, taking care to exhibit no suspicion of the Pasha's object, and no desire to see the holy city. But the guide himself proposed that they should pass through Mecca in order to save travel; the journey was hurried, however, and only a rapid observation was possible. Pushing eastward, they reached, on the third night, the Mountain of Kora, which divides the territory of Mecca from that of Tayf. Burckhardt was astonished at the change in the scenery, produced by the greater elevation of the interior of Arabia above the sea. His description is a striking contrast to that of the scenery about Mecca.

"This," he says, "is the most beautiful spot in the Hedjaz, and more picturesque and delightful than anything I had seen since my departure from Lebanon, in Syria. The top of Djebel Kora is flat, but large masses of granite lie scattered over it, the surface of which, like that of the granite rocks near the second cataract of the Nile, is blackened by the sun. Several small rivulets descend from this peak and irrigate the plain, which is covered with verdant fields and large shady trees beside the granite rocks. To those who have only known the dreary and scorching sands of the lower country of the Hedjaz, this scene is as surprising as the keen air which blows here is refreshing. Many of the fruit-trees of Europe are found here: figs, apricots, peaches, apples, the Egyptian sycamore, almonds, pomegranates; but particularly vines, the produce of which is of the best quality. After having passed through this delightful district for about half an hour, just as the sun was rising, when every leaf and blade of grass was covered with a balmy dew, and every tree and shrub diffused a fragrance as delicious to the smell as was the landscape to the eye, I halted near the largest of the rivulets, which, although not more than two paces across, nourishes upon its banks a green alpine turf, such as the mighty Nile, with all its luxuriance, can never produce in Egypt."

Burckhardt had an interview with Mohammed Ali on the evening of his arrival in Tayf. His suspicions were confirmed: the Kadi (Judge) of Mecca and two well-informed teachers of the Moslem faith were present, and although the Pasha professed to accept Burckhard's protestations of his Moslem character, it was very evident to the latter that he was cunningly tested by the teachers. Nevertheless, when the interview was over, they pronounced him to be not only a genuine Moslem, but one of unusual learning and piety. The Pasha was forced to submit to this decision, but he was evidently not entirely convinced, for he gave orders that Burckhardt should be the guest of his physician, in order that his speech and actions might be more closely observed. Burckhardt took a thoroughly Oriental way to release himself from this surveillance. He gave the physician so much trouble that the latter was very glad, at the end of ten days, to procure from the Pasha permission for him to return to Mecca, in order to get rid of him. Burckhardt thereupon travelled to the holy city in company with the Kadi himself.

At the valley of Mohram, nearly a day's journey from Mecca, Burckhardt changed his garb for the *ihram*, or costume worn by the pilgrims during their devotional services. It consists of two pieces of either linen, cotton, or woollen cloth; one is wrapped around the loins, while the other is thrown over the shoulder in such a manner as to leave the right arm entirely bare. On reaching Mecca he obeyed the Moslem injunction of first visiting the great mosque and performing all the requisite ceremonies before transacting any worldly business. When this had been accomplished he made a trip to Jedda for the purpose of procuring supplies, which were necessary for the later pilgrimage to Medina, and then established himself comfortably in an unfrequented part of Mecca, to await the arrival of the caravan of pilgrims from Damascus.

Burckhardt describes the great mosque of Mecca, which is called the *Beit Allah*, or "House of God," as "a large quadrangular building, in the centre of which stands the Kaaba, an oblong, massive structure eighteen paces in length, fourteen in breadth, and from thirty-five to forty feet in height. It is constructed of gray Mecca stone, in large blocks of different sizes, joined together in a very rough manner, and with bad cement. At the northeast corner of the Kaaba, near the door, is the famous Black Stone, which forms part of the sharp angle of the building at four or five feet above the ground. It is an irregular oval of about seven inches in diameter, with an undulating surface, composed of about a dozen smaller stones of different sizes and shapes, well joined together with a small quantity of cement, and perfectly smoothed. It is very difficult to determine accurately the quality of this stone, which has been worn to its present surface by the millions of touches and kisses it has received. It appears to me like a lava, containing several small extraneous particles. Its color is now a deep reddish brown, approaching to black. It is surrounded on all sides by a border, composed of a substance which I took to be a close cement of pitch and gravel; this border serves to support its detached pieces. Both the border and the stone itself are encircled by a silver band."

Toward the end of November the caravans from Syria and Egypt arrived, and at the same time Mohammed Ali, so that the *hadj*, or pilgrimage, assumed a character of unusual pomp and parade. The Pasha's *ihram* consisted of two of the finest Cashmere shawls; the horses and camels belonging to himself and his large retinue, with those of the Pasha of Damascus and other Moslem princes, were decorated with the most brilliant trappings. On arriving, the pilgrims did not halt in Mecca, but continued their march to the Sacred Mountain of Arafat, to the eastward of the city. A camp, several miles in extent, was formed upon the plain, at the foot of the mountain, and here Burckhardt joined the immense crowd, in order to take his share in the ceremonies of the following day.

In the morning he climbed to the top of Arafat,

which is an irregular, isolated mass of granite, rising only about two hundred feet above the plain. Overlooking thus the entire camp, he counted more than three thousand tents, and estimated that at least twenty-five thousand camels and seventy thousand human beings were there collected together. "The scene," he says, "was one of the most extraordinary which the earth affords. Every pilgrim issued from his tent to walk over the plain and take a view of the busy crowds assembled there. Long streets of tents, fitted up as bazaars, furnished them with all kinds of provisions. The Syrian and Egyptian cavalry were exercised by their chiefs early in the morning, while thousands of camels were seen feeding upon the dry shrubs of the plain all around the camp. The Syrian pilgrims were encamped upon the south and southwest sides of the mountain; the Egyptians upon the southeast. Mohammed Ali, and Soleyman, Pasha of Damascus, as well as several of their followers, had very handsome tents; but the most magnificent of all was that of the wife of Mohammed Ali, the mother of Toossoon Pasha and Ibrahim Pasha, who had lately arrived from Cairo with a truly royal equipage, five hundred camels being necessary to transport her baggage from Jedda to Mecca. Her tent was in fact an encampment, consisting of a dozen tents of different sizes, inhabited by her women; the whole enclosed by a wall of linen cloth, eight hundred paces in circuit, the single entrance to which was guarded by eunuchs in splendid dresses. The beautiful embroidery on the exterior of this linen palace, with the various colors displayed in every part of it, constituted an object which reminded me of some descriptions in the Arabian tales of the Thousand and One Nights."

Burckhardt also gives an interesting description of the sermon preached on Mount Arafat, the hearing of which is an indispensable part of the pilgrimage: unless a person is at least present during its delivery, he is not entitled to the name of *hadji*, or pilgrim. The great encampment broke up at three o'clock in the afternoon, and Mount Arafat was soon covered from top to bottom. "The two Pashas, with their whole cavalry drawn up in two squadrons behind them, took their posts in the rear of the deep line of camels of the pilgrims, to which those of the people of Hedjaz were also joined; and here they waited in solemn and respectful silence the conclusion of the sermon. Farther removed from the preacher was the Scherif of Mecca, with his small body of soldiers, distinguished by several green standards carried before him. The two *mahmals*, or holy camels, which carry on their backs the high structure which serves as the banner of their respective caravans, made way with difficulty through the ranks of camels that encircled the southern and eastern sides of the hill, opposite to the preacher, and took their station, surrounded by their guards, directly under the platform in front of him. The preacher, who is usually the Kadi of Mecca, was mounted upon a finely caparisoned camel, which had been led up the steps: it was traditionally said that Mohammed was always seated when he addressed his followers, a practice in which he was imitated by all the Caliphs who came to the pilgrimage, and who from this place addressed their subjects in person. The Turkish gentleman of Constantinople, however, unused to camel-riding, could not keep his seat so well as the hardy Bedouin prophet, and the camel becoming unruly, he was soon obliged to alight from it. He read his sermon from a book in Arabic, which he held in his hands: At intervals of every four or five minutes he paused and stretched forth his arms to implore blessings from above, while the assembled multitudes around and before him waved the skirts of their *ihrams* over their heads and rent the air with shouts of *Lebeyk, Allah, huma lebeyk!*—' Here we are at Thy bidding, oh God!' During the waving of the *ihrams* the sides of the mountain, thickly crowded as it was by the people in their white garments, had the appearance of a cataract of water; while the green umbrellas, with which several thousand pilgrims sitting on their camels below were provided, bore some resemblance to a verdant plain."

Burckhardt performed all the remaining ceremonies required of a pilgrim; but these have been more recently described and with greater minuteness by Captain Burton. He remained in Mecca for another month, unsuspected and unmolested, and completed his observations of a place which the Arabs believed they had safely sealed against all Christian travellers.

Leaving Mecca with a small caravan of pilgrims, on January 15, 1815, he reached Medina after a journey of thirteen days, during which he narrowly escaped being slain by the Bedouins.

Burckhardt was attacked with fever soon after his arrival at Medina, and remained there three months. The ceremonies prescribed for the pilgrims who visit the city are brief and unimportant; but the description of the tomb of Mohammed is of sufficient interest to quote. "The mausoleum," he says, "stands at the southeastern corner of the principal mosque, and is protected from the too near approach of visitors by an iron railing, painted green, about two-thirds the height of the pillars of the colonnade which runs around the interior of the mosque. The railing is of good workmanship, in imitation of filigree, and is interwoven with open-worked inscriptions of yellow bronze, supposed by the vulgar to be of gold, and of so close a texture that no view can be obtained of the interior except by several small windows, about six inches square, which are placed in the four sides of the railing, about five feet above the ground. On the south side, where are the two principal windows, before which the devout stand when praying, the railing is plated with silver, and the common inscription—'There is no god but God, the Evident Truth!'—is wrought in silver letters around the windows. The tomb itself, as well as those of Abu Bekr and Omar, which stand close to it, is concealed from the public gaze by a curtain of rich silk brocade of various colors, interwoven with silver flowers and arabesques, with inscriptions in characters of gold running across the midst of it, like that of the covering of the Kaaba. Behind this curtain, which, according to the historian of the city, was formerly changed every six years, and is now renewed by the Porte

VIEW OF EL MEDINA.

whenever the old one is decayed, or when a new Sultan ascends the throne, none but the chief eunuchs, the attendants of the mosque, are permitted to enter. This holy sanctuary once served, as the temple of Delphi did among the Greeks, as the public treasury of the nation. Here the money, jewels, and other precious articles of the people of Hedjaz were kept in chests, or suspended on silken ropes. Among these was a copy of the Koran in Cufic characters; a brilliant star set in diamonds and pearls, which was suspended directly over the Prophet's tomb; with all sorts of vessels filled with jewels, earrings, bracelets, necklaces, and other ornaments sent as presents from all parts of the empire. Most of these articles were carried away by the Wahabees when they sacked and plundered the sacred cities."

Burckhardt reached Yambo (the port of Medina), at the end of April, and, after running great danger from the plague, succeeded in obtaining passage to the Peninsula of Sinai, whence he slowly made his way back to Cairo. Here he waited for two years, vainly hoping for the departure of a caravan for Central Africa, and meanwhile assisting Belzoni in his explorations at Thebes. In October, 1817, he died, and the people who knew him only as Shekh Abdallah, laid his body in the Moslem burying-ground, on the eastern side of Cairo.

CHAPTER V.

WELLSTED'S EXPLORATIONS IN OMAN

PERHAPS the most satisfactory account of the interior of Oman—the southeastern portion of Arabia—has been given by Lieutenant Wellsted. While in the Indian Navy he was employed for several years in surveying the southern and eastern coasts of Arabia. Having become somewhat familiar with the language and habits of the people, he conceived the idea of undertaking a journey to Derreyeh, in Nedjed, the capital of the Wahabees, which no traveller had then reached. The governor of Bombay gave him the necessary leave of absence, and he landed at Muscat in November, 1835.

The Sultan, Sayid Saeed, received the young Englishman with great kindness, promised him all possible aid in his undertaking, and even arranged for him the route to be travelled. He was to sail first to the port of Sur, south of Muscat, thence penetrate to the country inhabited by the Beni-Abu-Ali tribe, and make his way northward to the Jebel Akhdar, or Green Mountains, which were described to him as lofty, fruitful, and populous. Having thus visited the most interesting portions of Oman, he was then to be at liberty, if the way was open, to take the northern route through the Desert toward Nedjed.

The Sultan presented him with a horse and sword, together with letters to the governors of the districts through which he should pass.

At Sur, which is a small, insignificant village, with a good harbor, the mountains of the interior approach the sea, but they are here divided by a valley which furnishes easy access to the country beyond them. After a journey of four days Wellsted reached the tents of the tribe of Ben-Abu-Ali, at a point to which the English troops had penetrated in 1821, to punish the tribe for acts of piracy. Although no Englishman had visited them since that time, they received him with every demonstration of friendship. Sheep were killed, a feast prepared, a guard of honor stationed around the tent, and, in the evening, all the men of the encampment, 250 in number, assembled for the purpose of exhibiting their war-dance. Wellsted thus describes the scene: "They formed a circle within which five of their number entered. After walking leisurely around for some time, each challenged one of the spectators by striking him gently with the flat of his sword. His adversary immediately leaped forth and a feigned combat ensued. They have but two cuts, one directly downward, at the head, the other horizontal, across the legs. They parry neither with the sword nor shield, but avoid the blows by leaping or bounding backward. The blade of their sword is three feet in length, thin, double-edged, and as sharp as a razor. As they carry it upright before them, by a peculiar motion of the wrist they cause it to vibrate in a very remarkable manner, which has a singularly striking effect when they are assembled in any considerable number. It was part of the entertainment to fire off their matchlocks under the legs of some one of the spectators who appeared too intent on watching the game to observe their approach, and any signs of alarm which incautiously escaped the individual added greatly to their mirth."

In the evening a party of the Geneba Bedouins came in from the desert, accompanied by one of their chiefs. The latter readily consented that Wellsted should accompany him on a short journey into his country, and they set out the following morning. It was December, and the morning air was cold and pure; the party swept rapidly across the broad, barren plains, the low hills, dotted with acacia trees, and the stony channels which carried the floods of the rainy season to the sea. After a day's journey of forty-four miles they encamped near some brackish wells. "You wished," said the chief to Wellsted, "to see the country of the Bedouins; *this*," he continued, striking his spear into the firm sand, "*this* is the country of the Bedouins." Neither he nor his companions wore any clothing except a single cloth around the loins. Their hair, which is permitted to grow until it reaches the waist, and is usually well plastered with grease, is the only covering which protects their heads from the sun.

The second day's journey brought Wellsted to a small encampment, where the chief's wives were abiding. They conversed with him, unveiled, gave him coffee, milk, and dates, and treated him with all the hospitality which their scanty means allowed.

The Beni Geneba tribe numbers about three thousand five hundred fighting men; they are spread over a large extent of Southern Arabia, and are divided into two distinct classes,—those who live by fishing, and those who follow pastoral pursuits. A race of fishermen, however, is found on all parts of the Arabian coast. In some districts they are considered a separate and degraded people, with whom the genuine Bedouins will neither eat, associate, nor intermarry; but among the Beni Geneba this distinction does not exist.

Wellsted might have penetrated much farther to the westward under the protection of this tribe, and was tempted to do so; but it seemed more important to move northward, and get upon some one of the caravan tracks leading into Central Arabia. He therefore returned to the camp of the Beni-Abu-Ali, where the friendly people would hardly suffer him to depart, promising to build a house for him if he would remain a month with them. For two days he travelled northward, over an undulating region of sand, sometimes dotted with stunted acacias, and reached a district called Bediah, consisting of seven villages, each seated in its little oasis of date palms. One striking feature of these towns is their low situation. They are erected in artificial hollows, which have been excavated to the depth of six or eight feet. Water is then conveyed to them in subterranean channels from wells in the neighboring hills, and the soil is so fertile that irrigation suffices to produce the richest harvest of fruit and vegetables. A single step carries the traveller from the glare and sand of the desert into a spot teeming with the most luxuriant vegetation, and embowered by lofty trees, whose foliage keeps out the sun. "Some idea," says Wellsted, "may be formed of the density of this shade by the effect it produces in lessening the terrestrial radiation. A Fahrenheit thermometer which within the house stood at 55°, six inches from the ground fell to 45°. From this cause and the abundance of water they are always saturated with damp, and even in the heat of the day possess a clammy coldness."

On approaching Ibrah, the next large town to the north, the country became hilly, and the valleys between the abrupt limestone ranges increased in fertility. Wellsted thus describes the place: "There are some handsome houses in Ibrah; but the style of building is quite peculiar to this part of Arabia. To avoid the damp and catch an occasional beam of the sun above the trees, they are usually very lofty. A parapet surrounding the upper part is turreted, and on some of the largest houses guns are mounted. The windows and doors have the Saracenic arch, and every part of the building is profusely decorated with ornaments of stucco in bas-relief, some in very good taste. The doors are also cased with brass, and have rings and other massive ornaments of the same metal.

"Ibrah is justly renowned for the beauty and fairness of its females. Those we met on the streets evinced but little shyness, and on my return to the tent I found it filled with them. They were in high glee at all they saw; every box I had was turned over for their inspection, and whenever I attempted to remonstrate against their proceedings they stopped my mouth with their hands. With such damsels there was nothing left but to laugh and look on."

Travelling two days farther in the northward, Wellsted reached the town of Semmed, where he found a fine stream of running water. The Shekh's house was a large fort, the rooms of which were spacious and lofty, but destitute of furniture. Suspended on pegs protruding from the walls were the saddles, cloths, and harness of the horses and camels. The ceilings were painted in various devices, but the floors were of mud, and only partially covered with mats. Lamps formed of shells, a species of murex, were suspended by lines from the ceiling. On returning to the tent, after this visit, the traveller found, as usual, a great crowd collected there, but kept in order by a boy about twelve years of age. He had taken possession of the tent, as its guardian, and allowed none to enter without his permission. He carried a sword longer than himself, and also a stick, with which he occasionally laid about him. It is a part of the Arab system of education to cease treating boys as children at a very early age, and they acquire, therefore, the gravity and demeanor of men.

Beyond this place Wellsted was accompanied by a guard of seventy armed men, for the country was considered insecure. For two days and a half he passed many small villages, separated by desert tracts, and then reached the town of Minnà, near the foot of the Green Mountains. "Minnà," he says, "differs from the other towns in having its cultivation in the open fields. As we crossed these, with lofty almond, citron, and orange trees yielding a delicious fragrance on either hand, exclamations of astonishment and admiration burst from us. 'Is this Arabia?' we said; 'this the country we have looked on heretofore as a desert?' Verdant fields of grain and sugar-cane stretching along for miles are before us; streams of water, flowing in all directions, intersect our path; and the happy and contented appearance of the peasants agreeably helps to fill up the smiling picture. The atmosphere was delightfully clear and pure; and, as we trotted joyously along, giving or returning the salutations of peace or welcome, I could almost fancy that we had at last reached that 'Araby the Blessed' which I had been accustomed to regard as existing only in the fictions of our poets.

"Minnà is an old town, said to have been erected at the period of Narhirvan's invasion; but it bears, in common with the other towns, no indications of antiquity; its houses are lofty, but do not differ from those of Ibrah or Semmed. There are two square towers, about one hundred and seventy feet in height, nearly in the centre of the town; at their bases the breadth of the wall is not more than two feet, and neither side exceeds in length eight yards. It is therefore astonishing, considering the rudeness of the materials (they have nothing but unhewn stones and a coarse but apparently strong cement), that, with proportions so meagre, they should have been able to carry them to their present elevation. The guards, who are constantly on the lookout, ascend by means of a rude ladder, formed by placing bars of wood in a diagonal direction in one of the side angles within the interior of the building."

The important town of Neswah, at the western base of the Jebel Akdar, or Green Mountains, is a short day's journey from Minnà. On arriving there Wellsted was received in a friendly manner by the governor, and lodged, for the first time since leaving Muscat, in a substantial house. He was allowed to visit the fortress, which, in that region, is considered impregnable. He was admitted by an iron door of great strength, and, ascending through a vaulted passage, passed through six others equally massive before reaching the summit. The form of the fort is circular, its diameter being nearly one hundred yards, and to the height of ninety feet it has been filled up by a solid mass of earth and stones. Seven or eight wells have been bored through this, from several of which they obtain a plentiful supply of water, while those which are dry serve as magazines for their shot and ammunition. A wall forty feet high surrounds the summit, making the whole height of the fortress one hundred and fifty feet. It is a work of extraordinary labor, and from its appearance probably of considerable antiquity; but no certain intelligence could be obtained on this point.

On Christmas-day Wellsted left Neswah on an excursion to the celebrated Green Mountains. The Shekh of Tanuf, the first village where he encamped, endeavored in every possible way to dissuade him from undertaking the journey; but his resolute manner and a few gifts overcame the difficulty. Mounted on strong asses, the party commenced ascending a precipitous ridge by a track so narrow that they seemed at times to be suspended over precipices of unknown depth. On the second day they reached the village of Seyk. "By means of steps," he says, "we descended the steep side of a narrow glen, about four hundred feet in depth, passing in our progress several houses perched on crags or other acclivities, their walls built up in some places so as to appear but a continuation of the precipice. These small, snug, compact-looking dwellings have been erected by the natives one above the other, so that their appearance from the bottom of the glen, hanging as it were in mid-air, affords to the spectator a most novel and interesting picture. Here we found, amid a great variety of fruits and trees, pomegranates, citrons, almonds, nutmegs, and walnuts, with coffee-bushes and vines. In the summer, these together must yield a delicious fragrance; but it was now winter, and they were leafless. Water flows in many places from the upper part of the hills, and is received at the lower in small reservoirs, whence it is distributed all over the face of the country. From the narrowness of this glen, and the steepness of its sides, only the lower part of it receives the warmth of the sun's rays for a short period of the day; and even at the time of our arrival we found it so chilly, that, after a short halt, we were very happy to continue our journey."

They halted for the night at a village called Shirazi, in the heart of the mountains, the highest peaks of which here reach a height of 6,000 feet above the sea. The inhabitants belong to a tribe called the Beni Ryam, who are considered infidels by the people of

Neswah because they cultivate the grape for the purpose of making wine. The next day the Arabs who formed Wellsted's escort left him, and he had considerable difficulty in returning to Neswah by another road. From this point he had intended starting for Central Arabia, but the funds which he expected did not arrive from Muscat, the British agent there having refused to make the necessary advances. Wellsted thereupon applied directly to the Sultan, Sayd Saeed, for a loan, and while waiting an answer, made an excursion into the desert, fifty miles to the westward of Neswah. With a view to familiarize himself with the manners and domestic life of the Bedouins, he mixed with them during this trip, living and sleeping in their huts and tents. On all occasions he was treated with kindness, and often with a degree of hospitality above rather than below the means of those who gave it.

Although the Sultan of Muscat was willing to furnish the necessary supplies, and arrangements had been made which Wellsted felt sure would have enabled him to penetrate into the interior, he was prevented from going forward by a violent fever, from the effects of which he remained insensible for five days. Recovering sufficiently to travel, his only course was to return at once to the sea-coast, and on January 22, 1836, he left Neswah for the little port of Sib, where he arrived after a slow journey of eight days. He relates the following incident, which occurred at Semayel, the half-way station: "Weary and faint from the fatigue of the day's journey, in order to enjoy the freshness of the evening breeze I had my carpet spread beneath a tree. An Arab passing by paused to gaze upon me, and, touched by my condition and the melancholy which was depicted on my countenance, he proffered the salutation of peace, pointed to the crystal stream which sparkled at my feet, and said: 'Look, friend, for running water maketh the heart glad!' With his hands folded over his breast, that mute but most graceful of Eastern salutations, he bowed and passed on. I was in a situation to estimate sympathy; and so much of that feeling was exhibited in the manner of this son of the desert, that I have never since recurred to the incident, trifling as it is, without emotion."

A rest of four weeks at Sib recruited the traveller's strength, and he determined to make another effort to reach Central Arabia. He therefore applied to the Sultan for an escort to Bireimah, the first town of the Wahabees, beyond the northern frontier of Oman. The Sultan sent a guide, but objected to the undertaking, as word had just arrived that the Wahabees were preparing to invade his territory. Wellsted, however, was not willing to give up his design without at least making the attempt. He followed the coast, north of Muscat, as far as the port of Suweik, where he was most hospitably received by the wife of the governor, Seyd Hilal, who was absent. "A huge meal, consisting of a great variety of dishes, sufficient for thirty or forty people, was prepared in his kitchen, and brought to us, on large copper dishes, twice a day during the time we remained. On these occasions there was a great profusion of blue and gilt

A VALLEY IN OMAN.

chinaware, cut glass dishes, and decanters containing sherbet instead of wine."

"The Shekh," Wellsted continues, "after his return, usually spent the evening with us. On one occasion he was accompanied by a professional storyteller, who appeared to be a great favorite with him. 'Whenever I feel melancholy or out of order,' said he, 'I send for this man, who very soon restores me to my wonted spirits.' From the falsetto tone in which the story was chanted, I could not follow the thread of the tale, and, upon my mentioning this to him, the Shekh very kindly sent me the manuscript, of which the reciter had availed himself. With little variation I found it to be the identical Sindbad the Sailor, so familiar to the readers of the Arabian Nights. I little thought, when first I perused these fascinating tales in my own language, that it would ever be my lot to listen to the original in a spot so congenial and so remote."

Leaving Suweik on March 4th, Wellsted was deserted by his camel-men at the end of the first day's march, but succeeded in engaging others at a neighboring village. The road, which at first led between low hills, now entered a deep mountain-gorge, inclosed by abrupt mountains of rock several thousand feet in height.

For two days the party followed this winding defile, where the precipices frequently towered from three to four thousand feet over their heads. Then, having passed the main chain, the country became more open, and they reached the village of Muskin, in the territory of the Beni Kalban Arabs. Their progress beyond this point was slow and tedious, on account of the country being divided into separate districts, which are partly independent of each other. At the next town, Makiniyat, the Shekh urged them to go no farther, on account of the great risk, but finally consented to furnish an escort to Obri, the last town to the northward which acknowledges the sway of Muscat. This was distant two days' journey —the first through a broad valley between pyramidal hills, the second over sandy plains, which indicated their approach to the Desert.

Obri is one of the largest and most populous towns in Oman. The inhabitants devote themselves almost exclusively to agriculture, and export large quantities of indigo, sugar, and dates. On arriving Wellsted went immediately to the residence of the Shekh, whom he found to be a very different character from the officials whom he had hitherto encountered. "Upon my producing the Imâm's letters," says he, "he read them, and took his leave without returning any answer. About an hour afterward he sent a verbal message to request that I should lose no time in quitting his town, as he begged to inform me, what he supposed I could not have been aware of, that it was then filled with nearly two thousand Wahabees. This was indeed news to us; it was somewhat earlier than we anticipated falling in with them, but we put a good face on the matter, and behaved as coolly as we could."

The next morning the Shekh returned, with a positive refusal to allow them to proceed farther. Wellsted demanded a written refusal, as evidence which he could present to the Sultan, and this the Shekh at once promised to give. His object was evidently to force the traveller away from the place, and such was the threatening appearance of things that the latter had no wish to remain. The Wahabees crowded around the party in great numbers, and seemed only waiting for some pretext to commence an affray. "When the Shekh came and presented me with the letter for the Sultan," says Wellsted, "I knew it would be in vain to make any further effort to shake his resolution, and therefore did not attempt it. In the meantime news had spread far and wide that two Englishmen, with a box of 'dollars,' but in reality containing only the few clothes that we carried with us, had halted in the town. The Wahabees and other tribes had met in deliberation, while the lower classes of the townsfolk were creating noise and confusion. The Shekh either had not the shadow of any influence, or was afraid to exercise it, and his followers evidently wished to share in the plunder. It was time to act. I called Ali on one side, told him to make neither noise nor confusion, but to collect the camels without delay. In the meantime we had packed up the tent, the crowd increasing every minute; the camels were ready, and we mounted on them. A leader, or some trifling incident, was now only wanting to furnish them with a pretext for an onset. They followed us with hisses and various other noises until we got sufficiently clear to push briskly forward; and, beyond a few stones being thrown, we reached the outskirts of the town without further molestation. I had often before heard of the inhospitable character of the inhabitants of this place. The neighboring Arabs observe that to enter Obri a man must either go armed to the teeth, or as a beggar with a cloth, and that not of decent quality, around his waist. Thus, for a second time, ended my hopes of reaching Derreyeh from this quarter."

Wellsted was forced to return to Suweik, narrowly escaping a Bedouin ambush on the way. As a last attempt he followed the coast as far as Schinas, near the mouth of the Straits of Ormuz, and thence despatched a messenger to the Wahabees at Birsimah. This plan also failed, and he then returned to India. He has given us, however, the only authentic account of the scenery and inhabitants of the interior of Oman, and his travels are thus an important contribution to our knowledge of Arabia.

It is a sufficient commentary on the exclusive character of Interior Arabia, and the difficulties that bar the way there to free and thorough exploration, that, although Lieutenant Wellsted's journey was in 1835, we still (1892) have to turn to his very interesting narrative for almost all we know of the interior of Oman.

CHAPTER VI.

WELLSTED'S DISCOVERY OF AN ANCIENT CITY IN HADRAMAUT

WHILE employed in the survey of the southern coast of Arabia in the spring of 1835, Lieutenant Wellsted was occupied for a time near the cape called Ras el-Aseïda, in Hadramaut, about one hundred miles east of Aden. On this cape there is a watch-tower, with the guardian of which, an officer named Hamed, he became acquainted; and on learning from the Bedouins of the neighborhood that extensive ruins, which they described as having been built by infidels, and of great antiquity, were to be found at some distance inland, he prevailed upon the officer to procure him camels and guides.

One day, having landed with a midshipman in order to visit some inscriptions at a few hours' distance, the Bedouins who brought the camels refused to go to the place, but expressed their willingness to convey the two Europeans to the ruined city. Hamed declined to accompany them, on the plea of sickness, and they were unsupplied with provisions or presents for the Shekhs of the villages on the way. Still the chance was too tempting to be lost. Wellsted decided to trust himself to the uncertain protection of the Bedouins, sent his boat to the surveying vessel with a message that it should meet him at a point farther to the westward at the end of three days, and set out for the ruins late in the afternoon.

Leaving the sea-shore at sunset, they struck northward into the interior, and travelled until after midnight, passing several villages of the Diyabi Bedouins, a very fierce and powerful tribe, who are dreaded by all their neighbors. Scraping for themselves beds in the sand, the travellers slept until daybreak without being disturbed. The path soon after mounted a ledge about four hundred feet in height, from the summit of which they obtained an extensive but dreary view of the surrounding country. Their route lay along a broad valley, skirted on each side by a lofty range of mountains. By eight o'clock the sun became so oppressive that the Bedouins halted under the shade of some stunted tamarisk trees. "Within these burning hollows," says Wellsted, "the sun's rays are concentrated and thrown off as from a mirror; the herbs around were scorched to a cindery blackness; not a cloud obscured the firmament, and the breeze which moaned past us was of a glowing heat, like that escaping from the mouth of a furnace. Our guides dug hollows in the sand, and thrust their blistered feet within them. Although we were not long in availing ourselves of the practical lesson they had taught us, I began to be far from pleased with their churlish demeanor."

During the day they travelled over sandy and stony ridges, and late in the afternoon entered the Wady Meifah, where they found wells of good water

DISCOVERY OF AN ANCIENT CITY 57

and scanty vegetation. "The country now began to assume a far different aspect. Numerous hamlets, interspersed amid extensive date groves, verdant fields of grain, and herds of sleek cattle, showed themselves in every direction, and we now fell in with parties of inhabitants for the first time since leaving the sea-shore. Astonishment was depicted on their countenances, but as we did not halt they had no opportunity of gratifying their curiosity by gazing at us for any length of time."

One of the Bedouins, however, in spite of Wellsted's remonstrances, told the people that the travellers were in search of buried treasure. When the latter attempted to encamp near a village, the inhabitants requested them to remove; the guides proved to be ignorant of the road in the night, and they would have been suffered to wander about without shelter but for the kindness of an old woman, who conducted them to her house. This proved to be a kind of khan for travellers, and was already so crowded that the travellers were obliged to sleep in an open courtyard.

They were hardly prepared for the scene which daylight disclosed to them. "The dark verdure of fields of millet, sorghum, tobacco, etc., extended as far as the eye could reach. Mingled with these we had the soft acacia and the stately but more sombre foliage of the date palm; while the creaking of numerous wheels with which the grounds were irrigated, and in the distance several rude ploughs drawn by oxen, the ruddy and lively appearance of the people, who now flocked toward us from all quarters, and the delightful and refreshing coolness of the morning air, combined to form a scene which he who gazes on the barren aspect of the coast could never anticipate.

After three hours' travel through this bright and populous region, they came in sight of the ruins, which the inhabitants call *Nakab el-Hadjar* (meaning "The Excavation from the Rock"). According to Wellsted's estimate, they are about fifty miles from the coast.

The following is Wellsted's description of the place: "The hill upon which these ruins are situated stands out in the centre of the valley, and divides a stream which passes, during floods, on either side of it. It is nearly eight hundred yards in length, and about three hundred and fifty yards at its extreme breadth. About a third of the height from its base a massive wall, averaging from thirty to forty feet in height, is carried completely around the eminence, and flanked by square towers, erected at equal distances. There are but two entrances, north and south; a hollow, square tower, measuring fourteen feet, stands on both sides of these. Their bases extend to the plain below, and are carried out considerably beyond the rest of the building. Between the towers, at an elevation of twenty feet from the plain, there is an oblong platform which projects about eighteen feet without and within the walls. A flight of steps was apparently once attached to either extremity of the building.

"Within the entrance, at an elevation of ten feet from the platform, we found inscriptions. They are

RUINS OF NAKAB-EL-HADJAR, IN HADRAMAUT.

executed with extreme care, in two horizontal lines, on the smooth face of the stones, the letters being about eight inches long. Attempts have been made, though without success, to obliterate them. From the conspicuous situation which they occupy, there can be but little doubt but that, when deciphered, they will be found to contain the name of the founder of the building, as well as the date and purport of its erection.* The whole of the walls and towers, and some of the edifices within, are built of the same material—a compact grayish-colored marble, hewn to the required shape with the utmost nicety. The dimensions of the slabs at the base were from five to seven feet in length, two to three in height, and three to four in breadth.

"Let us now visit the interior, where the most conspicuous object is an oblong square building, the walls of which face the cardinal points: its dimensions are twenty-seven by seventeen yards. The walls are fronted with a kind of freestone, each slab being cut of the same size, and the whole so beautifully put together that I endeavored in vain to insert the blade of a small penknife between them. The outer, unpolished surface is covered with small chisel-marks, which the Bedouins have mistaken for writing. From the extreme care displayed in the construction of this building, I have no doubt that it is a temple, and my disappointment at finding the in-

* The inscription, which is copied in Lieutenant Wellsted's work, appears to be in the Himyaritic character. If any translation of it has ever been made, the compiler is unable to say where it can be found.

terior filled up with the ruins of the fallen roof was very great. Had it remained entire, we might have obtained some clew to guide us in our researches respecting the form of religion professed by the earlier Arabs. Above and beyond this building there are several other edifices, with nothing peculiar in their form or appearance.

"In no portion of the ruins did we succeed in tracing any remains of arches or columns, nor could we discover on their surface any of those fragments of pottery, colored glass, or metals, which are always found in old Egyptian towns, and which I also saw in those we discovered on the northwest coast of Arabia. Except the attempts to deface the inscriptions, there is no other appearance of the buildings having suffered from any ravages besides those of time; and owing to the dryness of the climate, as well as the hardness of the material, every stone, even to the marking of the chisel, remains as perfect as the day it was hewn. We were anxious to ascertain if the Arabs had preserved any tradition concerning the building, but they refer them, like other Arabs, to their pagan ancestors. 'Do you believe,' said one of the Bedouins to me upon my telling him that his ancestors were then capable of greater works than themselves, 'that these stones were raised by the unassisted hands of the Kafirs? No! no! They had devils, legions of devils (God preserve us from them!), to aid them.'"

On his return to the sea, which occupied a day and a half, Wellsted was kindly treated by the natives, and suffered only from the intense heat. The vessel was fortunately waiting at the appointed place. Since the journey was made (in 1836) Baron von Wrede, a German traveller, has succeeded in exploring a portion of Hadramaut, penetrating as far as Wady Doan, a large and populous valley, more than a hundred miles from the coast. But a thorough exploration of both Yemen and Hadramaut is still wanting, and when made, it will undoubtedly result in many important discoveries.

CHAPTER VII.

BURTON'S PILGRIMAGE

CAPTAIN RICHARD F. BURTON, the discoverer of the great Lake Tanganyika, in Central Africa, first became known to the world by his daring and entirely successful visit to Medina and Mecca, in the year 1853, in the disguise of a Moslem pilgrim. Although his journey was that of Burckhardt, reversed, and he describes the same ceremonies, his account supplies many deficiencies in the narrative of his predecessor, and has the merit of a livelier and more graphic style.

Burton's original design was to cross the Arabian Peninsula from west to east, as Palgrave has since done, and the Royal Geographical Society was disposed to accept his services. But he failed to obtain a sufficient leave of absence from the East India Company, which only granted him a furlough of one year—a period quite insufficient for the undertaking. He therefore determined to prove at least his fitness for the task, by making the pilgrimage to the holy cities. He was already familiar with the Arabic and Persian languages, and had the advantage of an Eastern cast of countenance.

Like Burckhardt, he assumed an Oriental character at the start, and during the voyage from Southampton to Alexandria was supposed to be a Persian prince. For two or three months he laboriously applied himself in Egypt to the necessary religious studies, joined a society of dervishes, under the name of Shekh Abdullah, kept the severe fast of Ramazan, and familiarized himself with all the orthodox forms of ablution, prayer, and prostration. He gave himself out to be an Afghan by birth, but long absent from his native country, a character which was well adapted to secure him against detection. During his stay in Cairo he made the acquaintance of a boy named Mohammed el-Basyuni, a native of Mecca, who became his companion for the journey, and who seems not to have suspected his real character until the pilgrimage was over.

Having purchased a tent and laid in an ample supply of provisions, with about four hundred dollars in money, he went to Suez about July 1st, with the avowed purpose of proceeding to Mecca by way of Jedda, yet with the secret intention of visiting Medina on the way. Here he became acquainted with a company of pilgrims, whose good-will he secured by small loans of money, and joined them in taking passage in a large Arab boat bound for Yembo. The vessel was called the Golden Wire. "Immense was the confusion," says Burton, "on the eventful day of our departure. Suppose us standing on the beach, on the morning of a fiery July day, carefully watching our hurriedly-packed goods and chattels, surrounded by a mob of idlers who are not too proud to pick up waifs and strays, while pilgrims rush about apparently mad, and friends are weeping, acquaintances vociferating adieux, boatmen demanding fees, shopmen claiming debts, women shrieking and talking with inconceivable power, children crying—in short, for an hour or so we were in the thick of a human storm. To confound confusion, the boatmen have moored their skiff half a dozen yards away from the shore, lest the porters should be unable to make more than double their fare from the pilgrims."

They sailed on July 6th, and were five days in reaching the mouth of the Gulf of Akaba. While crossing to the Arabian shore, the pilgrims are accustomed to repeat the following prayer, which is a good example of Moslem invocation: "O Allah, O Exalted, O Almighty, O All-pitiful, O All-powerful, thou art my God, and sufficeth to me the knowledge of it! Glorified be the Lord my Lord, and glorified be the faith my faith! Thou givest victory to whom thou pleaseth, and thou art the glorious, the merciful! We pray thee for safety in our goings-forth and in our standings-still, in our words and our designs, in our dangers of temptation and doubts, and the secret designs of our hearts. Subject unto us this sea, even as thou didst subject the deep to Moses, and as thou didst subject the fire to Abraham, and as thou didst subject the iron to David, and as thou didst subject the wind, and devils, and genii, and mankind to Solomon, and as thou didst subject the moon and El-Burak to Mohammed, upon whom be Allah's mercy and His blessing! And subject unto us all the seas in earth and heaven, in the visible and in thine invisible worlds, the sea of this life, and the sea of futurity. O thou who reignest over everything, and unto whom all things return, Khyar! Khyar!"

A further voyage of another week, uncomfortable and devoid of incident, brought the vessel to Yembo. As the pilgrims were desirous of pushing on to Medina, camels were hired on the day of arrival, and, a week's provisions having been purchased, the little caravan started the next afternoon. Burton, by the advice of his companions, assumed the Arab dress, but travelled in a litter, both because of an injury to his foot, and because he could thus take notes on the way without being observed. On account of the heat the caravan travelled mostly by night; the country, thus dimly seen, was low and barren for the first two days, but on the third day they reached a wilder region, which Burton thus describes: "We travelled through a country fantastic in its desolation —a mass of huge hills, barren plains, and desert vales. Even the sturdy acacias here failed, and in some places the camel grass could not find earth enough to take root in. The road wound among mountains, rocks, and hills of granite, over broken ground, flanked by huge blocks and bowlders, piled up as if man's art had aided nature to disfigure herself. Vast clefts seemed like scars on the hideous face of earth; here they widened into dark caves, there they were choked up with glistening drift sand. Not a bird or a beast was to be seen or heard; their presence would have argued the vicinity of water, and though my companions opined that Bedouins were lurking among the rocks, I decided that these Bedouins were the creatures of their fears. Above, a sky like polished blue steel, with a tremendous blaze of yellow light, glared upon us, without the thinnest veil of mist or cloud. The distant prospect, indeed, was more attractive than the near view, because it borrowed a bright azure tinge from the intervening atmosphere; but the jagged peaks and the perpendicular streaks of shadow down the flanks of the mountainous background showed that no change for the better was yet in store for us."

At the little towns of El-Hamra and Bir Abbas the caravan rested a day, suffering much from the intense heat, and with continual quarrels between the pilgrims and the Arabs to whom the camels belonged. At the latter place they were threatened with a detention of several days, but the difficulty was settled, and they set out upon the most dangerous portion of the road. "We travelled that night," says Burton "up a dry river-course in an easterly direction, and at early dawn found ourselves in an ill-famed gorge, called *Shuab el-Hadj* (the 'Pilgrim's Pass'). The loudest talkers became silent as we neared it, and their countenances showed apprehension written in legible characters. Presently, from the high, precipitous cliff on our left, thin blue curls of smoke—somehow or other they caught every eye—rose in the air, and instantly afterward rang the loud, sharp cracks of the hill-men's matchlocks, echoed by the rocks on the right. My shugduf had been broken by the camel's falling during the night, so I called out to Mansúr that we had better splice the frame-work with a bit of rope; he looked up, saw me laughing,

and with an ejaculation of disgust disappeared. A
number of Bedouins were to be seen swarming like
hornets over the crests of the rocks, boys as well as
men carrying huge weapons, and climbing with the
agility of cats. They took up comfortable places in
the cut-throat eminence, and began firing upon us
with perfect convenience to themselves. The height
of the hills and the glare of the rising sun prevented
my seeing objects very distinctly, but my companions
pointed out to me places where the rock had been
scarped, and a kind of breastwork of rough stones—
the Sangah of Afghanistan, piled up as a defence,
and a rest for the long barrel of the matchlock. It
was useless to challenge the Bedouins to come down
and fight us upon the plain like men; and it was
equally unprofitable for our escort to fire upon a foe
ensconced behind stones. We had, therefore, nothing
to do but to blaze away as much powder and to
veil ourselves in as much smoke as possible; the result of the affair was that we lost twelve men, besides camels and other beasts of burden. Though
the bandits showed no symptoms of bravery, and
confined themselves to slaughtering the enemy from
their hill-top, my companions seemed to consider
this questionable affair a most gallant exploit."

After two more days of severe travel, the pilgrims,
at early dawn, came in sight of the holy city of Medina. Burton thus describes the approach, and the
view from the western ridge: "Half an hour after
leaving the Wady el-Akik, or 'Blessed Valley,' we
came to a huge flight of steps, roughly cut in a long,
broad line of black, scoriaceous basalt. This is

called the *Mudarraj*, or flight of steps over the western ridge of the so-called El-Harratain; it is holy ground, for the Prophet spoke well of it. Arrived at the top, we passed through a lane of black scoria, with deep banks on both sides, and, after a few minutes a full view of the city suddenly opened on us. We halted our beasts as if by word of command. All of us descended, in imitation of the pious of old, and sat down, jaded and hungry as we were, to feast our eyes with a view of the Holy City. The prayer was, ' O Allah! this is the *Haram* (sanctuary) of the Prophet; make it to us a protection from hell fire, and a refuge from eternal punishment! O, open the gates of thy mercy, and let us pass through them to the land of joy!'

"As we looked eastward, the sun arose out of the horizon of low hills, blurred and dotted with small tufted trees, which gained a giant stature from the morning mists, and the earth was stained with gold and purple. Before us lay a spacious plain, bounded in front by the undulating ground of Nedjed; on the left was a grim barrier of rocks, the celebrated Mount Ohod, with a clump of verdure and a white dome or two nestling at its base. Rightward, broad streaks of lilac-colored mists were thick with gathered dew, there pierced and thinned by the morning rays, stretched over the date-groves and the gardens of Kuba, which stood out in emerald green from the dull tawny surface of the plain. Below, at the distance of about two miles, lay El Medina; at first sight it appeared a large place, but a closer inspection proved the impression to be an erroneous one."

VIEW OF MEDINA FROM THE WEST.

On arriving at Medina, Burton became the guest of one of the company he had met at Suez, and during his stay of a month in the city performed all the religious ceremonies and visitations which are prescribed for the pilgrim. He gives the following description of the Prophet's mosque: "Passing through muddy streets—they had been freshly watered before evening time—I came suddenly upon the mosque. Like that at Mecca, the approach is choked up by ignoble buildings, some actually touching the holy 'enceinte,' others separated by a lane compared with which the road around St. Paul's is a Vatican square. There is no outer front, no general aspect of the Prophet's mosque; consequently, as a building it has neither beauty nor dignity. And entering the Bab el-Rahmah—the Gate of Pity—by a diminutive flight of steps, I was astonished at the mean and tawdry appearance of a place so universally venerated in the Moslem world. It is not like the Meccan mosque, grand and simple—the expression of a single sublime idea; the longer I looked at it the more it suggested the resemblance of a museum of second-rate art, a curiosity-shop, full of ornaments that are not accessories, and decorated with pauper splendor."

We must also quote the traveller's account of his manner of spending the day during his residence in Medina: "At dawn we arose, washed, prayed, and broke our fast upon a crust of stale bread, before smoking a pipe, and drinking a cup of coffee. Then it was time to dress, to mount, and to visit the Haram in one of the holy places outside the city. Returning before the sun became intolerable, we sat together, and with conversation, shishas and chibouques, coffee and cold water perfumed with mastich-smoke, we whiled away the time till our *ariston*, an early dinner which appeared at the primitive hour of 11 A.M. The meal was served in the *majlis* on a large copper tray sent from the upper apartments. Ejaculating 'Bismillah'—the Moslem grace—we all sat round it, and dipped equal hands in the dishes set before us. We had usually unleavened bread, different kinds of meat and vegetable stews, and at the end of the first course plain boiled rice, eaten with spoons; then came the fruits, fresh dates, grapes, and pomegranates. After dinner I used invariably to find some excuse—such as the habit of a 'Kaylúlah' (midday siesta), or the being a 'Saudawi,' or person of melancholy temperament, to have a rug spread in the dark passage, and there to lie reading, dozing, smoking, or writing, all through the worst part of the day, from noon to sunset. Then came the hour for receiving and paying visits. The evening prayers ensued, either at home or in the Haram, followed by our supper, another substantial meal like the dinner, but more plentiful, of bread, meat, vegetables, rice, and fruits. In the evening we sometimes dressed in common clothes and went to the café; sometimes on festive occasions we indulged in a late supper of sweetmeats, pomegranates, and dried fruits. Usually we sat upon mattresses spread upon the ground in the open air, at the Shekh's door, receiving evening visits, chatting, telling stories, and making merry, till each, as he felt the approach of the drowsy god, sank down into his proper place, and fell asleep."

Burton was charmed with the garden and date-groves about Medina, and enjoyed the excursions, which were enjoined upon him as a pilgrim, to Jebel Ohod, the mosque of Kuba, and other places in the vicinity of the city. On August 28th the caravan of pilgrims from Damascus arrived, and, on account of danger from the Bedouins, decided to leave on the fourth day afterward, taking the Desert road to Mecca, the same travelled by the Caliph Haroun El-Raschid and his wife Zobeida, instead of the longer road nearer the coast, which Burckhardt had followed. When this plan was announced, Burton and his companions had but twenty-four hours to make the necessary preparations; but by hard work they were ready. Leaving Medina, they hastened onward to secure good places in the caravan, which was composed of about seven thousand pilgrims, and extended over many miles of the road.

For the first four days they travelled southward over a wild, desolate country, almost destitute of water and vegetation. On account of heat, as well as for greater security, the journey was made chiefly by night, although the forced marches between the wells obliged them sometimes to endure the greatest heat of the day. Burton says: "I can scarcely find words to express the weary horrors of a long night's march, during which the hapless traveller, fuming, if a European, with disappointment in his hopes of 'seeing the country,' is compelled to sit upon the back of a creeping camel. The day sleep, too, is a kind of lethargy, and it is all but impossible to preserve an appetite during the hours of heat."

After making ninety-nine miles from Medina, they reached the village of El Suwayrkiyah, which is included within the Meccan territory. The town, consisting of about one hundred houses, is built at the base and on the sides of a basaltic mass which rises abruptly from the hard clayey plain. The summit is converted into a rude fortalice by a bulwark of uncut stone, piled up so as to make a parapet. The lower part of the town is protected by a mud wall, with the usual semicircular towers. Inside there is a bazaar, well supplied with meat (principally mutton) by the neighboring Bedouins, and wheat, barley, and dates are grown near the town. There is little to describe in the narrow streets and the mud houses, which are essentially Arab. The fields around are divided into little square plots by earthen ridges and stone walls; some of the palms are fine grown trees, and the wells appeared numerous. The water is near the surface and plentiful, but it has a brackish taste, highly disagreeable after a few days' use, and the effects are the reverse of chalybeate.

Seventeen miles beyond El Suwayrkiyah is the small village of Sufayuah, beyond which the country becomes again very wild and barren. Burton thus describes the scenery the day after leaving Sufayuah: "This day's march was peculiarly Arabia. It was a desert peopled only with echoes—a place of death for what little there is to die in it— a wilderness where, to use my companion's phrase, there is nothing but He (Allah). Nature, scalped, flayed, discovered her anatomy to the gazer's eye. The horizon was a sea of mirage; gigantic sand-columns whirled over the plain; and on both sides of our road were huge piles of bare rock standing detached upon the surface of sand and clay. Here they appeared in oval lumps, heaped up with a semblance of symmetry; there a single bowlder stood, with its narrow foundation based upon a pedestal of low, dome-shaped rock. All are of a pink coarse-grained granite, which flakes off in large crusts under the influence of the atmosphere."

After four more long marches the caravan reached a station called El Zaribah, where the pilgrims halted a day to assume the *ihram*, or costume which they wear on approaching Mecca. They were now in the country of the Utaybah Bedouins, the most fierce and hostile of all the tribes on the road. Although only two marches, or fifty miles, from Mecca, the pilgrims were by no means safe, as the night after they left Zaribah testified. While threading a narrow pass between high rocks, in the twilight, there was a sudden discharge of musketry and some camels dropped dead. The Utaybah, hidden behind the rocks crowning the pass, poured down an irregular fire upon the pilgrims, who were panic-stricken and fell into great disorder. The Wahabees, however, commenced scaling the rocks, and very soon drove the robbers from their ambush. The caravan then hurried forward in great disorder, leaving the dead and severely wounded lying on the ground.

"At the beginning of the skirmish," says Burton, "I had primed my pistols, and sat with them ready for use. But soon seeing that there was nothing to be done, and, wishing to make an impression—nowhere does Bobadil now 'go down' but in the East—I called aloud for my supper. Shekh Nur, exanimate with fear, could not move. The boy Mohammed ejaculated only an 'Oh, sir!' and the people around exclaimed in disgust, 'By Allah! he eats!' Shekh Abdullah, the Meccan, being a man of spirit, was amused by the spectacle. 'Are these Afghan manners, Effendim?' he inquired from the shugduf behind me. 'Yes,' I replied aloud, 'in my country we always dine before an attack of robbers, because that gentry is in the habit of sending men to bed supperless.' The Shekh laughed aloud, but those around him looked offended."

The morning after this adventure the pilgrims reached the Wady Laymun, or Valley of Limes, a beautiful region of gardens and orchards, only twenty-four miles from Mecca. Here they halted four hours to rest and enjoy the fruits and fresh water; then the line of march was resumed toward the Holy City. In the afternoon the range of Jebel Kora, in the southeast, became visible, and as evening approached all eyes were strained, but in vain, for a sight of Mecca. Night came down, and the pilgrims moved slowly onward in the darkness. An hour after midnight Burton was roused by a general excitement in the caravan. "Mecca! Mecca!" cried some voices; "The Sanctuary, O the Sanctuary!" exclaimed others, and all burst into loud cries of "*Labeyk!*" not unfrequently broken by sobs. Looking out from his litter the traveller saw by the light of the southern stars the dim outlines of a large city. They were passing over the last rocky ridge by an artificial cut. The winding path was flanked on both sides by high watch-towers; a short distance farther they entered the northern suburb.

The Meccan boy Mohammed, who had been Burton's companion during the pilgrimage, conducted the latter to his mother's house, where he remained during his stay. A meal of vermicelli and sugar was prepared on their arrival in the night, and after an hour or two of sleep they rose at dawn, in order to perform the ceremonies of arrival. After having bathed, they walked in their pilgrim garb to the *Beit Allah*, or " House of God."

"There," says Burton, " there at last it lay, the bourne of my long and weary pilgrimage, realizing the plans and hopes of many and many a year. The mirage medium of fancy invested the huge catafalque and its gloomy pall with peculiar charms. There were no giant fragments of hoar antiquity as in Egypt, no remains of graceful and harmonious beauty as in Greece and Italy, no barbaric gorgeousness as in the buildings of India; yet the view was strange, unique, and how few have looked upon the celebrated shrine! I may truly say, that, of all the worshippers who clung weeping to the curtain, or who pressed their beating hearts to the stone, none felt for the moment a deeper emotion than did the Hadji from the far north. It was as if the poetical legends of the Arab spoke truth, and that the waving wings of angels, not the sweet breezes of morning, were agitating and swelling the black covering of the shrine. But, to confess humbling truth, theirs was the high feeling of religious enthusiasm, mine was the ecstasy of gratified pride."

Burton's description of the Beit Allah and the Kaaba is more minute and careful than that of Burckhardt, but does not differ from it in any important particular. Neither is it necessary to quote his account of the ceremonies to be performed by each individual pilgrim, with all their mechanical prostrations and repetitions. His account of the visit to the famous Black Stone, however, is both curious and amusing: "For a long time I stood looking in despair at the swarming crowd of Bedouin and other pilgrims that besieged it. But the boy Mohammed was equal to the occasion. During our circuit he had displayed a fiery zeal against heresy and schism by foully abusing every Persian in his path, and the inopportune introduction of hard words into his prayers made the latter a strange patchwork. He might, for instance, be repeating 'and I take refuge with thee from ignominy in this world,' when, 'O thou rejected one, son of the rejected!' would be the interpolation addressed to some long-bearded Khorassani, 'and in that to come—O hog and brother of a hoggess!' And so he continued till I wondered that no one dared to turn and rend him. After vainly addressing the pilgrims, of whom nothing could be seen but a mosaic of occiputs and shoulder-blades, the boy Mohammed collected about half a dozen stalwart Meccans, with whose assistance, by sheer strength, we wedged our way into the thin and light-legged crowd. The Bedouins turned round upon us like wildcats, but they had no daggers. The

TIA-G

CAMP AT MOUNT ARAFAT.

season being autumn, they had not swelled themselves with milk for six months; and they had become such living mummies that I could have managed single-handed half a dozen of them. After thus reaching the stone, despite popular indignation, testified by impatient shouts, we monopolized the use of it for at least ten minutes. Whilst kissing it and rubbing hands and forehead upon it I narrowly observed it, and came away persuaded that it is a big aërolite."

On September 12th the pilgrims set out for Mount Arafat. Three miles from Mecca there is a large village called Muna, noted for three standing miracles—the pebbles, there thrown at the Devil, return by angelic agency to whence they came; during the three days of drying meat rapacious birds and beasts cannot prey there, and flies do not settle upon the articles of food exposed in the bazaars. Beyond the place there is a mosque called El Khayf, where, according to some traditions, Adam is buried, his head being at one end of the long wall and his feet at the other, while the dome is built over his navel.

"Arafat," says Burton, "is about a six hours' march, or twelve miles, on the Taif road, due east of Mecca. We arrived there in a shorter time, but our weary camels, during the last third of the way, frequently threw themselves upon the ground. Human beings suffered more. Between Muna and Arafat I saw no less than five men fall down and die upon the highway; exhausted and moribund, they had dragged themselves out to give up the ghost where it departs to instant beatitude. The spectacle showed how easy it is to die in these latitudes; each man suddenly staggered, fell as if shot, and, after a brief convulsion, lay still as marble. The corpses were carefully taken up, and carelessly buried that same evening, in a vacant space amongst the crowds encamped upon the Arafat plain.

"Nothing can be more picturesque than the view the mountain affords of the blue peaks behind, and the vast encampment scattered over the barren yellow plain below. On the north lay the regularly pitched camp of the guards that defend the unarmed pilgrims. To the eastward was the Scherif's encampment with the bright mahmals and the gilt knobs of the grander pavilions; whilst, on the southern and western sides, the tents of the vulgar crowded the ground, disposed in dowars, or circles, for penning cattle. After many calculations, I estimated the number to be not less than fifty thousand, of all ages and both sexes."

After the sermon on Arafat, which Burton describes in the same manner as Burckhardt, the former gives an account of the subsequent ceremony of "stoning the Great Devil" near the village of Muna: "'The Shaytan el-Kabir' is a dwarf buttress of rude masonry, about eight feet high by two and a half broad, placed against a rough wall of stones, at the Meccan entrance to Muna. As the ceremony of 'Ramy,' or Lapidation, must be performed on the first day by all pilgrims between sunrise and sunset, and as the Fiend was malicious enough to appear in a rugged pass, the crowd makes the place dangerous.

On one side of the road, which is not forty feet broad, stood a row of shops belonging principally to barbers. On the other side is the rugged wall of the pillar, with a *chevaux de frise* of Bedouins and naked boys. The narrow space was crowded with pilgrims, all struggling like drowning men to approach as near as possible to the Devil; it would have been easy to run over the heads of the mass. Amongst them were horsemen with rearing chargers. Bedouins on wild camels, and grandees on mules and asses, with outrunners, were breaking a way by assault and battery. I had read Ali Bey's self-felicitations upon escaping this place with 'only two wounds in the left leg,' and had duly provided myself with a hidden dagger. The precaution was not useless. Scarcely had my donkey entered the crowd than he was overthrown by a dromedary, and I found myself under the stamping and roaring beast's stomach. By a judicious use of the knife, I avoided being trampled upon, and lost no time in escaping from a place so ignobly dangerous. Finding an opening at last, we approached within about five cubits of the place, and holding each stone between the thumb and forefinger of the ring hand, cast it at the pillar, exclaiming: 'In the name of Allah, and Allah is Almighty, I do this in hatred of the Fiend and to his shame.' The seven stones being duly thrown, we retired, and entering the barber's booth, took our places upon one of the earthen benches around it. This was the time to remove the *ihram* or pilgrim's garb, and to return to *ihlal*, the normal state of El Islam. The barber shaved our heads, and, after trimming our beards

and cutting our nails, made us repeat these words:
'I purpose loosening my *ihram* according to the
practice of the Prophet, whom may Allah bless and
preserve! O Allah, make unto me in every hair a
light, a purity, and a generous reward! In the name
of Allah, and Allah is Almighty!' At the conclusion of his labor the barber politely addressed to us a
'Naiman'—Pleasure to you! To which we as
ceremoniously replied, 'Allah give thee pleasure!'"

We will conclude these quotations from Burton's
narrative with his description of a sermon in the
great mosque of Mecca. "After returning to the
city from the sacrifice of sheep in the valley of Muna,
we bathed, and when noon drew nigh we repaired to
the Haram for the purpose of hearing the sermon.
Descending to the cloisters below the Bab el-Ziyadah,
I stood wonderstruck by the scene before me. The
vast quadrangle was crowded with worshippers sitting
in long rows, and everywhere facing the central black
tower; the showy colors of their dresses were not to
be surpassed by a garden of the most brilliant flowers, and such diversity of detail would probably not
be seen massed together in any other building upon
earth. The women, a dull and sombre-looking group,
sat apart in their peculiar place. The Pasha stood on
the roof of Zem Zem, surrounded by guards in Nizam uniform. Where the principal ulema stationed
themselves the crowd was thicker; and in the more
auspicious spots naught was to be seen but a pavement of heads and shoulders. Nothing seemed to
move but a few dervishes, who, censer in hand, sidled
through the rows and received the unsolicited alms

COSTUME OF PILGRIMS TO MECCA.

of the faithful. Apparently in the midst, and raised above the crowd by the tall, pointed pulpit, whose gilt spire flamed in the sun, sat the preacher, an old man with snowy beard. The style of head-dress called '*taylasan*' covered his turban, which was white as his robes, and a short staff supported his left hand. Presently he arose, took the staff in his right hand, pronounced a few inaudible words, and sat down again on one of the lower steps, whilst a Muezzin, at the foot of the pulpit, recited the call to sermon. Then the old man stood up and began to preach. As the majestic figure began to exert itself there was a deep silence. Presently a general 'Amin' was intoned by the crowd at the conclusion of some long sentence. And at last, toward the end of the sermon, every third or fourth word was followed by the simultaneous rise and fall of thousands of voices.

"I have seen the religious ceremonies of many lands, but never—nowhere—aught so solemn, so impressive as this spectacle."

Finding that it was impossible for him to undertake the journey across Central Arabia, both for lack of time and the menacing attitude of the Desert tribes, Burton left Mecca for Jedda at the end of September. Starting in the afternoon, the chance caravan of returning pilgrims reached, about midnight, a mass of huts called El Hadda, which is the usual half-way halting-place. It is maintained solely for the purpose of supplying travellers with coffee and water. Here the country slopes gradually toward the sea, the hills recede, and every feature denotes departure from the upland plateau of Mecca. After reaching here, and at some solitary coffee-houses farther on the way, the pilgrims reached Jedda safely at eight in the morning.

From this place Burton took passage on a steamer for Suez, and returned to Cairo, but without the Meccan boy, Mohammed, who began to have a suspicion of his true character, after seeing him in company with some English officers, and who left him before embarking.

CHAPTER VIII.

PALGRAVE'S TRAVELS IN CENTRAL ARABIA: FROM PALESTINE TO THE DJOWF

MR. WILLIAM GIFFORD PALGRAVE, son of Sir Francis Palgrave, the historian, performed, in 1862–63, a journey in Arabia, which gives us the first clear and full account of the interior of the country, including the great Wahabee state of Nedjed, the early home of Arabian poetry and also of the famous Arabian breed of horses. Mr. Palgrave's qualifications for the undertaking were in some respects superior to those of either Burckhardt or Burton. To a high degree of general culture and a vigorous and picturesque style as a writer, he added a knowledge of the Arabic language and literature equal to that of any native scholar; he spoke the language as well as his mother tongue; his features were sufficiently Oriental to disarm suspicion, and years of residence in the East had rendered him entirely familiar with the habits of the people and even with all those minor forms of etiquette which are so rarely acquired by a stranger. His narrative, therefore, is as admirable and satisfactory in its character as the fields he traversed were new and fascinating. It throws, indeed, so much indirect light upon the experiences of all his predecessors, and is so much richer in its illustrations of Arab life and character that no brief summary of its contents can do justice to its importance.

Of the first stage of the journey, from Gaza on the Mediterranean to the little town of Ma'an, which lies

William Gifford Palgrave.

on the route of the caravans from Damascus to Mecca, a short distance to the northeast of Petra, and thus nearly on the boundary between the country of Moab and Edom, Palgrave gives us no account. Yet, in spite of the comparatively brief distance traversed, it must have been both laborious and dangerous. His narrative commences as follows, at the moment of his departure from Ma'an:

"Once for all let us attempt to acquire a fairly correct and comprehensive knowledge of the Arabian Peninsula. With its coasts we are already in great measure acquainted; several of its maritime provinces have been, if not thoroughly, at least sufficiently, explored; Yemen and Hedjaz, Mecca and Medina, are no longer mysteries to us, nor are we wholly without information on the districts of Hadramaut and Oman. But of the interior of the vast region, of its plains and mountains, its tribes and cities, of its governments and institutions, of its inhabitants, their ways and customs, of their social condition, how far advanced in civilization or sunk in barbarism, what do we as yet really know, save from accounts necessarily wanting in fulness and precision? It is time to fill up this blank in the map of Asia, and this, at whatever risks, we will now endeavor; either the land before us shall be our tomb, or we will traverse it in its fullest breadth, and know what it contains from shore to shore. *Vestigia nulla retrorsum.*"

"Such were my thoughts, and such, more or less, I should suppose, those of my companion, when we found ourselves at fall of night without the eastern gate of Ma'an, while the Arabs, our guides and fellow-travellers, filled their water-skins from a gushing source hard by the town walls, and adjusted the saddles and the burdens of their camels, in preparation for the long journey that lay before us and them. It was the evening of June 16, 1862; the largest stars were already visible in the deep blue depths of a cloudless sky, while the crescent moon, high to the west, shone as she shines in those heavens, and promised us assistance for some hours of our night march. We were soon mounted on our meagre long-necked beasts, 'as if,' according to the expression of an Arab poet, 'we and our men were at mast-heads,' and now we set our faces to the east. Behind us lay, in a mass of dark outline, the walls and castle of Ma'an, its houses and gardens, and farther back in the distance the high and barren range of the Sheraa' Mountains, merging into the coast chain of Hejaz. Before and around us extended a wide and level plain, blackened over with countless pebbles of basalt and flint, except where the moonbeams gleamed white on little intervening patches of clear sand, or on yellowish streaks of withered grass, the scanty product of the winter rains, and dried now into hay. Over all a deep silence, which even our Arab companions seemed fearful of breaking; when they spoke it was in a half whisper and in a few words, while the noiseless tread of our camels sped stealthily but rapidly through the gloom without disturbing its stillness.

"Some precaution was not indeed wholly out of place, for that stage of the journey on which we were now entering was anything but safe. We were bound for the Djowf, the nearest inhabited district of Central Arabia, its outlying station, in fact. Now the intervening tract offered for the most part the double danger of robbers and of thirst, of marauding bands and of the summer season. The distance itself to be traversed was near two hundred miles in a straight line, and unavoidable circumstances were likely to render it much longer."

Palgrave's companion was a native Syrian, named Barakat—a man on whom he could fully rely. Hardy, young, and enterprising, he belonged to a locality whose inhabitants are accustomed to danger. But the Bedouins who furnished the camels, and acted as guides, were of another class. They were three in number—Salim, their leader, a member of a powerful family of the Howeytat tribe, but outlawed for pillage and murder, and two men, Alee and Djordee, utter barbarians in appearance no less than in character. Even Salim advised the travellers to avoid all familiarities with the latter.

"Myself and my companion," says Palgrave, "were dressed like ordinary class travellers of inner Syria, an equipment in which we had already made our way from Gaza on the sea-coast to Ma'an without much remark or unseasonable questioning from those whom we fell in with, while we traversed a country so often described already by Pococke, Laborde, and downward, under the name of Arabia Petra, that it would be superfluous for me to enter into any new account of it in the present work. Our dress, then, consisted partly of a long stout blouse of Egyptian hemp, under which, unlike our Bedouin fellow-travellers, we indulged in the luxury of the loose cotton drawers common in the East, while our colored head-kerchiefs, though simple enough, were girt by 'akkals or headbands of some pretension to elegance; the loose red-leather boots of the country completed our toilet.

"But in the large travelling-sacks at our camels' sides were contained suits of a more elegant appearance, carefully concealed from Bedouin gaze, but destined for appearance when we should reach better inhabited and more civilized districts. This reserve toilet numbered articles like the following: colored overdresses, the Syrian combaz, handkerchiefs whose silk stripes relieved the plebeian cotton, and girdles of good material and tasteful coloring; such clothes being absolutely requisite to maintain our assumed character. Mine was that of a native travelling doctor, a quack if you will; and accordingly a tolerable dress was indispensable for the credit of my medical practice. My comrade, who in a general way passed for my brother-in-law, appeared sometimes as a retail merchant, such as not unfrequently visit these countries, and sometimes as pupil or associate in my assumed profession.

"Our pharmacopœia consisted of a few but well selected and efficacious drugs, inclosed in small tight-fitting tin boxes, stowed away for the present in the ample recesses of our travelling bags; about fifty of these little cases contained the wherewithal to kill or cure half the sick men of Arabia. Medicines of a liquid form had been as much as possible omitted, not only from the difficulty of insuring them a safe transport amid so rough a mode of journeying, but also on account of the rapid evaporation unavoidable in this dry and burning climate. In fact two or three small bottles whose contents had seemed to me of absolute necessity, soon retained nothing save their labels to indicate what they had held, in spite of airtight stoppers and double coverings. I record this, because the hint may be useful to anyone who should be inclined to embark in similar guise on the same adventures.

"Some other objects requisite in medical practice, two or three European books for my own private use, and kept carefully secret from Arab curiosity, with a couple of Esculapian treatises in good Arabic, intended for professional ostentation, completed this part of our fitting-out. But besides these, an ample provision of cloth handkerchiefs, glass necklaces, pipe-bowls, and the like, for sale in whatever localities might not offer sufficient facility for the healing art, filled up our saddle-bags wellnigh to bursting. Last, but not least, two large sacks of coffee, the sheet-anchor and main hope of our commerce, formed alone a sufficient load for a vigorous camel."

The first days of travel were a monotony of heat and desolation. The deceptive lakes of the mirage covered the tawny plain, and every dark basaltic block, lying here and there at random, was magnified into a mountain in the heated atmosphere. " Dreary land of death, in which even the face of an enemy were almost a relief amid such utter solitude. But for five whole days the little dried-up lizard of the plain that looks as if he had never a drop of moisture in his ugly body, and the jerboa, or field-rat of Arabia, were the only living creatures to console our view.

"It was a march during which we might have almost repented of our enterprise, had such a sentiment been any longer possible or availing. Day after day found us urging our camels to their utmost pace for fifteen or sixteen hours together out of the twenty-four, under a wellnigh vertical sun, which the Ethiopians of Herodotus might reasonably be excused for cursing, with nothing either in the landscape around or in the companions of our way to relieve for a moment the eye or the mind. Then an insufficient halt for rest or sleep, at most of two or three hours, soon interrupted by the oft-repeated admonition, 'if we linger here we all die of thirst,' sounding in our ears; and then to remount our jaded beasts and push them on through the dark night, amid the constant probability of attack and plunder from roving marauders. For myself, I was, to mend matters, under the depressing influence of a tertian fever contracted at Ma'an, and what between weariness and low spirits, began to imagine seriously that no waters remained before us except the waters of death for us and of oblivion for our friends. The days wore by like a delirious dream, till we were often almost unconscious of the ground we travelled over and the journey on which we were engaged. One only herb appeared at our feet to give some appearance of variety and life; it was the bitter and poisonous colocynth of the desert.

"Our order of road was this: Long before dawn we were on our way, and paced it till the sun, having attained about half-way between the horizon and the zenith, assigned the moment of alighting for our morning meal. This our Bedouins always took good care should be in some hollow or low ground, for concealment's sake; in every other respect we had ample liberty of choice, for one patch of black pebbles with a little sand and withered grass between was just like another; shade or shelter, or anything like them, was wholly out of the question in such 'nakedness of the land.' We then alighted, and my companion and myself would pile up the baggage into a sort of wall, to afford a half-screen from the scorching sun-rays, and here recline awhile. Next came the culinary preparations, in perfect accordance with our provisions, which were simple enough; namely, a bag of coarse flour mixed with salt and a few dried dates; there was no third item on the bill of fare. We now took a few handfuls of flour, and one of the Bedouins kneaded it with his unwashed hands or dirty bit of leather, pouring over it a little of the dingy water contained in the skins, and then patted out this exquisite paste into a large round cake, about an inch thick and five or six inches across. Meanwhile another had lighted a fire of dry grass, colocynth roots, and dried camels' dung, till he had prepared a bed of glowing embers; among these the cake was now cast, and immediately covered up with hot ashes, and so left for a few minutes, then taken out, turned, and covered again, till at last, half-kneaded, half-raw, half-roasted, and burnt all round, it was taken out to be broken up between the hungry band, and eaten scalding hot, before it should cool into an indescribable leathery substance, capable of defying the keenest appetite. A draught of dingy water was its sole but suitable accompaniment.

"The meal ended, we had again without loss of time to resume our way from mirage to mirage, till 'slowly flaming over all, from heat to heat, the day decreased,' and about an hour before sunset we would stagger off our camels as best we might, to prepare an evening feast of precisely the same description as that of the forenoon, or more often, for fear lest the smoke of our fire should give notice to some distant rover, to content ourselves with dry dates, and half an hour's rest on the sand. At last our dates, like Æsop's bread-sack, or that of Beyhas, his Arab prototype, came to an end; and then our supper was a soldier's one; what that is my military friends will know; but, grit and pebbles excepted, there was no bed in our case. After which, to remount, and travel on by moon or starlight, till a little before midnight we would lie down for just enough sleep to tantalize, not refresh.

"It was now the 22d of June, and the fifth day since our departure from the wells of Wokba. The water in the skins had little more to offer to our thirst than muddy dregs, and as yet no sign appeared of a fresh supply. At last about noon we drew near some hillocks of loose gravel and sandstone a little on our right; our Bedouins conversed together awhile, and then turned their course and ours in that direction. 'Hold fast on your camels, for they are going to be startled and jump about,' said Salim to us. Why the camels should be startled I could not understand; when, on crossing the mounds just mentioned, we suddenly came on five or six black tents, of the very poorest description, pitched near some wells excavated in the gravelly hollow below. The reason of Salim's precautionary hint now became evident, for our silly beasts started at first sight of the tents, as though they had never seen the like before, and then scampered about, bounding friskily here and there, till what between their jolting (for a camel's run much resembles that of a cow) and our own laughing, we could hardly keep on their backs. However, thirst soon prevailed over timidity, and they left off their pranks to approach the well's edge and sniff at the water below."

The inhabitants of the tents showed the ordinary curiosity, but were not unfriendly, and the little caravan rested there for the remainder of the day. A further journey of two days over a region of sand-hills, with an occasional well, still intervened before they could reach Wady Sirhan—a long valley running directly to the populated region of the Djowf. While passing over this intermediate region an incident occurred which had wellnigh put a premature end to the travels and the travellers together. "My readers, no less than myself," says Palgrave, "must have heard or read many a story of the simoom, or deadly wind of the desert, but for me I had never yet met it in full force; and its modified form, or *she-look*, to use the Arab phrase, that is, the sirocco of the Syrian waste, though disagreeable enough, can hardly ever be termed dangerous. Hence I had been almost inclined to set down the tales told of the strange phenomena and fatal effects of this 'poisoned gale' in the same category with the moving pillars of sand, recorded in many works of higher historical pretensions than 'Thalaba.' At those perambulatory columns and sand-smothered caravans the

Bedouins, whenever I interrogated them on the subject, laughed outright, and declared that beyond an occasional dust-storm, similar to those which anyone who has passed a summer in Scinde can hardly fail to have experienced, nothing of the romantic kind just alluded to occurred in Arabia. But when questioned about the simoom, they always treated it as a much more serious matter, and such in real earnest we now found it.

"It was about noon, the noon of a summer solstice in the unclouded Arabian sky over a scorched desert, when abrupt and burning gusts of wind began to blow by fits from the south, while the oppressiveness of the air increased every moment, till my companion and myself mutually asked each other what this could mean, and what was to be its result. We turned to inquire of Salim, but he had already wrapped up his face in his mantle, and bowed down and crouching on the neck of his camel, replied not a word. His comrades, the two Sherarat Bedouins, had adopted a similar position, and were equally silent. At last, after repeated interrogations, Salim, instead of replying directly to our questioning, pointed to a small black tent, providentially at no great distance in front, and said: 'Try to reach *that;* if we can get there we are saved.' He added: 'Take care that your camels do not stop and lie down;' and then, giving his own several vigorous blows, relapsed into muffled silence.

"We looked anxiously toward the tent; it was yet a hundred yards off, or more. Meanwhile the gusts grew hotter and more violent, and it was only by repeated efforts that we could urge our beasts forward. The horizon rapidly darkened to a deep violet hue, and seemed to draw in like a curtain on every side, while at the same time a stifling blast, as though from some enormous oven opening right on our path, blew steadily under the gloom; our camels, too, began, in spite of all we could do, to turn round and round and bend their knees, preparing to lie down. The simoom was fairly upon us.

"Of course we had followed our Arabs' example by muffling our faces, and now with blows and kicks we forced the staggering animals onward to the only asylum within reach. So dark was the atmosphere, and so burning the heat, that it seemed that hell had risen from the earth, or descended from above. But we were yet in time, and at the moment when the worst of the concentrated poison-blast was coming around, we were already prostrate, one and all, within the tent, with our heads well wrapped up, almost suffocated, indeed, but safe; while our camels lay without like dead, their long necks stretched out on the sand, awaiting the passing of the gale.

"On our first arrival the tent contained a solitary Bedouin woman, whose husband was away with his camels in the Wady Sirhan. When she saw five handsome men like us rush thus suddenly into her dwelling without a word of leave or salutation, she very properly set up a scream to the tune of the four crown pleas—murder, arson, robbery, and I know not what else. Salim hastened to reassure her by calling out 'friends,' and without more words threw himself flat on the ground. All followed his example in silence.

"We remained thus for about ten minutes, during which a still heat like that of red-hot iron slowly passing over us was alone to be felt. Then the tent walls began again to flap in the returning gusts, and announced that the worst of the simoom had gone by. We got up, half dead with exhaustion, and unmuffled our faces. My comrades appeared more like corpses than living men, and so, I suppose, did I. However, I could not forbear, in spite of warnings, to step out and look at the camels; they were still lying flat as though they had been shot. The air was yet darkish, but before long it brightened up to its usual dazzling clearness. During the whole time that the simoom lasted, the atmosphere was entirely free from sand or dust, so that I hardly know how to account for its singular obscurity."

"Late in the evening we continued our way, and next day early entered Wady Sirhan, where the character of our journey underwent a considerable modification; for the northerly Arabian desert, which we are now traversing, offers, in spite of all its dreariness, some spots of comparatively better cast, where water is less scanty and vegetation less niggard. These spots are the favorite resorts of Bedouins, and serve, too, to direct the ordinary routes of whatever travellers, trade-led or from other motives, may venture on this wilderness. These oases, if indeed they deserve the name, are formed by a slight depression in the surrounding desert surface, and take at times the form of a long valley, or of an oblong patch, where rock and pebble give place to a light soil more or less intermixed with sand, and concealing under its surface a tolerable supply of moisture at no great distance below ground. Here, in consequence, bushes and herbs spring up, and grass, if not green all the year round, is at least of somewhat longer duration than elsewhere; certain fruit-bearing plants, of a nature to suffice for meagre Bedouin existence, grow here spontaneously; in a word, man and beast find not exactly comfortable accommodation, but the absolutely needful supply. Such a spot is Wady Sirhan, literally, 'the Valley of the Wolf.'"

They entered Wady Sirhan on June 21st. "Passing tent after tent, and leaving behind us many a tattered Bedouin and grazing camel, Salim at last indicated to us a group of habitations, two or three of which seemed of somewhat more ample dimensions than the rest, and informed us that our supper that night (for the afternoon was already on the decline) would be at the cost of these dwellings. 'Ajaweed,' *i.e.*, 'generous fellow,' he subjoined, to encourage us by the prospect of a handsome reception. Of course we could only defer to his better judgment, and in a few minutes were alongside of the black goats' hair coverings where lodged our intended hosts.

"The chief or chieflet, for such he was, came out, and interchanged a few words of masonic laconism with Salim. The latter then came up to us where we remained halted in expectation, led our camels to a little distance from the tents, made them kneel down, helped us to disburden them, and while we installed ourselves on a sandy slope opposite to the abodes of the tribe, recommended us to keep a sharp lookout after our baggage, since there might be pickers and stealers among our hosts, for all 'Ajaweed' as they were. Disagreeable news! for 'Ajaweed' in an Arab mouth corresponds the nearest possible to our English 'gentlemen.' Now, if the gentlemen were thieves, what must the blackguards be? We put a good face on it, and then seated ourselves in dignified gravity on the sand awaiting the further results of our guide's negotiations.

"For some time we remained undisturbed, though not unnoticed; a group of Arabs had collected round our companions at the tent door, and were engaged in getting from them all possible information, especially about us and our baggage, which last was an object of much curiosity, not to say cupidity. Next came our turn. The chief, his family (women excepted), his intimate followers, and some twenty others, young and old, boys and men, came up, and, after a brief salutation, Bedouinwise seated themselves in a semicircle before us. Every man held a short crooked stick for camel-driving in his hand, to gesticulate with when speaking, or to play with in the intervals of conversation, while the younger members of society, less prompt in discourse, politely employed their leisure in staring at us, or in picking up dried pellets of dirt from the sand and tossing them about."

"'What are you? what is your business?' so runs the ordinary and unprefaced opening of the discourse. To which we answer, 'Physicians from Damascus, and our business is whatsoever God may put in our way.' The next question will be about the baggage; someone pokes it with a stick, to draw attention to it, and says, 'What is this? have you any little object to sell us?'

"We fight shy of selling; to open out our wares and chattels in full air, on the sand, and amid a crowd whose appearance and circumstances offer but a poor guarantee for the exact observance of the eighth commandment, would be hardly prudent or worth our while. After several fruitless trials they desist from their request. Another, who is troubled by some bodily infirmity, for which all the united faculties of London and Paris might prescribe in vain—a withered hand, for instance, or stone-blind of an eye—asks for medicine, which no sooner applied shall, in his expectation, suddenly restore him to perfect health and corporal integrity. But I had been already forewarned that to doctor a Bedouin, even under the most favorable circumstances, or a camel, is pretty much the same thing, and with about an equal chance of success or advantage. I politely decline. He insists; I turn him off with a joke.

"'So you laugh at us, O you inhabitants of towns. We are Bedouins, we do not know your customs,' replies he, in a whining tone; while the boys grin unconscionably at the discomfiture of their tribesman.

"'Ya woleyd,' or young fellow (for so they style every human male from eight to eighty without distinction), 'will you not fill my pipe?' says one, who has observed that mine was not idle, and who, though well provided with a good stock of dry tobacco tied up in a rag at his greasy waist-belt, thinks the moment a fair opportunity for a little begging, since neither medicine nor merchandise is to be had.

"But Salim, seated amid the circle, makes me a sign not to comply. Accordingly, I evade the demand. However, my petitioner goes on begging, and is imitated by two or three others, each of whom thrusts forward (a true Irish hint) a bit of marrow-bone with a hole drilled in one side to act for a pipe, or a porous stone, not uncommon throughout the desert, clumsily fashioned into a smoking apparatus, a sort of primitive meerschaum.

"As they grow rude, I pretend to become angry, thus to cut the matter short. 'We are your guests, O you Bedouins; are you not ashamed to beg of us?' 'Never mind, excuse us; those are ignorant fellows, ill-bred clowns,' etc., interposes one close by the chief's side; and whose dress is in somewhat better condition than that of the other half and three-quarter naked individuals who complete the assembly.

"'Will you not people the pipe for your little brother?' subjoins the chief himself, producing an empty one with a modest air. Bedouin language, like that of most Orientals, abounds with not ungraceful imagery, and accordingly, 'people' here means 'fill.' Salim gives me a wink of compliance. I take out a handful of tobacco and put it on his long shirt-sleeve, which he knots over it, and looks uncommonly well pleased. At any rate they are easily satisfied, these Bedouins.

"The night air in these wilds is life and health itself. We sleep soundly, unharassed by the anticipation of an early summons to march next morning, for both men and beasts have alike need of a full day's repose. When the sun has risen we are invited to enter the chief's tent and to bring our baggage under its shelter. A main object of our entertainer, in proposing this move, is to try whether he cannot render our visit some way profitable to himself, by present or purchase. Whatever politeness he can muster is accordingly brought into play, and a large bowl of fresh camel's milk, an excellent beverage, now appears on the stage. I leave to chemical analysis to decide why this milk will not furnish butter, for such is the fact, and content myself with bearing witness to its very nutritious and agreeable qualities.

"The day passes on. About noon our host naturally enough supposes us hungry, and accordingly a new dish is brought in: it looks much like a bowl full of coarse red paste, or bran mixed with ochre. This is samh, a main article of subsistence to the Bedouins of Northern Arabia. Throughout this part of the desert grows a small herbaceous and tufted plant, with juicy stalks and a little ovate yellow-tinted leaf; the flowers are of a brighter yellow, with many stamens and pistils. When the blossoms fall off there remains in place of each a four-leaved capsule about the size of an ordinary pea, and this, when ripe, opens to show a mass of minute reddish seeds, resembling grit in feel and appearance, but farinaceous in substance. The ripening season is in July, when old and young, men and women, all are out to collect the unsown and untoiled-for harvest.

"On the 27th of the month we passed with some difficulty a series of abrupt sand-hills that close in the direct course of Wady Sirhan. Here, for the first time, we saw the ghada, a shrub almost characteristic, from its very frequency, of the Arabian Peninsula, and often alluded to by its poets. It is of the genus *Euphorbia*, with a woody stem, often five or six feet in height, and innumerable round green twigs, very slender and flexible, forming a large feathery tuft, not ungraceful to the eye, while it affords some kind of shelter to the traveller and food to his camels. These last are passionately fond of ghada, and will continually turn right out of their way, in spite of blows and kicks, to crop a mouthful of it, and then swing back their long necks into the former direction, ready to repeat the same manœuvre at the next bush, as though they had never received a beating for their past voracity.

"I have, while in England, heard and read more than once of the 'docile camel.' If 'docile' means stupid, well and good; in such a case the camel is the very model of docility. But if the epithet is intended to designate an animal that takes an interest in its rider so far as a beast can, that in some way understands his intentions or shares them in a subordinate fashion, that obeys from a sort of submissive or half fellow-feeling with his master, like the horse and elephant, then I say that the camel is by no means docile, very much the contrary; he takes no heed of his rider, pays no attention whether he be on his back or not, walks straight on when once set a-going, merely because he is too stupid to turn aside; and then, should some tempting thorn or green branch allure him out of the path, continues to walk on in this new direction simply because he is too dull to turn back into the right road. His only care is to cross as much pasture as he conveniently can while pacing mechanically onward; and for effecting this, his long, flexible neck sets him at great advantage, and a hard blow or a downright kick alone has any influence on him whether to direct or impel. He will never attempt to throw you off his back, such a trick being far beyond his limited comprehension; but if you fall off, he will never dream of stopping for you, and walks on just the same, grazing while he goes, without knowing or caring an atom what has become of you. If turned loose, it is a thousand to one that he will never find his way back to his accustomed home or pasture, and the first comer who picks him up will have no particular shyness to get over; Jack or Tom is all the same to him, and the loss of his old master, and of his own kith and kin, gives him no regret, and occasions no endeavor to find them again."

On coming in sight of the mountains of Djowf the travellers were obliged to halt for two days at an encampment of the Sherarat Arabs, because Salim could not enter the Djowf with them in person, on account of a murder which he had committed there. He was therefore obliged to procure them another guide capable of conducting them safely the remainder of the journey. After much search and discussion, Salim ended by finding a good-natured, but somewhat timid, individual, who undertook their guidance to the Djowf.

Journeying one whole day and night over an open

plateau, where they saw a large troop of ostriches, they mounted again on the 30th, by the light of the morning star, anxious to enter the Djowf before the intense heat of noon should come on ; " but we had yet a long way to go, and our track followed endless windings among low hills and stony ledges, without any symptom of approach to cultivated regions. At last the slopes grew greener, and a small knot of houses, with traces of tillage close by, appeared. It was the little village of Djoon, the most westerly appendage of Djowf itself. I counted between twenty and thirty houses. We next entered a long and narrow pass, whose precipitous banks shut in the view on either side. Suddenly several horsemen appeared on the opposite cliff, and one of them, a handsome youth, with long, curling hair, well armed and well mounted (we shall make his more special acquaintance in the next chapter), called out to our guide to halt, and answer in his own behalf and ours. This Suleyman did, not without those marks of timidity in his voice and gesture which a Bedouin seldom fails to show on his approach to a town, for, when once in it, he is apt to sneak about much like a dog who has just received a beating for theft. On his answer, delivered in a most submissive tone, the horsemen held a brief consultation, and we then saw two of them turn their horses' heads and gallop off in the direction of the Djowf, while our original interlocutor called out to Suleyman, ' All right, go on, and fear nothing,' and then disappeared after the rest of the band behind the verge of the upland.

" We had yet to drag on for an hour of tedious

AN ARAB CHIEF.

march; my camel fairly broke down, and fell again and again; his bad example was followed by the coffee-laden beast; the heat was terrible in these gorges, and noon was approaching. At last we cleared the pass, but found the onward prospect still shut out by an intervening mass of rocks. The water in our skins was spent, and we had eaten nothing that morning. When shall we get in sight of the Djowf? or has it flown away from before us? While thus wearily laboring on our way we turned a huge pile of crags, and a new and beautiful scene burst upon our view.

"A broad, deep valley, descending ledge after ledge till its innermost depths are hidden from sight amid far-reaching shelves of reddish rock, below everywhere studded with tufts of palm-groves and clustering fruit-trees, in dark-green patches, down to the furthest end of its windings; a large brown mass of irregular masonry crowning a central hill; beyond, a tall and solitary tower overlooking the opposite bank of the hollow, and further down small round turrets and flat house-tops, half buried amid the garden foliage, the whole plunged in a perpendicular flood of light and heat; such was the first aspect of the Djowf as we now approached it from the west. It was a lovely scene, and seemed yet more so to our eyes, weary of the long desolation through which we had, with hardly an exception, journeyed day after day, since our last farewell glimpse of Gaza and Palestine, up to the first entrance on inhabited Arabia. 'Like the Paradise of eternity, none can enter it till after having previously passed over hell-bridge,' says an Arab poet, describing some similar locality in Algerian lands.

"Reanimated by the view, we pushed on our jaded beasts, and were already descending the first craggy slope of the valley when two horsemen, well dressed and fully armed after the fashion of these parts, came up toward us from the town, and at once saluted us with a loud and hearty 'Marhaba,' or 'welcome;' and without further preface they added, 'Alight and eat,' giving themselves the example of the former by descending briskly from their light-limbed horses and untying a large leather bag full of excellent dates and a water-skin filled from the running spring; then, spreading out these most opportune refreshments on the rock, and adding, 'we were sure that you must be hungry and thirsty, so we have come ready provided,' they invited us once more to sit down and begin."

CHAPTER IX.

PALGRAVE'S TRAVELS—RESIDENCE IN THE DJOWF

THE elder of the two cavaliers who welcomed the travellers proved to be Ghafil-el-Haboob, the chief of the most important family of the Djowf. Ghafil, and also his companion, Dafee, invited the travellers to be his guests, and the former, it afterward appeared, had intended that they should reside in his house, hoping to make some profit from the merchandise which they might have brought. They felt bound, at least, to accompany him to his house and partake of coffee, before going elsewhere. Palgrave thus describes the manner of their reception:

"The k'hawah was a large, oblong hall, about twenty feet in height, fifty in length, and sixteen, or thereabouts, in breadth; the walls were colored in a rudely decorative manner, with brown and white wash, and sunk here and there into small triangular recesses, destined to the reception of books—though of these Ghafil at least had no over-abundance—lamps, and other such like objects. The roof of timber, and flat; the floor was strewed with fine clean sand, and garnished all round alongside of the walls with long strips of carpet, upon which cushions, covered with faded silk, were disposed at suitable intervals.

"We enter. On passing the threshold it is proper to say, '*Bismillah*,' *i.e.*, 'in the name of God;' not to do so would be looked on as a bad augury, alike for him who enters and for those within. The visitor next advances in silence, till, on coming about half-way across the room, he gives to all present, but looking specially at the master of the house, the customary '*Es-salamu'aleykum*,' or 'Peace be with you,' literally, 'on you.' All this while everyone else in the room has kept his place, motionless, and without saying a word. But on receiving the salaam of etiquette, the master of the house rises, and if a strict Wahabee, or at any rate desirous of seeming such, replies with the full-length traditionary formula: 'And with (or, on) you be peace, and the mercy of God, and his blessings.' But should he happen to be of anti-Wahabee tendencies, the odds are that he will say 'Marhaba,' or 'Ahlan w'sahlan,' *i.e.*, 'welcome,' or 'worthy and pleasurable,' or the like; for of such phrases there is an infinite but elegant variety. All present follow the example thus given by rising and saluting. The guest then goes up to the master of the house, who has also made a step or two forward, and places his open hand in the palm of his host's, but without grasping or shaking, which would hardly pass as decorous, and, at the same time each repeats once more his greeting, followed by the set phrases of polite inquiry, 'How are you?' 'How goes the world with you?' and so forth, all in a tone of great interest, and to be gone over three or four times, till one or other has the discretion to say 'El hamdu l'illah,' 'Praise be to

God,' or, in equivalent value, 'all right,' and this is a signal for a seasonable diversion to the ceremonious interrogatory.

"Meantime we have become engaged in active conversation with our host and his friends. But our Sherarat guide, Suleyman, like a true Bedouin, feels too awkward when among townsfolk to venture on the upper places, though repeatedly invited, and accordingly has squatted down on the sand near the entrance. Many of Ghafil's relations are present; their silver-decorated swords proclaim the importance of the family. Others, too, have come to receive us, for our arrival, announced beforehand by those we had met at the entrance pass, is a sort of event in the town; the dress of some betokens poverty, others are better clad, but all have a very polite and decorous manner. Many a question is asked about our native land and town, that is to say, Syria and Damascus, conformably to the disguise already adopted, and which it was highly important to keep well up; then follow inquiries regarding our journey, our business, what we have brought with us, about our medicines, our goods and wares, etc. From the very first it is easy for us to perceive that patients and purchasers are likely to abound. Very few travelling merchants, if any, visit the Djowf at this time of year, for one must be mad, or next door to it, to rush into the vast desert around during the heats of June and July; I for one have certainly no intention of doing it again. Hence we had small danger of competitors, and found the market almost at our absolute disposal.

"But before a quarter of an hour has passed, and while blacky is still roasting or pounding his coffee, a tall, thin lad, Ghafil's eldest son, appears, charged with a large circular dish, grass-platted like the rest, and throws it with a graceful jerk on the sandy floor close before us. He then produces a large wooden bowlful of dates, bearing in the midst of the heap a cupful of melted butter; all this he places on the circular mat, and says, '*Semmoo*,' literally, 'pronounce the Name,' of God, understood; this means 'set to work at it.' Hereon the master of the house quits his place by the fireside and seats himself on the sand opposite to us; we draw nearer to the dish, and four or five others, after some respectful coyness, join the circle. Everyone then picks out a date or two from the juicy, half-amalgamated mass, dips them into the butter, and thus goes on eating till he has had enough, when he rises and washes his hands."

"I will take the opportunity of leading my readers over the whole of the Djowf, as a general view will help better to understand what follows in the narrative, besides offering much that will be in part new, I should fancy, to the greater number.

"This province is a sort of oasis, a large oval depression of sixty or seventy miles long, by ten or twelve broad, lying between the northern desert that separates it from Syria and the Euphrates, and the southern Nefood, or sandy waste, and interposed between it and the nearest mountains of the central Arabian plateau. However, from its comparative proximity to the latter, no less than from the character of its climate and productions, it belongs hardly so much to Northern as to Central Arabia, of which it is a kind of porch or vestibule. If an equilateral triangle were to be drawn, having its base from Damascus to Bagdad, the vertex would find itself pretty exactly as the Djowf, which is thus at a nearly equal distance, southeast and southwest, from the two localities just mentioned, while the same cross-line, if continued, will give at about the same intervals of space in the opposite direction, Medina on the one hand, and Zulphah, the great commercial door of Eastern Nedjed, on the other. Djebel Shomer lies almost due south, and much nearer than any other of the places above specified. Partly to this central position, and partly to its own excavated form, the province owes its appropriate name of Djowf, or 'belly.'

"The principal, or rather the only, town of the district, all the rest being mere hamlets, bears the name of the entire region. It is composed of eight villages, once distinct, but which have in process of time coalesced into one, and exchanged their separate existence and name for that of Sook, or 'quarter,' of the common borough. Of these Sooks, the principal is that belonging to the family Haboob, and in which we were now lodged. It includes the central castle already mentioned, and numbers about four hundred houses. The other quarters, some larger, others smaller, stretch up and down the valley, but are connected together by their extensive gardens. The entire length of the town thus formed, with the cultivation immediately annexed, is full four miles, but the average breadth does not exceed half a mile, and sometimes falls short of it.

"The size of the domiciles varies with the condition of their occupants, and the poor are contented with narrow lodgings, though always separate; for I doubt if throughout the whole of Arabia two families, however needy, inhabit the same dwelling. Ghafil's abode, already described, may give a fair idea of the better kind; in such we have an outer court, for unlading camels and the like, an inner court, a large reception-room, and several other smaller apartments, to which entrance is given by a private door, and where the family itself is lodged.

"But another and a very characteristic feature of domestic architecture is the frequent addition, throughout the Djowf, of a round tower, from thirty to forty feet in height and twelve or more in breadth, with a narrow entrance and loop-holes above. This construction is sometimes contiguous to the dwelling-place, and sometimes isolated in a neighboring garden belonging to the same master. These towers once answered exactly the same purposes as the 'torri,' well known to travellers in many cities of Italy, at Bologna, Siena, Rome, and elsewhere, and denoted a somewhat analogous state of society to what formerly prevailed there. Hither, in time of the ever-recurring feuds between rival chiefs and factions, the leaders and their partisans used to retire for refuge and defence, and hence they would make their sallies to burn and destroy. These towers, like all the modern edifices of the Djowf, are of unbaked bricks; their great thickness and solidity of make, along with the extreme tenacity of the soil, joined to a very dry climate, renders the material a rival almost of stone-work in strength and endurance. Since the final occupation of this region by the forces of Telal, all these towers have, without exception, been rendered unfit for defence, and some are even half-ruined. Here again the phenomena of Europe have repeated themselves in Arabia.

"The houses are not unfrequently isolated each from the other by their gardens and plantations; and this is especially the case with the dwellings of chiefs and their families. What has just been said about the towers renders the reasons of this isolation sufficiently obvious. But the dwellings of the commoner sort are generally clustered together, though without symmetry or method.

"The gardens of the Djowf are much celebrated in this part of the East, and justly so. They are of a productiveness and variety superior to those of Djebel Shomer or of Upper Nedjed, and far beyond whatever the Hedjaz and its neighborhood can offer. Here, for the first time in our southward course, we found the date-palm a main object of cultivation; and if its produce be inferior to that of the same tree in Nedjed and Hasa, it is far, very far, above whatever Egypt, Africa, or the valley of the Tigris from Bagdad to Bassora can show. However, the palm is by no means alone here. The apricot and the peach, the fig-tree and the vine, abound throughout these orchards, and their fruit surpasses in copiousness and flavor that supplied by the gardens of Damascus or the hills of Syria and Palestine. In the intervals between the trees or in the fields beyond, corn, leguminous plants, gourds, melons, etc., etc., are widely cultivated. Here, too, for the last time, the traveller bound for the interior sees the irrigation indispensable to all growth and tillage in this droughty climate kept up by running streams of clear water, whereas in the Nedjed and its neighborhood it has to be laboriously procured from wells and cisterns.

"Besides the Djowf itself, or capital, there exist several other villages belonging to the same homonymous province, and all subject to the same central governor. Of these the largest is Sekakah; it lies at about twelve miles distant to the northeast, and though inferior to the principal town in importance and fertility of soil, almost equals it in the number of its inhabitants. I should reckon the united population of these two localities—men, women, and children—at about thirty-three or thirty-four thousand souls. This calculation, like many others before us in the course of the work, rests partly on an approximate survey of the number of dwellings, partly on the military muster, and partly on what I heard on the subject from the natives themselves. A census is here unknown, and no register records birth, marriage, or death. Yet, by aid of the war list, which generally represents about one-tenth of the entire population, a fair though not absolute idea may be obtained on this point.

"Lastly, around and at no great distance from these main centres, are several small villages or hamlets, eight or ten in number, as I was told, and containing each of them from twenty to fifty or sixty houses. But I had neither time nor opportunity to visit each separately. They cluster round lesser water springs, and offer in miniature features much resembling those of the capital. The entire population of the province cannot exceed forty or forty-two thousand, but it is a brave one, and very liberally provided with the physical endowments of which it has been acutely said that they are seldom despised save by those who do not themselves possess them. Tall, well-proportioned, of a tolerably fair complexion, set off by long curling locks of jet-black hair, with features for the most part regular and intelligent, and a dignified carriage, the Djowfites are eminently good specimens of what may be called the pure northern or Ishmaelitish Arab type, and in all these respects they yield the palm to the inhabitants of Djebel Shomer alone. Their large-developed forms and open countenance contrast strongly with the somewhat dwarfish stature and suspicious under-glance of the Bedouin. They are, besides, a very healthy people, and keep up their strength and activity even to an advanced age. It is no uncommon occurrence here, to see an old man of seventy set out full-armed among a band of youths; though, by the way, such "green old age" is often to be met with also in the central province farther south, as I have had frequent opportunity of witnessing. The climate, too, is good and dry, and habits of out-door life contribute not a little to the maintenance of health and vigor.

"In manners, as in locality, the worthies of Djowf occupy a sort of half-way position between Bedouins and the inhabitants of the cultivated districts. Thus they partake largely in the nomad's aversion to mechanical occupations, in his indifference to literary acquirements, in his aimless fickleness too, and even in his treacherous ways. I have said, in the preceding chapter, that while we were yet threading the narrow gorge near the first entrance of the valley, several horsemen appeared on the upper margin of the pass, and one of them questioned our guide, and then, after a short consultation with his companions, called out to us to go on and fear nothing. Now, the name of this individual was Suliman-ebn-Dahir, a very adventurous and fairly intelligent young fellow, with whom next-door neighborhood and frequent intercourse rendered us intimate during our stay at the Djowf. One day, while we were engaged in friendly conversation, he said, half laughing, 'Do you know what we were consulting about while you were in the pass below on the morning of your arrival? It was whether we should make you a good reception, and thus procure ourselves the advantage of having you residents among us, or whether we should not do better to kill you all three, and take our gain from the booty to be found in your baggage.' I replied with equal coolness, 'It might have proved an awkward affair for yourself and your friends, since Hamood your governor could hardly have failed to get wind of the matter, and would have taken it out of you.' 'Pooh!' replied our friend, 'never a bit; as if a present out of the plunder would not have tied Hamood's tongue.' 'Bedouins that you are,' said I, laughing. 'Of course we are,' answered

Suliman, 'for such we all were till quite lately, and the present system is too recent to have much changed us.' However, he admitted that they all had, on second thoughts, congratulated themselves on not having preferred bloodshed to hospitality, though perhaps the better resolution was rather owing to interested than to moral motives.

"The most distinctive good feature of the inhabitants of Djowf is their liberality. Nowhere else, even in Arabia, is the guest, so at least he be not murdered before admittance, better treated, or more cordially invited to become in every way one of themselves. Courage, too, no one denies them, and they are equally lavish of their own lives and property as of their neighbors'.

"Let us now resume the narrative. On the morning after our arrival—it was now the 1st of July—Ghafil caused a small house in the neighborhood, belonging to one of his dependents, to be put at our entire disposal, according to our previous request. This, our new abode, consisted of a small court with two rooms, one on each side, for warehouse and habitation, the whole being surrounded with an outer wall, whose door was closed by lock and bolt. Of a kitchen-room there was small need, so constant and hospitable are the invitations of the good folks here to strangers; and if our house was not over capacious, it afforded at least what we most desired, namely, seclusion and privacy at will; it was, moreover, at our host's cost, rent and reparations.

"Hither, accordingly, we transferred baggage and chattels, and arranged everything as comfortably as we best could. And as we had already concluded, from the style and conversation of those around us, that their state of society was hardly far enough advanced to offer a sufficiently good prospect for medical art, whose exercise, to be generally advantageous, requires a certain amount of culture and aptitude in the patient, no less than of skill in the physician, we resolved to make commerce our main affair here, trusting that by so doing we should gain a second advantage, that of lightening our more bulky goods, such as coffee and cloth, whose transport had already annoyed us not a little.

"But in fact we were not more desirous to sell than the men, women, and children of the Djowf were to buy. From the very outset our little courtyard was crowded with customers, and the most amusing scenes of Arab haggling, in all its mixed shrewdness and simplicity, diverted us through the week. Handkerchief after handkerchief, yard after yard of cloth, beads for the women, knives, combs, looking-glasses, and what not? (for our stock was a thorough miscellany) were soon sold off, some for ready money, others on credit; and it is but justice to say that all debts so contracted were soon paid in very honestly; Oxford High Street tradesmen, at least in former times, were not always equally fortunate.

"Meanwhile we had the very best opportunity of becoming acquainted with and appreciating all classes, nay, almost all individuals, of the place. Peasants, too, from various hamlets arrived, led by rumor, whose trumpet, prone to exaggerate under every sky, had proclaimed us throughout the valley of Djowf for much more important characters, and possessed of a much larger stock in hand, than was really the case. All crowded in, and before long there were more customers than wares assembled in the store-room.

"Our manner of passing the time was as follows: We used to rise at early dawn, lock up the house, and go out in the pure cool air of the morning to some quiet spot among the neighboring palm-groves, or scale the wall of some garden, or pass right on through the by-lanes to where cultivation merges in the adjoining sands of the valley; in short, to any convenient place where we might hope to pass an hour of quiet, undisturbed by Arab sociability, and have leisure to plan our work for the day. We would then return home about sunrise, and find outside the door some tall lad sent by his father, generally one of the wealthier and more influential inhabitants of the quarter yet unvisited by us, waiting our return, to invite us to an early breakfast. We would now accompany our Mercury to his domicile, where a hearty reception, and some neighbors collected for the occasion, or attracted by a cup of good coffee, were sure to be in attendance. Here an hour or so would wear away, and some medical or mercantile transaction be sketched out. We, of course, would bring the conversation, whenever it was possible, on local topics, according as those present seemed likely to afford us exact knowledge and insight into the real state and circumstances of the land. We would then return to our own quarters, where a crowd of customers, awaiting us, would allow us neither rest nor pause till noon. Then a short interval for date or pumpkin eating in some neighbor's house would occur, and after that business be again resumed for three or four hours. A walk among the gardens, rarely alone, more often in company with friends and acquaintances, would follow; and meanwhile an invitation to supper somewhere had unfailingly been given and accepted."

"After supper all rise, wash their hands, and then go out into the open air to sit and smoke a quiet pipe under the still transparent sky of the summer evening. Neither mist nor vapor, much less a cloud, appears; the moon dips down in silvery whiteness to the very verge of the palm-tree tops, and the last rays of daylight are almost as sharp and clear as the dawn itself. Chat and society continue for an hour or two, and then everyone goes home, most to sleep, I fancy, for few Penseroso lamps are here to be seen at midnight hour, nor does the spirit of Plato stand much risk of unsphering from the nocturnal studies of the Djowf; we, to write our journal, or to compare observations and estimate characters.

"Sometimes a comfortable landed proprietor would invite us to pass an extemporary holiday morning in his garden, or rather orchard, there to eat grapes and enjoy ourselves at will, seated under clustering vine-trellises, with palm-trees above and running streams around. How pleasant it was after the desert! At other times visits of patients, prescriptions, and similar duties would take up a part of the day; or some young fellow, particularly desirous of information about Syria or Egypt, or perhaps curious after history and moral science, would hold us for a couple of hours in serious and sensible talk, at any rate to our advantage."

It was necessary that the travellers should not delay in paying their official visit to Hamood, the vicegerent of Telal. His residence is in the centre of the garden region, near a solitary round tower, whose massive stone walls are mentioned in Arabian poetry. Hamood's residence is an irregular structure, of more recent date, with no distinguishing feature except a tower about fifty feet in height. Palgrave and his companion were accompanied by a large number of their newly-found friends. After passing through an outer court, filled with armed guards, they found the ruler seated in his large reception-hall:

"There, in the place of distinction, which he never yields to any individual of Djowf, whatever be his birth or wealth, appeared the governor, a strong, broad-shouldered, dark-browed, dark-eyed man, clad in the long white shirt of the country, and over it a handsome black cloak, embroidered with crimson silk; on his august head a silken handkerchief or *keffee'yeh*, girt by a white band of finely woven camel's hair; and in his fingers a grass fan. He rose graciously on our approach, extended to us the palm of his hand, and made us sit down near his side, keeping, however, Ghafil, as an old acquaintance, between himself and us, perhaps as a precautionary arrangement against any sudden assault or treasonable intention on our part, for an Arab, be he who he may, is never off his guard when new faces are in presence. In other respects he showed us much courtesy and good-will, made many civil inquiries about our health after so fatiguing a journey, praised Damascus and the Damascenes, by way of an indirect compliment, and offered us a lodging in the castle. But here Ghafil availed himself of the privileges conceded by Arab custom to priority of hostship to put in his negative on our behalf; nor were we anxious to press the matter. A pound or so of our choicest coffee, with which we on this occasion presented his excellency, both as a mute witness to the object of our journey, and the better to secure his good-will, was accepted very readily by the great man, who in due return offered us his best services. We replied that we stood in need of nothing save his long life, this being the Arab formula for rejoinder to such fair speeches; and, next in order, of means to get safe on to Ha'yel so soon as our business at the Djowf should permit, being desirous to establish ourselves under the immediate patronage of Telal. In this he promised to aid us, and kept his word."

Hamood afterward politely returned their visit, and they frequently went to his castle for the purpose of studying the many interesting scenes presented by the exercise of the very primitive Arab system of justice. Palgrave gives the following case as a specimen:

"One day my comrade and myself were on a visit of mere politeness at the castle; the customary ceremonies had been gone through, and business, at first interrupted by our entrance, had resumed its course. A Bedouin of the Ma'az tribe was pleading his cause before Hamood, and accusing someone of having forcibly taken away his camel. The governor was seated with an air of intense gravity in his corner, half leaning on a cushion, while the Bedouin, cross-legged on the ground before him, and within six feet of his person, flourished in his hand a large reaping-hook, identically that which is here used for cutting grass. Energetically gesticulating with this graceful implement, he thus challenged his judge's attention: 'You, Hamood, do you hear?' (stretching out at the same time the hook toward the governor, so as almost to reach his body, as though he meant to rip him open); 'he has taken from me my camel; have you called God to mind?' (again putting his weapon close to the unflinching magistrate). 'The camel is my camel; do you hear?' (with another reminder from the reaping-hook); 'he is mine, by God's award, and yours too; do you hear, child?' and so on, while Hamood sat without moving a muscle of face or limb, imperturbable and impassible till some one of the counsellors quieted the plaintiff with 'Remember God, child; it is of no consequence, you shall not be wronged.' Then the judge called on the witnesses, men of the Djowf, to say their say, and on their confirmation of the Bedouin's statement, gave orders to two of his satellites to search for and bring before him the accused party; while he added to the Ma'azee, 'All right, daddy, you shall have your own; put your confidence in God,' and composedly motioned him back to his place.

"A fortnight and more went by, and found us still in the Djowf, 'honored guests' in Arab phrase, and well rested from the bygone fatigues of the desert. Ghafil's dwelling was still, so to speak, our official home; but there were two other houses where we were still more at our ease; that of Dafee, the same who along with Ghafil came to meet us on our first arrival; and that of Salim, a respectable and, in his way, a literary old man, our near neighbor, and surrounded by a large family of fine strapping youths, all of them brought up more or less in the fear of Allah and in good example. Hither we used to retire when wearied of Ghafil and his like, and pass a quiet hour in their k'hawah, reciting or hearing Arab poety, talking over the condition of the country and its future prospects, discussing points of morality, or commenting on the ways and fashions of the day."

The important question for the travellers was how they should get to Djebel Shomer, the great fertile oasis to the south, under the rule of the famous Prince Telal. The terrible *Nefood*, or sand-passes, which the Arabs themselves look upon with dread, must be crossed, and it was now the middle of summer. The hospitable people of the Djowf begged Palgrave and his friends to remain until September, and they probably would have been delayed for some time but for a lucky chance. The Azzam tribe of Bedouins, which had been attacked by Prince Telal, submitted, and a dozen of their chiefs arrived at the Djowf, on their way to Djebel Shomer, where they purposed to win Telal's good graces by tendering him their allegiance in his very capital. Hamood received them and lodged them for several days, while they rested from their past fatigues, and prepared themselves for what yet lay before them. Some inhabitants of the Djowf, whose business required their presence at Ha'yel, were to join the party. "Hamood sent for us," Palgrave continues, "and gave us notice of this expedition, and on our declaring that we desired to profit by it, he handed us a scrap of paper, addressed to Telal himself, wherein he certified that we had duly paid the entrance fee exacted from strangers on their coming within the limits of Shomer rule, and that we were indeed respectable individuals, worthy of all good treatment. We then, in presence of Hamood, struck our bargain with one of the band for a couple of camels, whose price, including all the services of their master as guide and companion for ten days of July travelling, was not extravagant either; it came up to just a hundred and ten piastres, equivalent to eighteen or nineteen shillings of English money.

"Many delays occurred, and it was not till the 18th of July, when the figs were fully ripe—a circumstance which furnished the natives of Djowf with new cause of wonder at our rushing away, in lieu of waiting like rational beings to enjoy the good things of the land—that we received our final 'Son of Hodeirah, depart.' This was intimated to us, not by a locust, but by a creature almost as queer, namely, our new conductor, a half-cracked Arab, neither peasant nor Bedouin, but something anomalous between the two, hight Djedey', and a native of the outskirts of Djebel Shomer, who darkened our door in the forenoon, and warned us to make our final packing up, and get ready for starting the same day.

"When once clear of the houses and gardens, Djedey' led us by a road skirting the southern side of the valley, till we arrived, before sunset, at the other, or eastern, extremity of the town. Here was the rendezvous agreed on by our companions; but they did not appear, and reason good, for they had right to a supper more under Hamood's roof, and were loath to lose it. So we halted and alighted alone. The chief of this quarter, which is above two miles distant from the castle, invited us to supper, and thence we returned to our baggage, there to sleep. To pass a summer's night in the open air on a soft sand bed implies no great privation in these countries, nor is anyone looked on as a hero for so doing.

"Early next morning, while Venus yet shone like a drop of melted silver on the slaty blue, three of our party arrived and announced that the rest of our companions would soon come up. Encouraged by the news, we determined to march on without further tarrying, and ere sunrise we climbed the steep ascent of the southerly bank, whence we had a magnificent view of the whole length of the Djowf, its castle and towers, and groves and gardens, in the ruddy light of morning, and beyond the drear northern deserts stretching far away. We then dipped down the other side of the bordering hill, not again to see the Djowf till—who knows when?"

CHAPTER X.

PALGRAVE'S TRAVELS—CROSSING THE NEFOOD

"OUR way was now to the southeast, across a large plain varied with sand-mounds and covered with the ghada-bush, already described, so that our camels were much more inclined to crop pasture than to do their business in journeying ahead. About noon we halted near a large tuft of this shrub, at least ten feet high. We constructed a sort of cabin with boughs broken off the neighboring plants and suitably arranged shedwise, and thus passed the noon hours of intolerable heat till the whole band came in sight.

"They were barbarous, nay, almost savage, fellows, like most Sherarat, whether chiefs or people; but they had been somewhat awed by the grandeurs of Hamood, and yet more so by the prospect of coming so soon before the terrible majesty of Telal himself. All were duly armed, and had put on their best suits of apparel, an equipment worthy of a scarecrow or of an Irishman at a wake. Tattered red overalls; cloaks with more patches than original substance, or, worse yet, which opened large mouths to cry for patching, but had not got it; little broken tobacco pipes, and no trousers soever (by the way, all genuine Arabs are *sans-culottes*); faces meagre with habitual hunger, and black with dirt and weather stains—such were the high-born chiefs of Azzam, on their way to the king's levee. Along with them were two Bedouins of the Shomer tribe, a degree better in guise and person than the Sherarat; and lastly, three men of Djowf, who looked almost like gentlemen among such ragamuffins. As to my comrade and myself, I trust that the reader will charitably suppose us the exquisites of the party. So we rode on together.

"Next morning, a little after sunrise, we arrived at a white calcareous valley, girt round with low hills of marl and sand. Here was the famous Be'er Shekeek, or 'well of Shekeek,' whence we were to fill our water-skins, and that thoroughly, since no other source lay before us for four days' march amid the sand passes, up to the very verge of Djebel Shomer.

"Daughters of the Great Desert, to use an Arab phrase, the 'Nefood,' or sand-passes, bear but too strong a family resemblance to their unamiable mother. What has been said elsewhere about their origin, their extent, their bearings, and their connection with the Dhana, or main sand-waste of the south, may exempt me from here entering on a minute enarration of all their geographical details; let it suffice for the present that they are offshoots—inlets, one might not unsuitably call them—of the great ocean of sand that covers about one-third of the peninsula, into whose central and comparatively fertile plateau they make deep inroads, nay, in some places almost intersect it. Their general character, of which

CAPTAIN BURTON AS A PILGRIM.

the following pages will, I trust, give a tolerably correct idea, is also that of Dahna, or 'red desert,' itself. The Arabs, always prone to localize rather than generalize, count these sand-streams by scores, but they may all be referred to four principal courses, and he who would traverse the centre must necessarily cross two of them, perhaps even three, as we did.

"The general type of Arabia is that of a central table-land, surrounded by a desert ring, sandy to the south, west, and east, and stony to the north. This outlying circle is in its turn girt by a line of mountains, low and sterile for the most, but attaining in Yemen and Oman considerable height, breadth, and fertility, while beyond these a narrow rim of coast is bordered by the sea. The surface of the midmost table-land equals somewhat less than one-half of the entire peninsula, and its special demarcations are much affected, nay, often absolutely fixed, by the windings and in-runnings of the Nefood. If to these central highlands, or Nedjed, taking that word in its wider sense, we add the Djowf, the Ta'yif, Djebel 'Aaseer, Yemen, Oman, and Hasa, in short, whatever spots of fertility belong to the outer circles, we shall find that Arabia contains about two-thirds of cultivated, or at least of cultivable, land, with a remaining third of irreclaimable desert, chiefly to the south. In most other directions the great blank spaces often left in maps of this country are quite as frequently indications of non-information as of real non-inhabitation. However, we have just now a strip, though fortunately only a strip, of pure, unmitigated desert before us, after which better lands await us; and in this hope let us take courage and boldly enter the Nefood.

"Much had we heard of them from Bedouins and countrymen, so that we had made up our minds to something very terrible and very impracticable. But the reality, especially in these dog days, proved worse than aught heard or imagined.

"We were now traversing an immense ocean of loose reddish sand, unlimited to the eye, and heaped up in enormous ridges, running parallel to each other from north to south, undulation after undulation, each swell two or three hundred feet in average height, with slant sides and rounded crests furrowed in every direction by the capricious gales of the desert. In the depths between the traveller finds himself as it were imprisoned in a suffocating sand-pit, hemmed in by burning walls on every side; while at other times, while laboring up the slope, he overlooks what seems a vast sea of fire, swelling under a heavy monsoon wind, and ruffled by a cross blast into little red-hot waves."

Palgrave devotes several pages to his journey across the Nefood, bearing out in his general description its character, as above.

Lady Anne Blunt, who with her husband and native followers crossed the Nefood sixteen years later, however, takes issue with Mr. Palgrave as to its character, as will be found in Chapter XVII., largely devoted to her travels in Arabia.

Arriving at the eastern edge of the Nefood Palgrave continues:

"The morning broke on us still toiling amid the

sands. By daylight we saw our straggling companions like black specks here and there, one far ahead on a yet vigorous dromedary, another in the rear dismounted, and urging his fallen beast to rise by plunging a knife a good inch deep into its haunches, a third lagging in the extreme distance. Everyone for himself and God for us all!—so we quickened our pace, looking anxiously before us for the hills of Djobbah, which could not now be distant. At noon we came in sight of them all at once, close on our right, wild and fantastic cliffs, rising sheer on the margin of the sand sea. We coasted them awhile, till at a turn the whole plain of Djobbah and its landscape opened on our view.

"Here we had before us a cluster of black granite rock, streaked with red, and about seven hundred feet, at a rough guess, in height; beyond them a large barren plain, partly white and encrusted with salt, partly green with tillage, and studded with palmgroves, amongst which we could discern, not far off, the village of Djobbah, much resembling that of Djowf in arrangement and general appearance, only smaller, and without castle or tower. Beyond the valley glistened a second line of sand-hills, but less wild and desolate-looking than those behind us, and far in the distance the main range of Djebel Shomer, a long purple sierra of most picturesque outline. Had we there and then mounted, as we afterward did, the heights on our right, we should have also seen in the extreme southwest a green patch near the horizon, where cluster the palm plantations of Teymah, a place famed in Arab history, and by some supposed identical with the Teman of Holy Writ.

"But for the moment a drop of fresh water and a shelter from the July sun was much more in our thoughts than all the Teymahs or Temans that ever existed. My camel, too, was—not at the end of his wits, for he never had any—but of his legs, and hardly capable of advance, while I was myself too tired to urge him on vigorously, and we took a fair hour to cross a narrow white strip of mingled salt and sand that yet intervened between us and the village.

"Without its garden walls was pitched the very identical tent of our noble guide, and here his wife and family were anxiously awaiting their lord. Djedey' invited us—indeed he could not conformably with Shomer customs do less—to partake of his board and lodging, and we had no better course than to accept of both. So we let our camels fling themselves out like dead or dying alongside of the tabernacle, and entered to drink water mixed with sour milk." Here the caravan rested for a day.

"About sunrise on the 25th of July we left Djobbah, crossed the valley to the southeast, and entered once more on a sandy desert, but a desert, as I have before hinted, of a milder and less inhospitable character than the dreary Nefood of two days back. Here the sand is thickly sprinkled with shrubs and not altogether devoid of herbs and grass; while the undulations of the surface, running invariably from north to south, according to the general rule of that phenomenon, are much less deeply traced, though never wholly absent. We paced on all day; at nightfall we found ourselves on the edge of a vast funnel-like depression, where the sand recedes on all sides to leave bare the chalky bottom-strata below; here lights glimmering amid Bedouin tents in the depths of the valley invited us to try our chance of a preliminary supper before the repose of the night. We had, however, much ado to descend the cavity, so steep was the sandy slope; while its circular form and spiral marking reminded me of Edgar Poe's imaginative 'Maelstrom.' The Arabs to whom the watch-fires belonged were shepherds of the numerous Shomer tribe, whence the district, plain and mountain, takes its name. They welcomed us to a share of their supper; and a good dish of rice, instead of insipid samh or pasty, augured a certain approach to civilization.

"At break of day we resumed our march, and met with camels and camel-drivers in abundance, besides a few sheep and goats. Before noon we had got clear of the sandy patch, and entered in its stead on a firm gravelly soil. Here we enjoyed an hour of midday halt and shade in a natural cavern, hollowed out in a high granite rock, itself an advanced guard of the main body of Djebel Shomer. This mountain range now rose before us, wholly unlike any other that I had ever seen; a huge mass of crag and stone, piled up in fantastic disorder, with green valleys and habitations intervening. The sun had not yet set when we reached the pretty village of Kenah, amid groves and waters—no more, however, running streams like those of Djowf, but an artificial irrigation by means of wells and buckets. At some distance from the houses stood a cluster of three or four large overshadowing trees, objects of peasant veneration here, as once in Palestine. The welcome of the inhabitants, when we dismounted at their doors, was hearty and hospitable, nay, even polite and considerate; and a good meal, with a dish of fresh grapes for dessert, was soon set before us in the veranda of a pleasant little house, much reminding me of an English farm-cottage, whither the good man of the dwelling had invited us for the evening. All expressed great desire to profit by our medical skill; and on our reply that we could not conveniently open shop except at the capital, Ha'yel, several announced their resolution to visit us there; and subsequently kept their word, though at the cost of about twenty-four miles of journey.

"We rose very early. Our path, well tracked and trodden, now lay between ridges of precipitous rock, rising abruptly from a level and grassy plain; sometimes the road was sunk in deep gorges, sometimes it opened out on wider spaces, where trees and villages appeared, while the number of wayfarers, on foot or mounted, single or in bands, still increased as we drew nearer to the capital. There was an air of newness and security about the dwellings and plantations hardly to be found nowadays in any other part of Arabia, Oman alone excepted. I may add also the great frequency of young trees and ground newly enclosed, a cheerful sight, yet further enhanced by the total absence of ruins, so common in the East; hence the general effect produced by Djebel Shomer, when contrasted with most other provinces or kingdoms around, near and far, is that of a newly coined piece, in all its sharpness and shine, amid a dingy heap of defaced currency. It is a fresh creation, and shows what Arabia might be under better rule than it enjoys for the most part: an inference rendered the more conclusive by the fact that in natural and unaided fertility Djebel Shomer is perhaps the least favored district in the entire central peninsula.

"We were here close under the backbone of Djebel Shomer, whose reddish crags rose in the strangest forms on our right and left, while a narrow cleft down to the plain-level below gave opening to the capital. Very hard to bring an army through this against the will of the inhabitants thought I; fifty resolute men could, in fact, hold the pass against thousands; nor is there any other approach to Ha'yel from the northern direction. The town is situated near the very centre of the mountains; it was as yet entirely concealed from our view by the windings of the road amid huge piles of rock. Meanwhile from Djobbah to Ha'yel the whole plain gradually rises, running up between the sierras, whose course from northeast to southwest crosses two-thirds of the upper peninsula, and forms the outwork of the central high country. Hence the name of Nedjed, literally 'highland,' in contradistinction to the coast and the outlying provinces of lesser elevation.

"The sun was yet two hours' distance above the western horizon, when we threaded the narrow and winding defile, till we arrived at its farther end.

Here we found ourselves on the verge of a large plain, many miles in length and breadth, and girt on every side by a high mountain rampart, while right in front of us, at scarce a quarter of an hour's march, lay the town of Ha'yel, surrounded by fortifications of about twenty feet in height, with bastion towers, some round, some square, and large folding gates at intervals; it offered the same show of freshness, and even of something like irregular elegance, that had before struck us in the villages on our way. This, however, was a full-grown town, and its area might readily hold three hundred thousand inhabitants or more, were its streets and houses close packed like those of Brussels or Paris. But the number of citizens does not, in fact, exceed twenty or twenty-two thousand, thanks to the many large gardens, open spaces, and even plantations, included within the outer walls, while the immense palace of the monarch alone, with its pleasure-grounds annexed, occupies about one-tenth of the entire city. Our attention was attracted by a lofty tower, some seventy feet in height, of recent construction and oval form, belonging to the royal residence. The plain all around the town is studded with isolated houses and gardens, the property of wealthy citizens, or of members of the kingly family, and on the far-off skirts of the plain appear the groves belonging to Kafar, 'Adwah, and other villages, placed at the openings of the mountain gorges that conduct to the capital. The town walls and buildings shone yellow in the evening sun, and the whole prospect was one of thriving security, delightful to view, though wanting in the peculiar luxuriance of vegetation offered by the valley of Djowf. A few Bedouin tents lay clustered close by the ramparts, and the great number of horsemen, footmen, camels, asses, peasants, townsmen, boys, women, and other like, all passing to and fro on their various avocations, gave cheerfulness and animation to the scene.

"We crossed the plain and made for the town gate, opposite the castle; next, with no little difficulty, prevailed on our camels to pace the high-walled street, and at last arrived at the open space in front of the palace. It was yet an hour before sunset, or rather more; the business of the day was over in Ha'yel, and the outer courtyard where we now stood was crowded with loiterers of all shapes and sizes. We made our camels kneel down close by the palace gate, alongside of some forty or fifty others, and then stepped back to repose our very weary limbs on a stone bench opposite the portal, and awaited what might next occur."

CHAPTER XI.

PALGRAVE'S TRAVELS—LIFE IN HA'YEL

"AT our first appearance a slight stir takes place. The customary salutations are given and returned by those nearest at hand; and a small knot of inquisitive idlers, come up to see what and whence we are, soon thickens into a dense circle. Many questions are asked, first of our conductor, Djedey, and next of ourselves; our answers are tolerably laconic. Meanwhile a thin, middle-sized individual, whose countenance bears the type of smiling urbanity and precise etiquette, befitting his office at court, approaches us. His neat and simple dress, the long silver-circled staff in his hand, his respectful salutation, his politely important manner, all denote him one of the palace retinue. It is Seyf, the court chamberlain, whose special duty is the reception and presentation of strangers. We rise to receive him, and are greeted with a decorous 'Peace be with you, brothers,' in the fulness of every inflection and accent that the most scrupulous grammarian could desire. We return an equally Priscianic salutation. 'Whence have you come?' is the first question. 'May good attend you!' Of course we declare ourselves physicians from Syria, for our bulkier wares had been disposed of in the Djowf, and we were now resolved to depend on medical practice alone. 'And what do you desire here in our town? may God grant you success!' says Seyf. 'We desire the favor of God most high, and, secondly, that of Telal,' is our answer, conforming our style to the correctest formulas of the country, which we had already begun to pick up. Whereupon Seyf, looking very sweet the while, begins, as in duty bound, a little encomium on his master's generosity and other excellent qualities, and assures us that we have exactly reached right quarters.

"But alas! while my comrade and myself were exchanging side-glances of mutual felicitation at such fair beginnings, Nemesis suddenly awoke to claim her due, and the serenity of our horizon was at once overcast by an unexpected and most unwelcome cloud. My readers are doubtless already aware that nothing was of higher importance for us than the most absolute incognito, above all in whatever regarded European origin and character. In fact, once known for Europeans, all intimate access and sincerity of intercourse with the people of the land would have been irretrievably lost, and our onward progress to Nedjed rendered totally impossible. These were the very least inconveniences that could follow such a detection; others much more disagreeable might also be well apprehended. Now thus far nothing had occurred capable of exciting serious suspicion; no one had recognized us, or pretended to recognize. We, too, on our part, had thought that Gaza, Ma'an, and perhaps the Djowf, were the only localities

where this kind of recognition had to be feared. But
we had reckoned without our host; the first real danger was reserved for Ha'yel, within the very limits
of Nedjed, and with all the desert-belt between us
and our old acquaintances.

"For while Seyf was running through the preliminaries of his politeness, I saw to my horror, amid
the circle of bystanders, a figure, a face well known
to me scarce six months before in Damascus, and
well known to many others also, now merchant, now
trader, now post-contractor, shrewd, enterprising, and
active, though nigh fifty years of age, and intimate
with many Europeans of considerable standing in
Syria and Bagdad—one, in short, accustomed to all
kinds of men, and not to be easily imposed on by
any.

"While I involuntarily stared dismay on my
friend, and yet doubted if it could possibly be he, all
incertitude was dispelled by his cheerful salutation,
in the confidential tone of an old acquaintance, followed by wondering inquiries as to what wind had
blown me hither, and what I meant to do here in
Ha'yel.

"Wishing him most heartily somewhere else, I
had nothing for it but to 'fix a vacant stare,' to give
a formal return of greeting, and then silence.

"But misfortunes never come single. While I
was thus on my defensive against so dangerous an
antagonist in the person of my free-and-easy friend,
lo! a tall, sinister-featured individual comes up,
clad in the dress of an inhabitant of Kaseem, and
abruptly breaks in with, 'And I too have seen him

at Damascus,' naming at the same time the place and date of the meeting, and specifying exactly the circumstances most calculated to set me down for a genuine European.

"Had he really met me as he said? I cannot precisely say; the place he mentioned was one whither men, half-spies, half-travellers, and whole intriguers from the interior districts, nay, even from Nedjed itself, not unfrequently resort; and, as I myself was conscious of having paid more than one visit there, my officious interlocutor might very possibly have been one of those present on some such occasion. So that although I did not now recognize him in particular, there was a strong intrinsic probability in favor of his ill-timed veracity; and his thus coming in to support the first witness in his assertions rendered my predicament, already unsafe, yet worse.

"But ere I could frame an answer or resolve what course to hold, up came a third, who, by overshooting the mark, put the game into our hands. He too salaams me as an old friend, and then, turning to those around, now worked up to a most extraordinary pitch of amazed curiosity, says, 'And I also know him perfectly well; I have often met him at Cairo, where he lives in great wealth in a large house near the Kasr-el-'Eynee; his name is 'Abd-es-Saleeb; he is married, and has a very beautiful daughter, who rides an expensive horse,' etc.

"Here at last was a pure invention or mistake (for I know not which it was) that admitted of a flat denial. 'Aslahek Allah,' 'May Heaven set you right,' said I; 'never did I live at Cairo, nor have I the blessing of any horse-riding young ladies for daughters.' Then, looking very hard at my second detector, toward whom I had all the right of doubt, 'I do not remember having ever seen you; think well as to what you say; many a man besides myself has a reddish beard and straw-colored mustaches,' taking pains, however, not to seem particularly 'careful to answer him in this matter,' but as if merely questioning the precise identity. But for the first of the trio I knew not what to do or to reply, so I continued to look at him with a killing air of inquisitive stupidity, as though not fully understanding his meaning.

"But Seyf, though himself at first somewhat staggered by this sudden downpour of recognition, was now reassured by the discomfiture of the third witness, and came to the convenient conclusion that the two others were no better worthy of credit. 'Never mind them,' exclaimed he, addressing himself to us, 'they are talkative liars, mere gossipers; let them alone, they do not deserve attention; come along with me to the k'hawah in the palace, and rest yourselves.' Then turning to my poor Damascene friend, whose only wrong was to have been overmuch in the right, he sharply chid him, and next the rest, and led us off, most glad to follow the leader, through the narrow and dark portal into the royal residence.

"Here we remained whilst coffee was, as wont, prepared and served. Seyf, who had left us awhile, now came back to say that Telal would soon return from his afternoon walk in a garden where he had been taking the air, and that if we would pass into the outer court we should then and there have the opportunity of paying him our introductory respects. He added that we should afterward find our supper ready, and be provided also with good lodgings for the night; finally, that the k'hawah and what it contained were always at our disposition so long as we should honor Ha'yel by our presence.

"We rose accordingly and returned with Seyf to the outside area. It was fuller than ever, on account of the expected appearance of the monarch. A few minutes later we saw a crowd approach from the upper extremity of the place, namely, that toward the market. When the new-comers drew near, we saw them to be almost exclusively armed men, with some of the more important-looking citizens, but all on foot. In the midst of this circle, though detached from those around them, slowly advanced three personages, whose dress and deportment, together with the respectful distance observed by the rest, announced superior rank. 'Here comes Telal,' said Seyf, in an undertone.

"The midmost figure was in fact that of the prince himself. Short of stature, broad-shouldered, and strongly built, of a very dusky complexion, with long black hair, dark and piercing eyes, and a countenance rather severe than open, Telal might readily be supposed above forty years in age, though he is in fact thirty-seven or thirty-eight at most. His step was measured, his demeanor grave and somewhat haughty. His dress, a long robe of cashmere shawl, covered the white Arab shirt, and over all he wore a delicately worked cloak of camel's-hair from Oman, a great rarity, and highly valued in this part of Arabia. His head was adorned by a broidered handkerchief, in which silk and gold thread had not been spared, and girt by a broad band of camel's-hair entwined with red silk, the manufacture of Meshid 'Alee. A gold-mounted sword hung by his side, and his dress was perfumed with musk, in a degree better adapted to Arab than to European nostrils. His glance never rested for a moment; sometimes it turned on his nearer companions, sometimes on the crowd; I have seldom seen so truly an 'eagle eye,' in rapidity and in brilliancy.

"By his side walked a tall, thin individual, clad in garments of somewhat less costly material, but of gayer colors and embroidery than those of the king himself. His face announced unusual intelligence and courtly politeness; his sword was not, however, adorned with gold, the exclusive privilege of the royal family, but with silver only.

This was Zamil, the treasurer and prime minister —sole minister, indeed, of the autocrat. Raised from beggary by Abdallah, the late king, who had seen in the ragged orphan signs of rare capacity, he continued to merit the uninterrupted favor of his patron, and after his death had become equally, or yet more, dear to Telal, who raised him from post to post, till he at last occupied the highest position in the kingdom after the monarch himself. Of the demurely smiling Abd-el-Mahsin, the second companion of the king's evening walk, I will say nothing for the moment; we shall have him before long for a very intimate acquaintance and a steady friend.

"Everyone stood up as Telal drew nigh. Seyf gave us a sign to follow him, made way through the crowd, and saluted his sovereign with the authorized formula of 'Peace be with you, O the Protected of God!' Telal at once cast on us a penetrating glance, and addressed a question in a low voice to Seyf, whose answer was in the same tone. The prince then looked again toward us, but with a friendlier expression of face. We approached and touched his open hand, repeating the same salutation as that used by Seyf. No bow, hand-kissing, or other ceremony is customary on these occasions. Telal returned our greeting, and then, without a word more to us, whispered a moment to Seyf, and passed on through the palace gate.

"'He will give you a private audience to-morrow,' said Seyf, 'and I will take care that you have notice of it in due time; meanwhile come to supper.' The sun had already set when we re-entered the palace. This time, after passing the arsenal, we turned aside into a large square court, distinct from the former, and surrounded by an open veranda, spread with mats. Two large ostriches, presents offered to Telal by some chiefs of the Solibah tribe, strutted about the enclosure, and afforded much amusement to the negro boys and scullions of the establishment. Seyf conducted us to the further side of the court, where we seated ourselves under the portico.

"Hither some black slaves immediately brought the supper; the 'pièce de résistance' was, as usual, a huge dish of rice and boiled meat, with some thin cakes of unleavened bread and dates, and small onions with chopped gourds intermixed. The cookery was better than what we had heretofore tasted, though it would, perhaps, have hardly passed muster with a Vatel. We made a hearty meal, took coffee in the k'hawah, and then returned to sit awhile and smoke our pipes in the open air. Needs not say how lovely are the summer evenings, how cool the breeze, how pure the sky, in these mountainous districts."

Palgrave gives a historical sketch of the rise of Prince Telal to a position of power and importance in Central Arabia, scarcely secondary to that of the Wahabee ruler of Nedjed. The region of Djebel Shomer was subjected to the Wahabee rule during the last century, and the severe discipline of the new creed was forced upon its inhabitants. But, after the taking of Derreyeh by Ibrahim Pasha, the people regained a partial independence, and a rivalry for the chieftainship ensued between the two noble houses of Djaaper and Beyt Alee. The leader of the former was a young man named Abdallah, of more than ordinary character and intelligence, wealthy and popular. But he was defeated in the struggle, and about the year 1820 was driven into exile.

With a small band of followers he reached the Wady Sirhan (traversed by Palgrave on his way to the Djowf), where they were attacked by the Aneyzeh Bedouins, all the rest slain, and Abdallah left for dead on the sands. The Arab story is that the locusts came around them, scattered the sand with their wings and feet upon his wounds and thus stopped the flow of blood, while a flock of partridges hung above him to screen him from the burning sun. A merchant of Damascus, passing by with his caravan, beheld the miracle, took the youth, bound up his wounds, and restored him to health by the most tender care. When he had recovered his vigor in Damascus, the generous merchant sent him back to Arabia.

He went first to the Nedjed, entered the service of the Wahabee chief, rose to high military rank, and finally, by his own personal bravery, secured the sovereignty to Feysul, the present (1863) ruler. The latter then gave him an army to recover his heritage of Djebel Shomer, and about the year 1830 his sway was secured in his native country. The rival clan of Beyt Alee was extirpated, only one child being left, whom Telal afterward, with a rare but politic generosity, restored to wealth and honors.

Abdallah took every means to strengthen his power. He found it necessary, through his dependence on Feysul, to establish the Wahabee creed; he used the Bedouins as allies, in order to repress the rivalry of the nobles, and thus gained power at the expense of popularity. Many plots were formed against him, many attempts made to assassinate him, but they all failed: his lucky star attended him throughout. Up to this time he had dwelt in a quarter of the capital which the old chieftains and the nobility had mainly chosen for their domicile, and where the new monarch was surrounded by men his equals in birth and of even more ancient title to command. But now he added a new quarter to the town, and there laid the foundations of a vast palace destined for the future abode of the king and the display of all his grandeur, amid streets and nobles of his own creation. The walls of the projected edifice were fast rising when he died, almost suddenly, in 1844 or 1845, leaving three sons—Telal, Meta'ab, and Mohammed—the eldest scarce twenty years of age, besides his only surviving brother Obeyd, who could not then have been much under fifty.

"Telal was already highly popular," says Palgrave, "much more so than his father, and had given early tokens of those superior qualities which accompanied him to the throne. All parties united to proclaim him sole heir to the kingdom and lawful successor to the regal power, and thus the rival pretensions of Obeyd, hated by many and feared by all, were smothered at the outset and put aside without a contest.

"The young sovereign possessed, in fact, all that Arab ideas require to insure good government and lasting popularity. Affable toward the common people, reserved and haughty with the aristocracy, courageous and skilful in war, a lover of commerce and building in time of peace, liberal even to profusion, yet always careful to maintain and augment the state revenue, neither over-strict nor yet scandalously lax in religion, secret in his designs, but never known to break a promise once given, or violate a plighted faith; severe in administration, yet averse to bloodshed, he offered the very type of what an Arab prince should be. I might add, that among all rulers or governors, European or Asiatic, with whose acquaintance I have ever chanced to be honored, I know few equal in the true art of government to Telal, son of Abdallah-ebn-Rasheed.

"His first cares were directed to adorn and civilize the capital. Under his orders, enforced by personal superintendence, the palace commenced by his father was soon brought to completion. But he added, what probably his father would hardly have thought of, a long row of warehouses, the dependencies and property of the same palace; next he built a market-place consisting of about eighty shops or magazines, destined for public commerce and trade, and lastly constructed a large mosque for the official prayers of Friday. Round the palace, and in many other parts of the town, he opened streets, dug wells, and laid out extensive gardens, besides strengthening the old fortifications all round and adding new ones. At the same time he managed to secure at once the fidelity and the absence of his dangerous uncle by giving him charge of those military expeditions which best satisfied the restless energy of Obeyd. The first of these wars was directed, I know not on what pretext, against Kheybar. But as Telal intended rather to enforce submission than to inflict ruin, he associated with Obeyd in the military com mand his own brother Meta'ab, to put a check on the ferocity of the former. Kheybar was conquered, and Telal sent thither, as governor in his name, a young man of Ha'yel, prudent and gentle, whom I subsequently met when he was on a visit at the capital.

"Not long after, the inhabitants of Kaseem, weary of Wahabee tyranny, turned their eyes toward Telal, who had already given a generous and inviolable asylum to the numerous political exiles of that district. Secret negotiations took place, and at a favorable moment the entire uplands of that province—after a fashion not indeed peculiar to Arabia—annexed themselves to the kingdom of Shomer by universal and unanimous suffrage. Telal made suitable apologies to the Nedjean monarch, the original sovereign of the annexed district; he could not resist the popular wish; it had been forced on him, etc.—but Western Europe is familiar with the style. Feysul felt the inopportuneness of a quarrel with the rapidly growing power to which he himself had given origin only a few years before, and, after a wry face or two, swallowed the pill. Meanwhile Telal knowing the necessity of a high military reputation, both at home and abroad, undertook in person a series of operations againts Teyma' and its neighborhood, and at last against the Djowf itself. Everywhere his arms were successful, and his moderation in victory secured the attachment of the vanquished themselves.

"Toward his own subjects his conduct is uniformly of a nature to merit their obedience and attachment, and few sovereigns have here met with better success. Once a day, often twice, he gives public audience, hears patiently, and decides in person, the minutest causes with great good sense. To the Bedouins, no insignificant portion of his rule, he makes up for the restraint he imposes, and the tribute he levies from them, by a profusion of hospitality not to be found elsewhere in the whole of Arabia from Akabah to Aden. His guests at the midday and evening meal are never less than fifty or sixty, and I have often counted up to two hundred at a banquet, while presents of dress and arms are of frequent if not daily occurrence. It is hard for Europeans to estimate how much popularity such conduct brings an Asiatic prince. Meanwhile the townsfolk and villagers love him for the more solid advantages of undisturbed peace at home, of flourishing commerce, of extended dominion, and military glory.

"To capital punishment he is decidedly adverse, and the severest penalty with which he has hitherto chastised political offences is banishment or prison. Indeed, even in cases of homicide or murder, he has been known not unfrequently to avail himself of the option allowed by Arab custom between a fine and retaliation, and to buy off the offender, by bestowing on the family of the deceased the allotted price of blood from his own private treasury, and that from a pure motive of humanity. When execution does take place, it is always by beheading; nor is indeed any other mode of putting to death customary in Arabia. Stripes, however, are not uncommon, though administered on the broad back, not on the sole of the foot. They are the common chastisement for minor offences, like stealing, cursing, or quarrelling; in this last case both parties usually come in for their share.

"With his numerous retainers he is almost over-indulgent, and readily pardons a mistake or a negligence; falsehood alone he never forgives; and it is notorious that whoever has once lied to Telal must give up all hopes of future favor."

After describing the public audience which is daily given by this excellent prince, Palgrave describes the more private reception which was accorded to himself and his companion:

"Telal, once free from the mixed crowd, pauses a moment till we rejoin him. The simple and customary salutations are given and returned. I then present him with our only available testimonial, the scrap written by Hamood from the Djowf. He opens it, and hands it over to Zamil, better skilled in reading than his master. Then laying aside all his wonted gravity, and assuming a good-humored smile, he takes my hand in his right and my companion's in his left, and thus walks on with us through the court, past the mosque, and down the market-place, while his attendants form a moving wall behind and on either side.

"He was in his own mind thoroughly persuaded that we were, as we appeared, Syrians; but imagined, nor was he entirely in the wrong thus far, that we had other objects in view than mere medical practice. But if he was right in so much, he was less fortunate in the interpretation he chose to put on our riddle, having imagined that our real scope must be to buy horses for some government, of which we must be the agents; a conjecture which had certainly the merit of plausibility. However, Telal had, I believe, no doubt on the matter, and had already determined to treat us well in the horse business, and to let us have a good bargain, as it shortly appeared.

"Accordingly he began a series of questions and cross-questions, all in a jocose way, but so that the very drift of his inquiries soon allowed us to perceive what he really esteemed us. We, following our previous resolution, stuck to medicine, a family in want, hopes of good success under the royal patronage, and much of the same tenor. But Telal was not so easily to be blinkered, and kept to his first judgment. Meanwhile we passed down the street, lined with starers at the king and us, and at last arrived at the outer door of a large house near the farther end of the Sook or market-place; it belonged to Hasan, the merchant from Meshid 'Alee.

"Three of the retinue stationed themselves by way of guard at the street door, sword in hand. The rest entered with the king and ourselves; we traversed the court-yard, where the remainder of the armed men took position, while we went on to the k'hawah. It was small, but well furnished and carpeted. Here Telal placed us amicably by his side in the highest place; his brother Mohammed and five or six others were admitted, and seated themselves each according to his rank, while Hasan, being master of the house, did the honors.

"Coffee was brought and pipes lighted. Meantime Ebn-Rasheed renewed his interrogatory, skilfully throwing out side remarks, now on the government of Syria, now on that of Egypt, then on the Bedouins to the north of Djowf, or on the tribes of Hedjaz, or on the banks of the Euphrates, thus to gain light whence and to what end we had in fact come. Next he questioned us on medicine, perhaps to discover whether we had the right professional tone; then on horses, about which same noble animals we affected an ignorance unnatural and very unpardonable in an Englishman; but for which I hope afterward to make amends to my readers. All was in vain; and after a full hour our noble friend had only managed by his cleverness to get himself farther off the right track than he had been at the outset. He felt it, and determined to let matters have their own course, and to await the result of time. So he ended by assuring us of his entire confidence and protection, offering us, to boot, a lodging on the palace grounds. But this we declined, being desirous of studying the country as it was in itself, not through the medium of a court atmosphere; so we begged that an abode might be assigned us as near the market-place as possible; and this he promised, though evidently rather put out by our independent ways.

" "Excellent water-melons, ready peeled and cut up, with peaches hardly ripe, for it was the beginning of the season, were now brought in, and we all partook in common. This was the signal for breaking up; Telal renewed his proffers of favor and patronage; and we were at last reconducted to our lodgings by one of the royal guard.

"Seyf now went in search of a permanent dwelling-place wherein to install us; and, before evening, succeeded in finding one situated in a street leading at right angles to the market, and at no unreasonable distance from the palace. Every door was provided with its own distinct lock; the keys here are made of iron, and in this respect Ha'yel has the better of any other Arab town it was my chance to visit, where the keys were invariably wooden, and thus very liable to break and get out of order.

"The court-yard was soon thronged with visitors, some from the palace, others from the town. One had a sick relation, whom he begged us to come and see, another some personal ailment, a third had called out of mere politeness or curiosity; in short, men of all conditions and of all ages, but for the most part open and friendly in manner, so that we could already anticipate a very speedy acquaintance with the town and whatever it contained.

"The nature of our occupations now led to a certain daily routine, though it was often agreeably diversified by incidental occurrences. Perhaps a leaf taken at random from my journal, now regularly kept, may serve to set before my readers a tolerable sample of our ordinary course of life and society at Ha'yel, while it will at the same time give a more distinct idea of the town and people than we have yet supplied.

"Be it, then, the 10th of August, whose jotted notes I will put together and fill up the blanks. I might equally have taken the 9th or the 11th, they are all much the same; but the day I have chosen looks a little the closer written of the two, and for that sole reason I prefer giving it.

"On that day, then, in 1862, about a fortnight after our establishment at Ha'yel, and when we were, in consequence, fully inured to our town existence, Seleem Abou Mahmood-el-'Eys and Barakat-esh-Shamee, that is, my companion and myself, rose, not from our beds, for we had none, but from our roof-spread carpets, and took advantage of the silent hour of the first faint dawn, while the stars yet kept watch in the sky over the slumbering inhabitants of Shomer, to leave the house for a cool and undisturbed walk ere the sun should arise and man go forth unto his work and to his labor. We locked the outer door, and then passed into the still twilight gloom down the cross-street leading to the market-place, which we next followed up to its farther or southwestern end, where large folding-gates separate it from the rest of the town. The wolfish city-dogs, whose bark and bite, too, render walking the streets at night a rather precarious business, now tamely stalked away in the gloaming, while here and there a crouching camel, the packages yet on his back, and his sleeping driver close by, awaited the opening of the warehouse at whose door they had passed the night. Early though it was, the market gates were already unclosed, and the guardian sat wakeful in his niche. On leaving the market we had yet to go down a broad street of houses and gardens cheerfully intermixed, till at last we reached the western wall of the town, or, rather, of the new quarter added by 'Abdallah, where the high portal between round flanking towers gave us issue on the open plain, blown over at this hour by a light gale of life and coolness. To the west, but some four or five miles distant, rose the serrated mass of Djebel Shomer, throwing up its black fantastic peaks, now reddened by the reflected dawn, against the lead-blue sky. Northward the same chain bends round till it meets the town, and then stretches away for a length of ten or twelve days' journey, gradually losing in height on its approach to Meshid 'Alee and the valley of the Euphrates. On our south we have a little isolated knot of rocks, and far off the extreme ranges of Djebel Shomer, or 'Aja, to give it its historical name, intersected by the broad passes that lead on in the same direction to Djebel Solma. Behind us lies the capital. Telal's palace, with its high oval keep, houses, gardens, walls, and towers, all coming out black against the ruddy bars of eastern light, and behind, a huge pyramidal peak almost overhanging the town, and connected by lower rocks with the main mountain range to north and south, those stony ribs that protect the central heart of the kingdom. In the plain itself we can just distinguish by the doubtful twilight several blackish patches irregularly scattered over its face, or seen as though leaning upward against its craggy verge; these are the gardens and country houses of 'Obeyd and other chiefs, besides hamlets and villages, such as Kefar and 'Adwah, with their groves of palm and 'ithel' (the Arab larch), now blended in the dusk. One solitary traveller on his camel, a troop of jackals sneaking off to their rocky cavern, a few dingy tents of Shomer Bedouins, such are the last details of the landscape. Far away over the southern hills beams the glory of Canopus, and announces a new Arab year; the polestar to the north lies low over the mountain tops.

"We pace the pebble-strown flat to the south till we leave behind us the length of the town wall, and reach the little cluster of rocks already mentioned. We scramble up to a sort of niche near its summit, whence, at a height of a hundred feet or more, we can overlook the whole extent of the plain and wait the sunrise. Yet before the highest crags of Shomer are gilt with its first rays, or the long giant shadows of the easterly chain have crossed the level, we see groups of peasants, who, driving their fruit and vegetable-laden asses before them, issue like little bands of ants from the mountain gorges around, and slowly approach on the tracks converging to the capital. Horsemen from the town ride out to the gardens, and a long line of camels on the westerly Medina road winds up toward Ha'yel. We wait ensconced in our rocky lookout and enjoy the view till the sun has risen, and the coolness of the night air warms rapidly into the sultry day; it is time to return. So we quit our solitary perch and descend to the plain, where, keeping in the shadow of the western fortifications, we regain the town gate and thence the market.

"There all is now life and movement; some of the warehouses, filled with rice, flour, spices, or coffee, and often concealing in their inner recesses stores of the prohibited American weed, are already open; we salute the owners while we pass, and they return a polite and friendly greeting. Camels are unloading in the streets, and Bedouins standing by, looking anything but at home in the town. The shoemaker and the blacksmith, those two main props of Arab handicraft, are already at their work, and some gossiping bystanders are collected around them. At the corner where our cross-street falls into the market-place, three or four country women are seated, with piles of melons, gourds, egg-plant fruits, and the other garden produce before them for sale. My companion falls a haggling with one of these village nymphs, and ends by obtaining a dozen 'badinjans' and a couple of water-melons, each bigger than a man's head, for the equivalent of an English twopence. With this purchase we return home, where we shut and bolt the outer door, then take out of a flat basket what has remained from over night of our wafer-like Ha'yel bread, and with this and a melon make a hasty breakfast. I say a hasty one, for although it is only half an hour after sunrise, repeated knocks at our portal show the arrival of patients and visitors: early rising being here the fashion, and in reason must be wherever artificial lighting is scanty. However, we do not at once open to our friends, nor will they take offence at the delay, but remain where they are, chatting together before our door till we admit them; of so little value is time here.

"In comes a young man of good appearance, clad in the black cloak common to all of the middle or upper classes in Central Arabia; in his hand he bears a wand of the Sidr or lotos-wood. A silver-hilted sword and a glistening Kafee'yah announce him to be a person of some importance, while his long, black ringlets, handsome features, and slightly olive complexion, with a tall stature and easy gait, declare him a native of Djebel Shomer, and townsman of Ha'yel; it is 'Ojeyl, the eldest-born of a large family, and successor to the comfortable house and garden of his father, not long since deceased, in a quarter of the town some twenty minutes' walk distant. He leads by the hand his younger brother, a modest-looking lad of fair complexion and slim make, but almost blind, and evidently out of health also. After passing through the preliminary ceremonies of introduction to Barakat, he approaches my recess, and standing without, salutes me with the greatest deference. Thinking him a desirable acquaintance I receive him very graciously, and he begs me to see what is the matter with his brother. I examine the case, finding it to be within the limits of my skill, and not likely to require more than a very simple course of treatment. Accordingly I make my bargain for the chances of recovery, and find 'Ojeyl docile to the terms proposed, and with little disposition, all things considered, to backwardness in payment. Arabs, indeed, are in general close in driving a bargain and open in downright giving; they will chaffer half a day about a penny, while they will throw away the worth of pounds on the first asker. But 'Ojeyl was one of the best specimens of the Ha'-yel character, and of the clan Ta'i, renowned in all times for their liberal ways and high sense of honor. I next proceed to administer to my patient such drugs as his state requires, and he receives them with that air of absolute and half-religious confidence which well-educated Arabs show to their physician, whom they regard as possessed of an almost sacred and supernatural power—a feeling, by the way, hardly less advantageous to the patient than to the practitioner, and which may often contribute much to the success of the treatment.

"During the rest of my stay at Ha'yel, 'Ojeyl continued to be one of my best friends, I had almost said disciples; our mutual visits were frequent, and always pleasing and hearty. His brother's cure, which followed in less than a fortnight, confirmed his attachment, nor had I reason to complain of scantiness in his retribution.

"Meanwhile the court-yard has become full of visitors. Close by my door I see the intelligent and demurely smiling face of 'Abd-el-Mahsin, where he sits between two pretty and well-dressed boys; they are the two elder children of Telal—Bedr and Bander. Their guardsman, a negro slave with a handsome cloak and sword, is seated a little lower down; farther on are two townsmen, one armed, the other with a wand at his side. A rough, good-natured youth, of a bronzed complexion, and whose dingy clothes bespeak his mechanical profession, is talking with another of a dress somewhat different in form and coarser in material than that usually worn in Ha'yel; this latter must be a peasant from some one of the mountain villages. Two Bedouins, ragged and uncouth, have straggled in with the rest; while a tall, dark-featured youth, with a gilded hilt to his sword, and more silk about him than a Wahabee would approve, has taken his place opposite to 'Abd-el-Mahsin, and is trying to draw him into conversation. But this last has asked Barakat to lend him one of my Arabic books to read, and is deeply engaged in its perusal.

"'Ojeyl has taken leave, and I give the next turn of course to 'Abd-el-Mahsin. He informs me that Telal has sent me his two sons, Bedr and Bander, that

I may examine their state of health, and see if they require doctoring. This is in truth a little stroke of policy on Telal's part, who knows equally with myself that the boys are perfectly well and want nothing at all. But he wishes to give us a mark of his confidence, and at the same time to help us in establishing our medical reputation in the town; for though by no means himself persuaded of the reality of our doctoral title, he understands the expediency of saving appearances before the public.

"Well, the children are passed in review with all the seriousness due to a case of heart complaint or brain fever, while at a wink from me Barakat prepares in the kitchen a draught of cinnamon water, which, with sugar, named medicine for the occasion, pleases the young heirs of royalty and keeps up the farce; 'Abd-el-Mahsin expatiating all the time to the bystanders on the wonderful skill with which I have at once discovered the ailments and their cure, and the small boys thinking that if this be medicine they will do their best to be ill for it every day.

"'Abd-el-Mahsin now commits them to the negro, who, however, before taking them back to the palace, has his own story to tell of some personal ache, for which I prescribe without stipulating for payment, since he belongs to the palace, where it is important to have the greatest number of friends possible, even on the back stairs. But 'Abd-el-Mahsin remains, reading, chatting, quoting poetry, and talking history, recent events, natural philosophy, or medicine, as the case may be.

"Let us now see some of the other patients. The

gold-hilted swordsman has naturally a special claim on our attention. He is the son of Rosheyd, Telal's maternal uncle. His palace stands on the other side of the way, exactly opposite to our house; and I will say nothing more of him for the present, intending to pay him afterward a special visit, and thus become more thoroughly acquainted with the whole family.

"Next let us take notice of those two townsmen who are conversing, or rather 'chaffing,' together. Though both in plain apparel, and much alike in stature and features, there is yet much about them to distinguish the two; one has a civilian look, the other a military. He of the wand is no less a personage than Mohammed-el-Kadee, chief justice of Ha'yel, and of course a very important individual in the town. However, his exterior is that of an elderly, unpretentious, little man, and one, in spite of the proverb which attributes gravity to judges, very fond of a joke, besides being a tolerable representative of what may here be called the moderate party, neither participating in the fanaticism of the Wahabee, nor yet, like the most of the indigenous chiefs, hostile to Mahometanism; he takes his cue from the court direction and is popular with all factions because belonging properly to none.

"He requires some medical treatment for himself, and more for his son, a big, heavy lad with a swollen arm, who has accompanied him hither. Here, too, is a useful acquaintance, well up to all the scandal and small talk of the town, and willing to communicate it. Our visits were frequent, and I found his house well stored with books, partly manuscript, partly printed in Egypt, and mainly on legal or religious subjects.

"Of the country folks in the villages around, like Mogah, Delhemee'eh, and the rest, Mohammed-el-Kadee used to speak with a sort of half-contemptuous pity, much like a Parisian talking of Low Bretons; in fact, the difference between these rough and sturdy boors and the more refined inhabitants of the capital is, all due proportion allowed, no less remarkable here than in Europe itself. We will now let one of them come forward in his own behalf, and my readers shall be judges.

"It is accordingly a stout clown from Mogah, scantily dressed in working wear, and who has been occupied for the last half hour in tracing sundry diagrams on the ground before him with a thick peach-tree switch, thus to pass his time till his betters shall have been served. He now edges forward, and taking his seat in front of the door, calls my attention with an 'I say, doctor.' Whereon I suggest to him that his bulky corporation not being formed of glass or any other transparent material, he has by his position entirely intercepted whatever little light my recess might enjoy. He apologizes, and shuffles an inch or two sideways. Next I inquire what ails him, not without some curiosity to hear the answer, so little does the herculean frame before me announce disease. Whereto Do'cymis, or whatever may be his name, replies, 'I say, I am all made up of pain.' This statement, like many others, appears to me rather too general to be exactly true. So I proceed

LIFE IN HA'YEL

in my interrogatory: 'Does your head pain you?' 'No.' (I might have guessed that; these fellows never feel what our cross-Channel friends entitle '*le mal des beaux esprits*.') 'Does your back ache?' 'No.' 'Your arms?' 'No.' 'Your legs?' 'No.' 'Your body?' 'No.' 'But,' I conclude, 'if neither your head nor your body, back, arms, or legs pain you, how can you possibly be such a composition of suffering?' 'I am all made up of pain, doctor,' replies he, manfully intrenching himself within his first position. The fact is, that there is really something wrong with him, but he does not know how to localize his sensations. So I push forward my inquiries, till it appears that our man of Mogah has a chronic rheumatism; and on ulterior investigation, conducted with all the skill that Barakat and I can jointly muster, it comes out that three or four months before he had an attack of the disease in its acute form, accompanied by high fever, since which he has never been himself again.

"This might suffice for the diagnosis, but I wish to see how he will find his way out of more intricate questions; besides, the townsmen sitting by, and equally alive to the joke with myself, whisper, 'Try him again.' In consequence, I proceed with, 'What was the cause of your first illness?' 'I say, doctor, its cause was God,' replies the patient. 'No doubt of that,' say I; 'all things are caused by God: but what was the particular and immediate occasion?' 'Doctor, its cause was God, and secondly, that I ate camel's flesh when I was cold,' rejoins my scientific friend. 'But was there nothing else?' I suggest, not quite satisfied with the lucid explanation just given. 'Then, too, I drank camel's milk; but it was all, I say, from God, doctor,' answers he.

"Well, I consider the case, and make up my mind regarding the treatment. Next comes the grand question of payment, which must be agreed on beforehand, and rendered conditional on success; else no fees for the doctor, not at Ha'yel only, but throughout Arabia. I inquire what he will give me on recovery. 'Doctor,' answers the peasant, 'I will give you, do you hear? I say, I will give you a camel.' But I reply that I do not want one. 'I say, remember God,' which being interpreted here means, 'do not be unreasonable; I will give you a fat camel, everyone knows my camel; if you choose, I will bring witnesses, I say.' And while I persist in refusing the proffered camel, he talks of butter, meal, dates, and such like equivalents.

"There is a patient and a paymaster for you. However, all ends by his behaving reasonably enough; he follows my prescriptions with the ordinary docility, gets better, and gives me for my pains an eighteen-penny fee."

During this residence in Ha'yel, Palgrave made many friends, and soon established those relations of familiar intercourse which are so much easier in Moslem than in Christian lands—a natural result of the preservation of the old importance, which in the earliest Hebrew days was attached to "the stranger." Palgrave's intimacies embraced many families related to Telal, and others, whose knowledge of Arabian history or literature made their acquaintance welcome. His own knowledge of these subjects, fortunately, was equal to theirs, and, from the number of his invitations to dinners and suppers, he seems to have been a welcome guest to the better classes of Ha'yel. One of the aristocracy, by name Dohey, was his most agreeable acquaintance; and we quote the following pleasant account of his intercourse:

"Dohey's invitations were particularly welcome, both from the pleasantness of his dwelling-place, and from the varied and interesting conversation that I was sure to meet with there. This merchant, a tall and stately man of between fifty and sixty years of age, and whose thin features were lighted up by a lustre of more than ordinary intelligence, was a thorough Ha'yelite of the old caste, hating Wahabees from the bottom of his heart, eager for information on cause and effect, on lands and governments, and holding commerce and social life for the main props if not the ends of civil and national organization. His uncle, now near eighty years old, to judge by conjecture in a land where registers are not much in use, had journeyed to India, and traded at Bombay; in token whereof he still wore an Indian skull-cap and a cashmere shawl. The rest of the family were in keeping with the elder members, and seldom have I seen more dutiful children or a better educated household. My readers will naturally understand that by education I here imply its moral not its intellectual phase. The eldest son, himself a middle-aged man, would never venture into his father's presence without unbuckling his sword and leaving it in the vestibule, nor on any account presume to sit on a level with him or by his side in the divan.

"The divan itself was one of the prettiest I met with in these parts. It was a large square room, looking out on the large house-garden, and cheerfully lighted up by trellised windows on two sides, while the wall of the third had purposely been discontinued at about half its height, and the open space thus left between it and the roof propped by pillars, between which 'a fruitful vine by the sides of the house' was intertwined so as to fill up the interval with a gay net-work of green leaves and tendrils, transparent like stained glass in the eastern sunbeams. Facing this cheerful light, the floor of the apartment was raised about two feet above the rest, and covered with gay Persian carpets, silk cushions, and the best of Arab furniture. In the lower half of the k'hawah, and at its farthest angle, was the small stone coffee-stove, placed at a distance where its heat might not annoy the master and his guests. Many of the city nobility would here resort, and the talk generally turned on serious subjects, and above all on the parties and politics of Arabia; while Dohey would show himself a thorough Arab patriot, and at the same time a courteous and indulgent judge of foreigners, qualities seldom to be met with together in any notable degree, and therefore more welcome.

"Many a pleasant hour have I passed in this half greenhouse, half k'hawah, mid cheerful faces and varied talk, while inly commenting on the natural resources of this manly and vigorous people, and straining the eye of forethought to discern through the misty curtain of the future by what outlet their now unfruitful, because solitary, good may be brought into fertilizing contact with that of other more advanced nations, to the mutual benefit of each and all.

"Talk went on with the ease and decorum characteristic of good Eastern society, without the flippancy and excitement which occasionally mars it in some countries, no less than over-silence does in others. To my mind the Easterns are generally superior in the science of conversation to the inhabitants of the West; perhaps from a greater necessity of cultivating it, as the only means of general news and intercourse where newspapers and pamphlets are unknown.

"Or else some garden was the scene of our afternoon leisure, among fruit-trees and palms, by the side of a watercourse, whose constant supply from the well hid from view among thick foliage, seemed the work not of laborious art, but of unassisted nature. Here, stretched in the cool and welcome shade, would we for hours canvass with 'Abd-el-Mahsin, and others of similar pursuits, the respective merits of Arab poets and authors, of Omar-ebn-el-Farid or Aboo'l 'Ola, in meetings that had something of the Attic, yet with just enough of the Arab to render them more acceptable by their Semitic character of grave cheerfulness and mirthful composure.

"Or when the stars came out, Barakat and myself would stroll out of the heated air of the streets and market to the cool open plain, and there pass an hour or two alone, or in conversation with what chance passer-by might steal on us, half-unperceived and unperceiving in the dusk, and amuse ourselves with his simplicity if he were a Bedouin, or with his shrewdness if a townsman.

"Thus passed our ordinary life at Ha'yel. Many minor incidents occurred to diversify it, many of the little ups and downs that human intercourse never fails to furnish; sometimes the number of patients and the urgency of their attendance allowed of little leisure for aught except our professional duties; sometimes a day or two would pass with hardly any serious occupation. But of such incidents my readers have a sufficient sample in what has been already set down. Suffice to say, that from the 27th of July to the 8th of September we remained doctoring in the capital or in its immediate neighborhood."

By this time Palgrave had obtained sufficient knowledge of the country, and was anxious to advance farther eastward before the autumn—the best season for travel—should be spent. Now, the journey across the Shomer frontier could only be pursued with Telal's cognizance, and by his good will. In fact, a passport bearing the royal signature is indispensable for all who desire to cross the boundary, especially into the Wahabee territory; without such a document in hand no one would venture to conduct them.

"Accordingly," he says, "we requested and obtained a special audience at the palace. Telal, of whose good-will we had received frequent, indeed daily, proofs during our sojourn at Ha'yel, proved a sincere friend—patron would be a juster word—to the last; exemplifying the Scotch proverb about the guest not only who 'will stay,' but also who 'maun gang.' To this end he then dictated to Zamil, for Telal himself is no scribe, a passport or general letter of safe conduct, enough to insure us good treatment within the limits of his rule, and even beyond.

"When this was written, Telal affixed his seal, and rose to leave us alone with Zamil, after a parting shake of the hand, and wishing us a prosperous journey and speedy return. Yet with all these motives for going, I could not but feel reluctant to quit a pleasing town, where we certainly possessed many sincere friends and well-wishers, for countries in which we could by no means anticipate equal favor, or even equal safety. Indeed, so ominous was all that we heard about Wahabee Nedjed, so black did the landscape before us look, on nearer approach, that I almost repented of my resolution, and was considerably inclined to say, 'Thus far enough, and no farther.'

"'Obeyd, Telal's uncle, had left Ha'yel the day before on a military expedition against the Bedouins of the West. In common with all the sight-seers of the town, we had gone to witness his departure. It was a gay and interesting scene. 'Obeyd had caused his tent to be pitched in the plain without the northern walls, and there reviewed his forces. About one-third were on horseback, the rest were mounted on light and speedy camels; all had spears and matchlocks, to which the gentry added swords; and while they rode hither and thither in sham manœuvres over the parade ground, the whole appearance was very picturesque and tolerably martial. 'Obeyd now unfurled his own peculiar standard, in which the green color, distinctive of Islam, had been added border-wise to the white ground of the ancestral Nedjean banner, mentioned fourteen centuries back by 'Omar-ebn-Kelthoom, the poet of Taghleb, and many others. Barakat and myself mixed with the crowd of spectators. 'Obeyd saw us, and it was now several days since we had last met. Without hesitating he cantered up to us, and while he tendered his hand for a farewell shake, he said: 'I have heard that you intend going to Ri'ad; there you will meet with 'Abdallah, the eldest son of Feysul; he is my particular friend; I should much desire to see you high in his good graces, and to that end I have written him a letter in your behalf, of which you yourselves are to be the bearers; you will find it in my house, where I have left it for you with one of my servants.' He then assured us that if he found us still at Ha'yel on his return, he would continue to befriend us in every way; but that if we journeyed forward to Nedjed, we should meet with a sincere friend in 'Abdallah, especially if we gave him the letter in question.

"He then took his leave with a semblance of affectionate cordiality that made the bystanders stare; thus supporting to the last the profound dissimulation which he had only once belied for a moment.

The letter was duly handed over to us the same afternoon by his head steward, whom he had left to look after the house and garden in his absence. Doubtless my readers will be curious to know what sort of recommendation 'Obeyd had provided us with. It was written on a small scrap of thick paper, about four inches each way, carefully folded up and secured by three seals. However, 'our fears forgetting manners,' we thought best with Hamlet to make perusal of this grand commission before delivering it to its destination. So we undid the seals with precautions admitting of reclosing them in proper form, and read the royal knavery. I give it word for word; it ran thus: 'In the name of God the Merciful, the Compassionate, we, 'Obeyd-ebn-Rasheed, salute you, O 'Abdallah, son of Feysul-ebn-Sa'ood, and peace be on you, and the mercy of God and His blessings.' (This is the invariable commencement of all Wahabee epistles, to the entire omission of the complimentary formulas used by other Orientals.) 'After which,' so proceeded the document, 'we inform you that the bearers of this are one Seleem-el-'Eys, and his comrade, Barakat-esh-Shamee, who give themselves out for having some knowledge in'— here followed a word of equivocal import, capable of interpretation alike by 'medicine' or 'magic,' but generally used in Nedjed for the latter, which is at Ri'ad a capital crime. 'Now may God forbid that we should hear of any evil having befallen you. We salute also your father, Feysul, and your brothers, and all your family, and anxiously await your news in answer. Peace be with you.' Here followed the signet impression.

"A pretty recommendation, especially under the actual circumstances! However, not content with this, 'Obeyd found means to transmit further information regarding us, and all in the same tenor, to Ri'ad, as we afterward discovered. For his letter, I need hardly say that it never passed from our possession, where it yet remains as an interesting autograph, to that of 'Abdallah; with whom it would inevitably have proved the one only thing wanting, as we shall subsequently see, to make us leave the forfeit of our lives in the Nedjean man-trap.

"Before evening three men knocked at our door; they were our future guides. The eldest bore the name of Mubarek, and was a native of the suburbs of Bereydah; all three were of the genuine Kaseem breed, darker and lower in stature than the inhabitants of Ha'yel, but not ill-looking, and extremely affable in their demeanor.

"We had soon made all necessary arrangements for our departure, got in a few scattered debts, packed up our pharmacopœia, and nothing now remained but the pleasurable pain of farewells. They were many and mutually sincere. Meta'ab had indeed made his a few days before, when he a second time left Ha'yel for the pastures; Telal we had already taken leave of, but there remained his younger brother Mohammed to give us a hearty adieu of good augury. Most of my old acquaintance or patients, Dohey the merchant, Mohammed the judge, Doheym and his family, not forgetting our earliest friend Seyf the chamberlain, Sa'eed, the cavalry officer, and others of the court, freemen and slaves, white or black (for negroes readily follow the direction indicated by their masters, and are not ungrateful if kindly treated, while kept in their due position), and many others of whose names Homer would have made a catalogue and I will not, heard of our near departure and came to express their regrets, with hopes of future meeting and return."

"Early next morning, before day, Mubarek and another of his countrymen, named Dahesh, were at our door with the camels. Some of our town friends had also come, even at this hour, to accompany us as far as the city gates. We mounted our beasts, and while the first sunbeams streamed level over the plain, passed through the southwestern portal beyond the market-place, the 8th of September, 1862, and left the city of Ha'yel."

CHAPTER XII.

PALGRAVE'S TRAVELS—JOURNEY TO BEREYDAH

ANOTHER stage of our way. From Gaza to Ma'an, from Ma'an to the Djowf, from the Djowf to Ha'yel, three such had now been gone over, not indeed without some fatigue or discomfort, yet at comparatively little personal risk, except what nature herself, not man, might occasion. For to cross the stony desert of the northern frontier, or the sandy Nefood in the very height of summer, could not be said to be entirely free from danger, where in these waterless wastes thirst, if nothing else, may alone, and often does, suffice to cause the disappearance of the over-venturous traveller, nay, even of many a Bedouin, no less effectually than a lance-thrust or a musket-ball. But if nature had been so far unkind, of man at least we had hitherto not much to complain; the Bedouins on the route, however rough and uncouth in their ways, had, with only one exception, meant us fairly well, and the townsmen in general had proved friendly and courteous beyond our expectation. Once within the established government limits of Telal, and among his subjects, we had enjoyed our share in the common security afforded to wayfarers and inhabitants for life and property, while good success had hitherto accompanied us.

'Judge of the day by its dawn,' say the Arabs; and although this proverb, like all proverbs, does not always hold exactly true, whether for sunshine or cloud, yet it has its value at times. And thus, whatever unfavorable predictions or dark forebodings our friends might hint regarding the inner Nedjed and its denizens, we trusted that so favorable a past augured somewhat better things for the future.

"From physical and material difficulties like those before met with, there was henceforward much less to fear. The great heats of summer were past, the cooler season had set in; besides, our path now lay through the elevated table-land of Central Arabia, whose northern rim we had already surmounted at our entrance on the Djebel Shomer. Nor did there remain any uncultivated or sandy track to cross comparable to the Nefood of Djowf between Ha'yel and Ri'ad; on the contrary, we were to expect pasture lands and culture, villages and habitations, cool mountain air, and a sufficiency, if not an abundance, of water. Nor were our fellow-companions now mere Bedouins and savages, but men from town or village life, members of organized society, and so far civilized beings.

"When adieus, lookings back, wavings of the hand, and all the customary signs of farewell and good omen were over between our Ha'yel friends and ourselves, we pursued our road by the plain which I have already described as having been the frequent scene of our morning walks; but instead of following the southwesterly path toward Kefar, whose groves and roof-tops now rose in a blended mass before us, we turned eastward, and rounded, though at some distance, the outer wall of Ha'yel for nearly half an hour, till we struck off by a southeasterly track across stony ground, diversified here and there by wells, each with a cluster of gardens and a few houses in its neighborhood. At last we reached a narrow winding pass among the cliffs of Djebel 'Aja', whose mid-loop encircles Ha'yel on all sides, and here turned our heads to take a last far-off view of what had been our home, or the agreeable semblance of a home, for several weeks.

"Our only companions as yet were Mubarek and Dahesh. We had outstripped the rest, whose baggage and equipments had required a more tedious arrangement than our own. Before long they came up—a motley crew. Ten or thereabouts of the Kaseem, some from Bereydah itself, others from neighboring towns; two individuals, who gave themselves out, but with more asseveration than truth, to be natives of Mecca itself; three Bedouins, two of whom belonged to the Shomer clan, the third an 'Anezah of the north; next a runaway negro, conducting four horses, destined to pass the whole breadth of Arabia, and to be shipped off at Koweyt, on the Persian Gulf, for Indian sale; two merchants, one from Zulphah, in the province of Sedeyr, the other from Zobeyr, near Bussora; lastly, two women, wives of I know not exactly whom in the caravan, with some small children; all this making up, ourselves included, a band of twenty-seven or twenty-eight persons, the most mounted on camels, a few on horseback, and accompanied by a few beasts of burden alongside—such was our Canterbury pilgrims' group.

"Thus assembled, on we went together, now amid granite rocks, now crossing grassy valleys, till near sunset we stopped under a high cliff, at the extreme southerly verge of Djebel 'Aja', or, in modern parlance, of Djebel Shomer. The mountain here extended far away to right and left, but in front a wide plain of full twenty miles across opened out before us, till bounded southward by the long bluish chain of Djebel Solma, whose line runs parallel to the heights we were now to leave, and belongs to the same formation and rocky mass denominated in a comprehensive way the mountains of Ta'i or Shomer.

"At about three in the afternoon, next day, we saw, some way off to our west, a troop of Bedouins coming up from the direction of Medina. While they were yet in the distance, and half-hidden from view by the shrubs and stunted acacias of the plain, we could not precisely distinguish their numbers; but they were evidently enough to make us desire, with Orlando, 'that we might be better strangers.' On our side we mustered about fifteen matchlocks, besides a few spears and swords. The Bedouins had already perceived us, and continued to approach, though in the desultory and circuitous way which they affect when doubtful of the strength of their opponent; still they gained on us more than was pleasant.

"Fourteen armed townsmen might stand for a reasonable match against double the number of Bedouins, and in any case we had certainly nothing better to do than to put a bold face on the matter. The 'Eyoon chief, Foleyh, with two of his countrymen and Ghashee, carefully primed their guns, and then set off at full gallop to meet the advancing enemy, brandishing their weapons over their heads, and looking extremely fierce. Under cover of this manœuvre the rest of our band set about getting their arms ready, and an amusing scene ensued. One had lost his match, and was hunting for it in his housings; another, in his haste to ram the bullet home had it stick midway in the barrel, and could neither get it up nor down; the lock of a third was rusty and would not do duty; the women began to whine piteously; the two Meccans, who for economy's sake were both riding one only camel, a circumstance which caused between them many international squabbles, tried to make their beast gallop off with them, and leave the others to their fate; while the more courageous animal, despising such cowardly measures, insisted on remaining with his companions and sharing their lot; all was thoroughly Arab, much hubbub and little done. Had the menacing feint of the four who protected our rear proved insufficient, we might all have been in a very bad predicament, and this feeling drew every face with reverted gaze in a backward direction. But the Harb banditti, intimidated by the bold countenance of Foleyh and his companions, wheeled about and commenced a skirmishing retreat, in which a few shots, guiltless of bloodshed, were fired for form's sake on either side, till at last our assailants fairly disappeared in the remote valley.

"Our valiant champions now returned from pursuit, much elated with their success, and we journeyed on together, skirting the last rocky spur of Solma, close by the spot where Hatim Ta'i, the well-known model, half mythic and half historical, of Arab hospitality and exaggerated generosity, is said to be buried. Here we crossed some low hills that form a sort of offshoot to the Solma mountain, and limit the valley; and the last rays of the setting sun gilding to our view, in a sandy bottom some way off, the palm-trees of Feyd.

"Feyd may be taken as a tolerable sample of the villages met with throughout Northern or Upper Kaseem, for they all bear a close likeness in their main features, though various in size. Imagine a little sandy hillock of about sixty or seventy feet high, in the midst of a wide and dusty valley; part of the eminence itself and the adjoining bottom is covered by low earth-built houses, intermixed with groups of the feathery ithel. The grounds in the neighborhood are divided by brick walls into green gardens, where gourds and melons, leguminous plants and maize, grow alongside of an artificial irrigation from the wells among them; palms in plenty—they were now heavy laden with red-brown fruits; and a few peach or apricot trees complete the general lineaments. The outer walls are low, and serve more for the protection of the gardens than of the dwellings; here are neither towers nor trenches, nor even, at least in many places, any central castle or distinguishable residence for the chief; his habitation is of the same one-storied construction as those of his neighbors, only a little larger. Some of the townlets are quite recent, and date from the Shomer annexation, which gave this part of the province a degree of quiet and prosperity unknown under their former Wahabee rulers.

"Next morning, the 10th of September, we were all up by moonlight, two or three hours before dawn, and off on our road to the southeast. The whole country that we had to traverse for the next four days was of so uniform a character that a few words of description may here serve for the landscape of this entire stage of our journey.

"Upper Kaseem is an elevated plateau or steppe, and forms part of a long upland belt, crossing diagonally the northern half of the peninsula; one extremity reaches the neighborhood of Zobeyr and the Euphrates, while the other extends downward to the vicinity of Medina. Its surface is in general covered with grass in the spring and summer seasons, and with shrubs and brushwood at all times, and thus affords excellent pasture for sheep and camels. Across it blows the fresh eastern gale, so celebrated in Arab poetry under the name of 'Seba Nedjin,' or 'Zephyr of Nedjed' (only it comes from precisely the opposite corner to the Greek or Roman Zephyr), and continually invoked by sentimental bards to bring them news of imaginary loves or pleasing reminiscences. No wonder; for most of these versifiers being themselves natives of the barren Hedjaz or the scorching Tehama, perhaps inhabitants of Egypt and Syria, and knowing little of Arabia, except what they have seen on the dreary Meccan pilgrim road, they naturally look back to with longing, and frequently record, whatever glimpses chance may have allowed them of the cooler and more fertile highlands of the centre, denominated by them Nedjed, in a general way, with their transient experience of its fresh and invigorating climate, of its courteous men and sprightly maidens.

"But when, nor is this seldom, the sweet smell of the aromatic thyme-like plants that here abound mixes with the light morning breeze and enhances its balmy influence, then indeed can one excuse the raptures of an Arab Ovid or Theocritus, and appreciate—at least I often did—their yearnings after Nedjed, and all the praises they lavish on its memory.

"Then said I to my companion, while the camels were hastening
To bear us down the pass between Meneefah and Demar,
'Enjoy while thou canst the sweets of the meadows of Nedjed:
With no such meadows and sweets shalt thou meet after this evening.
Ah! heaven's blessing on the scented gales of Nedjed,
And its greensward and groves glittering from the spring shower,
And thy dear friends, when thy lot was cast awhile in Nedjed,
Little hadst thou to complain of what the days brought thee;
Months flew past, they passed and we perceived not,
Nor when their moons were new, nor when they waned.'"

For three days more they travelled forward over this undulating table-land, making from sixty to seventy miles a day. The view was extensive, but rather monotonous. There were no high mountains, no rivers, no lakes, no deep valleys; but a constant repetition of stony uplands, shallow and sandy hollows, and villages surrounded by belts of palm-groves, the extent and direction of which indicated the subterranean water-courses.

On the third evening they reached Kowarah, the most southern station in Telal territory—a large village, lying in a wooded and well-watered hollow. Here they still found the order and security which that ruler had established, and maintained everywhere throughout his dominions. Leaving the next morning, the 14th of September, they crossed a few low hills, came to a sudden dip in the general level of the country, and then the extent of Southern Kaseem burst suddenly upon their view.

"Now, for the first time," says Palgrave, "we could in some measure appreciate the strength of the Wahabee in his mastery over such a land. Before us to the utmost horizon stretched an immense plain, studded with towns and villages, towers and groves, all steeped in the dazzling noon, and announcing everywhere life, opulence, and activity. The average breadth of this populous district is about sixty miles, its length twice as much, or more; it lies full two hundred feet below the level of the uplands, which here break off like a wall. Fifty or more good-sized villages and four or five large towns form the commercial and agricultural centres of the province, and its surface is moreover thickly strewn with smaller hamlets, isolated wells, and gardens, and traversed by a net-work of tracks in every direction. Here begin, and hence extend to Djebel Toweyk itself, the series of high watch-towers that afford the

THE VILLAGE OF EL SUWAYRKIYAH.

inhabitants a means, denied otherwise by their level flats, of discerning from afar the approach of foray or invasion, and thus preparing for resistance. For while no part of Central Arabia has an older or a better established title to civilization or wealth, no part also has been the starting-point and theatre of so many wars, or witnessed the gathering of such numerous armies.

"We halted for a moment on the verge of the uplands to enjoy the magnificent prospect before us. Below lay the wide plain; at a few miles' distance we saw the thick palm-groves of 'Eyoon, and what little of its towers and citadel the dense foliage permitted to the eye. Far off on our right, that is, to the west, a large dark patch marked the tillage and plantations which girdle the town of Rass; other villages and hamlets, too, were thickly scattered over the landscape. All along the ridge where we stood, and visible at various distances down the level, rose the tall, circular watch-towers of Kaseem. But immediately before us stood a more remarkable monument, one that fixed the attention and wonder even of our Arab companions themselves.

"For hardly had we descended the narrow path where it winds from ledge to ledge down to the bottom, when we saw before us several huge stones, like enormous bowlders, placed endways perpendicularly on the soil, while some of them yet upheld similar masses laid transversely over their summit. They were arranged in a curve, once forming part, it would appear, of a large circle, and many other like fragments lay rolled on the ground at a moderate distance; the number of those still upright was, to speak by memory, eight or nine. Two, at about ten or twelve feet apart one from the other, and resembling huge gate-posts, yet bore their horizontal lintel, a long block laid across them; a few were deprived of their upper traverse, the rest supported each its head-piece in defiance of time and of the more destructive efforts of man. So nicely balanced did one of these cross-bars appear that, in hope it might prove a rocking-stone, I guided my camel right under it, and then stretching up my riding-stick at arm's-length could just manage to touch and push it, but it did not stir. Meanwhile the respective heights of camel, rider, and stick taken together would place the stone in question full fifteen feet from the ground.

"These blocks seem, by their quality, to have been hewn from the neighboring limestone cliff, and roughly shaped, but present no further trace of art, no groove or cavity of sacrificial import, much less anything intended for figure or ornament. The people of the country attribute their erection to Darim, and by his own hands, too, seeing that he was a giant; perhaps, also, for some magical ceremony, since he was a magician. Pointing toward Rass, our companions affirmed that a second and similar stone circle, also of gigantic dimensions, existed there; and, lastly, they mentioned a third toward the southwest, that is, on the confines of Hedjaz.

"Here, as in most parts of Arabia, the staple article of cultivation is the date-palm. Of this tree there are, however, many widely differing species, and Kaseem can boast of containing the best known anywhere, the Khalas of Hasa alone excepted. The ripening season coincides with the latter half of August and the first of September, and we had thus an ample opportunity for testing the produce. Those who, like most Europeans at home, only know the date from the dried specimens of that fruit shown beneath a label in shop-windows, can hardly imagine how delicious it is when eaten fresh and in Central Arabia. Nor is it, when newly gathered, heating, a defect inherent to the preserved fruit everywhere; nor does its richness, however great, bring satiety: in short, it is an article of food alike pleasant and healthy. Its cheapness in its native land might astonish a Londoner. Enough of the very best dates from the Bereydah gardens to fill a large Arab handkerchief, about fifteen inches each way, almost to bursting, cost Barakat and myself the moderate sum of three farthings. We hung it up from the roof-beam of our apartment to preserve the luscious fruit from the ants, and it continued to drip molten sweetness into a sugary pool on the floor below for three days together, before we had demolished the contents, though it figured at every dinner and supper during that period.

"We were soon under the outer walls of 'Eyoon, a good-sized town containing at least ten thousand inhabitants according to my rough computation. Its central site, at the very juncture of the great northern and western lines of communication, renders it important, and for this reason it is carefully fortified, that is, for the country, and furnished with watchtowers much resembling manufactory chimneys in size and shape, beside a massive and capacious citadel. My readers may anticipate analogous, though proportionate, features in most other towns and villages of this province.

"Between the town-walls and the sand-hills close by was a sheltered spot, where we took about four hours of sleep, till the waning moon rose. Then all were once more in movement, camels gnarling, men loading, and the doctor and his apprentice mounting their beasts, all for Bereydah. But that town was distant, and when day broke at last there was yet a long road to traverse. This now lay amid mounds and valleys, thick with the vegetation already described; and somewhat after sunrise we took a full hour to pass the gardens and fields of Ghat, a straggling village, where a dozen wells supplied the valley with copious irrigation. On the adjoining hillocks— I may not call them heights—was continued the series of watch-towers, corresponding with others farther off that belonged to villages seen by glimpses in the landscape; I heard, but soon forgot, their names.

"A march of ten or twelve hours had tired us, and the weather was oppressively close, no uncommon phenomenon in Kaseem, where, what between low sandy ground and a southerly latitude, the climate is much more sultry than in Djebel Shomer, or the mountains of Toweyk. So that we were very glad when the ascent of a slight eminence discovered to our gaze the long-desired town of Bereydah, whose oval fortifications rose to view amid an open and cultivated plain. It was a view for Turner. An enormous watch-tower, near a hundred feet in height, a minaret of scarce inferior proportions, a mass of bastioned walls, such as we had not yet witnessed in Arabia, green groves around and thickets of ithel, all under the dreamy glare of noon, offered a striking spectacle, far surpassing whatever I had anticipated, and announced populousness and wealth. We longed to enter those gates and walk those streets. But we had yet a delay to wear out. At about a league from the town our guide, Mubarek, led us off the main road to the right, up and down several little but steep sand-hills, and hot declivities, till about two in the afternoon, half-roasted with the sun, we reached, never so weary, his garden gate.

"The morning was bright, yet cool, when we got free of the maze of ithel and sand-slopes, and entered the lanes that traverse the garden circle round the town, in all quiet and security. But our approach to Bereydah was destined to furnish us an unexpected and undesired surprise, though indeed less startling than that which discomposed our first arrival at Ha'yel. We had just passed a well near the angle of a garden wall, when we saw a man whose garb and appearance at once bespoke him for a muleteer of the north, watering a couple of mules at the pool hard by. Barakat and I stared with astonishment, and could hardly believe our eyes. For since the day we left Gaza for the southeastern desert we had never met with a like dress, nor with these animals; and how, then, came they here? But there was no mistaking either the man or the beasts, and as the muleteer raised his head to look at the passers-by, he also started at our sight, and evidently recognized in us something that took him unawares. But the riddle was soon solved. A few paces farther on, our way opened out on the great plain that lies immediately under the town walls to the north. This space was now covered with tents and thronged with men of foreign dress and bearing, mixed with Arabs of town and desert, women and children, talking and quarrelling, buying and selling, going and coming; everywhere baskets full of dates and vegetables, platters bearing eggs and butter, milk and whey, meat hung on poles, bundles of firewood, etc., stood ranged in rows, horsemen and camel-men were riding about between groups seated round fires or reclining against their baggage; in the midst of all this medley a gilt ball surmounted a large white pavilion of a make that I had not seen since last I left India, some eleven years before, and numerous smaller tents of striped cloth, and certainly not of Arab fashion, clustered around; a lively scene, especially of a clear morning, but requiring some explanation from its exotic and non-Arab character. These tents belonged to the great caravan of Persian pilgrims, on their return from Medina to Meshid 'Alee by the road of Kaseem, and hence all this unusual concourse and bustle.

"Passing a little on to the east, we left the crowded encampment on one side and turned to enter the city gates. Here, and this is generally the case in the larger Arab towns of old date, the fortifications surround houses alone, and the gardens all lie without, sometimes defended—at 'Oneyzah, for example—by a second outer girdle of walls and

AN ARAB ENCAMPMENT.

towers, but sometimes, as at Bereydah, devoid of any mural protection. The town itself is composed exclusively of streets, houses, and market-places, and bears in consequence a more regular appearance than the recent and village-like arrangements of the Djowf and even of Ha'yel. We passed a few streets, tolerably large but crooked, and then made the camels kneel down in a little square or public place, where I remained seated by them on the baggage, switch in hand, like an ordinary Arab traveller, and Barakat with Mubarek went in search of lodgings.

"Very long did the half-hour seem to me during which I had thus to mount guard till my companions returned from their quest; the streets were full of people, and a disagreeable crowd of the lower sort was every moment collecting round myself and my camels, with all the inquisitiveness of the idle and vulgar in every land. At last my companions came back to say that they had found what they wanted; a kick or two brought the camels on their legs again, and we moved off to our new quarters.

"The house in question was hardly more than five minutes' walk from the north gate, and at about an equal distance only from the great market-place on the other side. Its position was therefore good. It possessed two large rooms on the ground story, and three smaller, besides a spacious court-yard, surrounded by high walls. A winding stair of irregular steps and badly lighted, like all in the Nedjed, led up to an extent of flat roof, girt round by a parapet six feet high, and divided into two compartments by a cross-wall, thus affording a very tolerable place for occupation morning and evening, at the hours when the side-walls might yet project enough shade to shelter those seated alongside of them, besides an excellent sleeping-place for night."

The day after their arrival they made a call upon Mohanna, the ruler of Bereydah, in order to ask his assistance in proceeding to Nedjed. But he was too busy in devising means to exact more tribute-money from the Persian pilgrims to give any notice to two persons whose dress and appearance gave no token of wealth. This neglect afterward proved to be a piece of good fortune. They then spent several days in a vain attempt to find camels and guides; no one was willing to undertake the service. The central province of Nedjed, the genuine Wahabee country, is to the rest of Arabia a sort of lion's den, into which few venture and yet fewer return. An elderly man of Bereydah, of whom Palgrave demanded information, simply replied, "It is Nedjed; he who enters it does not come out again," and this is almost literally true. Its mountains, once the fastnesses of robbers and assassins, are at the present day equally, or even more, formidable as the stronghold of fanatics who consider everyone save themselves an infidel or a heretic, and who regard the slaughter of an infidel or a heretic as a duty, at least a merit. In addition to this general cause of anticipating a worse than cold reception in Nedjed, wars and bloodshed, aggression and tyranny, have heightened the original antipathy of the surrounding population into special and definite resentment for wrongs received, perhaps inflicted, till Nedjed has become for all but her born sons doubly dangerous and doubly hateful.

Another circumstance, which seemed to make Palgrave's situation more difficult, although it was equally fortunate in the end, was a rebellion which had broken out in the neighboring city of 'Oneyzah, headed by Zamil, a native chief. The town was at that time besieged by the Wahabees, yet held out gallantly, and the sympathy of the people of all Kaseem was so strongly on the side of Zamil, that only the presence of the Wahabee troops in Bereydah kept that city, also, from revolt. The rebels had sent deputations to Mecca and also to Djebel Shomer for assistance, and there seemed to be some possibility of a general Central Arabian revolt against the hated Wahabee supremacy. It seemed thus to be a most unpropitious time for penetrating the stronghold of Nedjed. Palgrave did not so much fear the suspicion of being a European, as that of being an Ottoman spy. His first need, however, was the means of going forward safely. He thus described how an apparent chance made him acquainted with the man to whom almost the entire success of his later travels was due:

"It was the sixth day after our arrival, and the 22d of September, when about noon I was sitting alone and rather melancholy, and trying to beguile the time with reading the incomparable Divan of Ebn-el-Farid, the favorite companion of my travels. Barakat had at my request betaken himself out of doors, less in hopes of success than to 'go to and fro in the earth and walk up and down in it;' nor did

I now dare to expect that he would return any wiser than he had set forth. When lo! after a long two hours' absence he came in with cheerful face, index of good tidings.

"Good, indeed, they were, none better. Their bearer said, that after roaming awhile to no purport through the streets and market-place, he had bethought him of a visit to the Persian camp. There, while straying among the tents, 'like a washerwoman's dog,' as a Hindoo would say, he noticed somewhat aloof from the crowd a small group of pilgrims seated near their baggage on the sand, while curls of smoke going up from amid the circle indicated the presence of a fire, which at that time of day could be for nothing else than coffee. Civilized though Barakat undoubtedly was, he was yet by blood and heart an Arab, and for an Arab to see coffee-making and not to put himself in the way of getting a share would be an act of self-restraint totally unheard of. So he approached the group, and was of course invited to sit down and drink. The party consisted of two wealthy Persians, accompanied by three or four of that class of men, half servants, half-companions, who often hook on to travellers at Bagdad or its neighborhood, besides a mulatto of Arabo-negrine origin, and his master, this last being the leader of the band, and the giver of the aromatic entertainment.

"Barakat's whole attention was at once engrossed by this personage. A remarkably handsome face, of a type evidently not belonging to the Arab peninsula, long hair curling down to the shoulders, an over-dress of fine spun silk, somewhat soiled by travel, a colored handkerchief of Syrian manufacture on the head, a manner and look indicating an education much superior to that ordinary in his class and occupation, a camel-driver's, were peculiarities sufficient of themselves to attract notice, and give rise to conjecture. But when these went along with a welcome and a salute in the forms and tone of Damascus or Aleppo, and a ready flow of that superabundant and overcharged politeness for which the Syrian subjects of the Turkish empire are renowned, Barakat could no longer doubt that he had a fellow-countryman, and one, too, of some note, before him.

"Such was in fact the case. Aboo-'Eysa, to give him the name by which he was commonly known in these parts, though in his own country he bears another denomination, was a native of Aleppo, and son of a not unimportant individual in that fair city. His education, and the circumstances of his early youth, had rendered him equally conversant with townsmen and herdsmen, with citizens and Bedouins, with Arabs and Europeans. By lineal descent he was a Bedouin, since his grandfather belonged to the Mejadimah, who are themselves an offshoot of the Benoo-Khalid; but in habits, thoughts, and manners he was a very son of Aleppo, where he had passed the greater part of his boyhood and youth. When about twenty-five years of age he became involved, culpably or not, in the great conspiracy against the Turkish government which broke out in the Aleppine insurrection of 1852. Like many others he was compelled to anticipate consequences by a prompt flight.

"After trying commerce in order to retrieve his ruined fortunes, but with ill success, Aboo-'Eysa engaged in the horse trade between Persia and Arabia, and also failed. He then went to Ri'ad, the capital of Nedjed, and by presents to Feysul, the chief, obtained a post as guide to the Persian caravans of pilgrims to Mecca, across Arabia. At this time he had followed that career for three years, and had amassed considerable wealth, for his politeness, easy manners, and strict probity made him popular with the pilgrims.

"He recognized a fellow-countryman in Barakat," says Palgrave, "received him with marked politeness, and carefully informed himself of our whence and whither. Barakat, overjoyed to find at last a kind of opening after difficulties that had appeared to obstruct all further progress, made no delay in inquiring whether he would undertake our guidance to Ri'ad. Aboo-'Eysa replied that he was just on the point of separating from his friends the Persians, whose departure would leave camels enough and to spare at his disposition, and that so far there was no hindrance to the proposal. As for the Wahabees and their unwillingness to admit strangers within their limits, he stated himself to be well known to them, and that in his company we should have nothing to fear from their suspicious criticism."

The agreement was made at once, and the travellers now only waited until their new companion should have made some final arrangements with the Persian pilgrims, who were to travel directly from Bereydah to Bagdad. In the meantime, the former took advantage of the delay to see as much as possible of the place, and even to make excursions in the neighborhood, especially in the direction of the beleaguered city of 'Oneyzah. Palgrave's description of the place shows that it possesses the same general features as the other Arabian towns, yet may be quoted for its intrinsic picturesqueness:

"Barakat and myself have made our morning household purchases at the fair, and the sun being now an hour or more above the horizon, we think it time to visit the market-place of the town, which would hardly be open sooner. We re-enter the city gate, and pass on our way by our house door, where we leave our bundle of eatables, and regain the high street of Bereydah. Before long we reach a high arch across the road; this gate divides the market from the rest of the quarter. We enter. First of all we see a long range of butchers' shops on either side, thick hung with flesh of sheep and camel, and very dirtily kept. Were not the air pure and the climate healthy, the plague would assuredly be endemic here; but in Arabia no special harm seems to follow. We hasten on, and next pass a series of cloth and linen warehouses, stocked partly with home manufacture, but more imported; Bagdad cloaks and head-gear, for instance, Syrian shawls and Egyptian slippers. Here markets follow the law general throughout the East, that all shops or stores of the same description should be clustered together, a system whose advantages on the whole outweigh its inconveniences, at least for small towns like these. In the large cities and capitals of Europe greater extent

of locality requires evidently a different method of
arrangement; it might be awkward for the inhabitants of Hyde Park were no hatters to be found
nearer than the Tower. But what is Bereydah compared even with a second-rate European city? However, in a crowd, it yields to none; the streets at
this time of the day are thronged to choking, and
to make matters worse, a huge, splay-footed camel
comes every now and then, heaving from side to side
like a lubber-rowed boat, with a long beam on his
back menacing the heads of those in the way, or
with two enormous loads of firewood, each as large
as himself, sweeping the road before him of men,
women, and children, while the driver, high-perched
on the hump, regards such trifles with the most supreme indifference, so long as he brushes his path
open. Sometimes there is a whole string of these
beasts, the head-rope of each tied to the crupper of
his precursor, very uncomfortable passengers when
met with at a narrow turning.

"Through such obstacles we have found or made
our way, and are now amid leather and shoemakers'
shops, then among coppersmiths and ironsmiths, whose
united clang might waken the dead or kill the living,
till at last we emerge on the central town-square, not
a bad one either, nor very irregular, considering that
it is in Kaseem.

The vegetable and fruit market is very extensive,
and kept almost exclusively by women; so are also
the shops for grocery and spices. Nor do the fair
sex of Bereydah seem a whit inferior to their rougher
partners in knowledge of business and thrifty dili-

gence. 'Close-handedness beseems a woman no less than generosity a man,' says an Arab poet, unconsciously coinciding with Lance of Verona in his comments on the catalogue of his future spouse's 'conditions.'

"The whole town has an aspect of old but declining prosperity. There are few new houses, but many falling into ruin. The faces, too, of most we meet are serious, and their voices in an undertone. Silk dresses are prohibited by the dominant faction, and tobacco can only be smoked within doors, and by stealth. Every now and then zealous Wahabee missionaries from Ri'ad pay a visit of reform and preaching to unwilling auditors, and disobedience to the customs of the Nedjean sect is noticed and punished, often severely.

"Enough of the town; the streets are narrow, hot, and dusty; the day, too, advances; but the gardens are yet cool. So we dash at a venture through a labyrinth of by-ways and cross-ways till we find ourselves in the wide street that, like a boulevard in France, runs immediately along but inside the walls.

"We stroll about in the shade, hide ourselves amid the high maize to smoke a quiet pipe unobserved by prying Nedjean eyes, and then walk on till at some distance we come under a high ridge of sand.

"While on one of our suburban excursions we took the direction of 'Oneyzah, but found it utterly impossible to arrive within its walls; so we contented ourselves with an outside and distant view of this large and populous town; the number of its houses, and their size, judging by the overtopping summits that marked out the dwelling of Zamil and his family, far surpassed anything in Bereydah. The outer fortifications are enormously thick, and the girdle of palm-trees between them and the town affords a considerable additional defence to the latter. For all I could see there is little stonework in the construction; they appear almost exclusively of unbaked bricks; yet even so they are formidable defences for Arabia. The whole country around, and whatever lay northeast toward Bereydah, was more or less ravaged by the war; and we were blamed by our friends as very rash in having ventured thus far; in fact, it was a mere chance that we did not fall in with skirmishers or plunderers; and in such a case the military discipline of Kaseem would hardly have insured our safety.

"When all was ready for the long-expected departure, it was definitely fixed for the 3d of October, a Friday, I think, at nightfall. Since our first interview Barakat and myself had not again presented ourselves before Mohanna, except in chance meetings, accompanied by distant salutations in the street or market-place; and we did not see any need for paying him a special farewell call. Indeed, after learning who and what he was, we did our best not to draw his gray eye on us, and thereby escaped some additional trouble and surplus duties to pay, nor did any one mention us to him. At star-rise we bade our host and householder Ahmed a final adieu, and left the town with Aboo-'Eysa for our guide."

CHAPTER XIII.

PALGRAVE'S TRAVELS—JOURNEY TO RI'AD THE CAPITAL OF NEDJED

TWO roads lay before us. The shorter, and for that reason the more frequented of the two, led southeast-by-east through Woshem and Wady Haneefah to Ri'ad. But this track passed through a district often visited at the present moment by the troops of 'Oneyzah and their allies, and hence our companions, not over-courageous for the most, were afraid to follow it. Another road, much more circuitous, but farther removed from the scene of military operations, led northeast to Zulphah, and thence entered the province of Sedeyr, which it traversed in a southeasterly or southern direction, and thus reached the 'Aared. Our council of war resolved on the latter itinerary, nor did we ourselves regret a roundabout which promised to procure us the sight of much that we might scarcely have otherwise an opportunity of visiting. Barakat and I were mounted on two excellent dromedaries of Aboo-'Eysa's stud; the Na'ib * was on a lovely gray she camel with

* "The Na'ib " was a Persian official, despatched by the Persian pilgrims to lay before Feysul, the ruler of Nedjed, a statement of the extortions to which they had been compelled to submit at Bereydah. He was thus equally under Aboo-'Eysa's

a handsome saddle, crimson and gold. The Meccans shared between them a long-backed black beast; the rest were also mounted on camels or dromedaries, since the road before us was impracticable for horses, at any rate at this time of year.

"Our road lay in Kaseem, whose highlands we rejoined once more, and traversed till sunset. The view was very beautiful from its extent and variety of ups and downs, in broad, grassy hills; little groups of trees stood in scattered detachments around; and had a river, that desideratum of Arabia, been in sight, one might almost have fancied one's self in the country bordering the Lower Rhine for some part of its course; readers may suppose, too, that there was less verdure here than in the European parallel—my comparison bears only on the general turn of the view. No river exists nearer Kaseem than Shatt (Euphrates), some hundred leagues off, and our eyes had been too long accustomed to the deceptive pools of the mirage to associate with them even a passing idea of aught save drought and heat.

"We journeyed on till dark, and then reached certain hillocks of a different character from the hard ground lately under our feet. Here began the Nefood, whose course from the southwest to northeast, and then north, parts between Kaseem, Woshem, and Sedeyr. I have already said something of these sandy inlets when describing that which we crossed three months ago between Djowf and Shomer.

charge, and his company was rather an advantage to Palgrave, since his mission was another cause of removing—or, at least, lessening—the prominence of the latter, after his arrival at Ri'ad.

"On the verge of the desert strip we now halted a little to eat a hasty supper, and to drink—the Arabs coffee and the Persians tea. But journeying in these sands, under the heat of the day, is alike killing to man and beast, and therefore Aboo-'Eysa had resolved that we should cross the greater portion under favor of the cooler hours of night.

"All night, a weary night, we waded up and down through waves of sand, in which the camels often sank up to their knees, and their riders were obliged to alight and help them on.

"Now by full daylight appeared the true character of the region which we were traversing; its aspect resembled the Nefood north of Djebel Shomer, but the undulations were here higher and deeper, and the sand itself lighter and less stable. In most spots neither shrub nor blade of grass could fix its root, in others a scanty vegetation struggled through, but no trace of man anywhere. The camels ploughed slowly on; the Persians, unaccustomed to such scenes, were downcast and silent; all were tired, and no wonder. At last, a little before noon, and just as the sun's heat was becoming intolerable, we reached the verge of an immense crater-like hollow, certainly three or four miles in circumference, where the sand-billows receded on every side, and left in the midst a pit seven or eight hundred feet in depth, at whose base we could discern a white gleam of limestone rock, and a small group of houses, trees, and gardens, thus capriciously isolated in the very heart of the desert.

"This was the little village and oasis of Wasit, or

'the intermediary,' so called because a central point between the three provinces of Kaseem, Sedeyr, and Woshem, yet belonging to none of them. Nor is it often visited by wayfarers, as we learned from the inhabitants, men simple and half-savage, from their little intercourse with the outer world, and unacquainted even with the common forms of Islamitic prayer, though dwelling in the midst of the Wahabee dominions.

"A long, winding descent brought us to the bottom of the valley, where on our arrival men and boys came out to stare at the Persians, and by exacting double prices for fruit and camel's milk proved themselves not altogether such fools as they looked. For us, regarded as Arabs, we enjoyed their hospitality—it was necessarily a limited one—gratis; whereupon the Na'ib grew jealous, and declaimed against the Arabs as 'infidels,' for not treating with suitable generosity pilgrims like themselves returning from the 'house of God.'

"To get out of this pit was no easy matter; *facilis descensus*, etc., thought I; no ascending path showed itself in the required direction, and every one tried to push up his floundering beast where the sand appeared at a manageable slope, and firm to the footing. Camels and men fell and rolled back down the declivity, till some of the party shed tears of vexation, and others, more successful, laughed at the annoyance of their companions. Aboo-'Eysa ran about from one to the other, attempting to direct and keep them together, till finally, as Heaven willed, we reached the upper rim to the north.

"Before us lay what seemed a storm-driven sea of fire in the red light of afternoon, and through it we wound our way, till about an hour before sunset we fell in with a sort of track or furrow. Next opened out on our road a long descent, at whose extreme base we discerned the important and commercial town of Zulphah. Beyond it róse the wall-like steeps of Djebel Toweyk, so often heard of, and now seen close at hand. Needless to say how joyfully we welcomed the first view of that strange ridge, the heart and central knot of Arabia, beyond which whatever lay might almost be reckoned as a return journey.

"We had now, in fact, crossed the Nefood, and had at our feet the great valley which constitutes the main line of communication between Nedjed and the north, reaching even to the Tigris and Bagdad.

"We passed the whole length of the town of Zulphah, several streets of which had been lately swept away by the winter torrents that pour at times their short-lived fury down this valley. Before us to the southeast stretched the long hollow; on our right was the Nefood, on our left Djebel Toweyk and the province of Sedeyr. The mountain air blew cool, and this day's journey was a far pleasanter one than its predecessor. We continued our march down the valley till the afternoon, when we turned aside into a narrow gorge running up at a sharp angle to the northeast, and thus entered between the heights of Djebel Toweyk itself.

"This mountain essentially constitutes Nedjed. It is a wide and flat chain, or rather plateau, whose general form is that of a huge crescent. If I may be permitted here to give my rough guess regarding the elevation of the main plateau, a guess grounded partly on the vegetation, climate, and similar local features, partly on an approximate estimate of the ascent itself, and of the subsequent descent on the other or sea side, I should say that it varies from a height of one to two thousand feet above the surrounding level of the peninsula, and may thus be about three thousand feet at most above the sea. Its loftiest ledges occur in the Sedeyr district, where we shall pass them before long; the centre and the southwesterly arm is certainly lower. Djebel Toweyk is the middle knot of Arabia, its Caucasus, so to say; and is still, as it has often been in former times, the turning-point of the whole, or almost the whole, peninsula in a political and national bearing.

"The climate of the northern part of Djebel Toweyk, whether plateau or valley, coincident with the province of Sedeyr, is perhaps one of the healthiest in the world; an exception might be made in favor of Djebel Shomer alone. The above-named districts resemble each other closely in dryness of atmosphere, and the inhabitants of Sedeyr, like those of Shomer, are remarkable for their ruddy complexion and well-developed stature. But when we approach the centre of the mountain crescent, where its whole level lowers, while the more southerly latitude brings it nearer to the prevailing influences of the tropical zone, the air becomes damper and more relaxing, and a less salubrious climate pictures itself in the sallower faces and slender make of its denizens.

"Two days later we attained the great plateau, of which I have a few pages since given an anticipated description.

"About noon we halted in a brushwood-covered plain to light fire and prepare coffee. After which we pursued our easterly way, still a little to the north, now and then meeting with travellers or peasants; but a European would find these roads very lonely in comparison with those of his own country. All the more did I admire the perfect submission and strict police enforced by the central government, so that even a casual robbery is very rare in the provinces, and highwaymen are totally out of the question. At last, near the same hour of afternoon that had brought us the day before to Ghat, we came in sight of Mejmaa', formerly capital of the province, and still a place of considerable importance, with a population, to judge by appearances and hearsay, of between ten and twelve thousand souls.

"We were up early next morning, for the night air was brisk, and a few hours of sleep had sufficed us.

"After sunrise we came on a phenomenon of a nature, I believe, without a second or a parallel in Central Arabia, yet withal most welcome, namely, a tolerably large source of running water, forming a wide and deepish stream, with grassy banks, and frogs croaking in the herbage. We opened our eyes in amazement; it was the first of the kind that we had beheld since leaving the valley of Djowf. But though a living, it is a short-lived rivulet, reaching only four or five hours' distance to Djelajil, where it is lost amid the plantations of the suburbs.

"We had not long traversed the Meteyr encampment, when we came in view of the walls of Toweym, a large town, containing between twelve and fifteen thousand inhabitants, according to the computation here in use, and which I follow for want of better. The houses are here built compactly, of two stories in general, sometimes three; the lower rooms are often fifteen or sixteen feet high, and the upper ten or twelve; while the roof itself is frequently surrounded by a blind wall of six feet or more, till the whole attains a fair altitude, and is not altogether unimposing.

"Early next day, at a short distance from Toweym, we passed another large village with battlemented walls, and on the opposite side of the road a square castle, looking very mediæval; this was Hafr. A couple of hours further on we reached Thomeyr, a straggling townlet, more abounding in broken walls than houses; close by was a tall white rock, crowned by the picturesque remains of an old outwork or fort, overlooking the place. Here our party halted for breakfast in the shadow of the ruins. Barakat and myself determined to try our fortune in the village itself; no guards appeared at its open gate; we entered unchallenged, and roamed through silent lanes and heaps of rubbish, vainly seeking news of milk and dates in this city of the dead. At last we met a meagre townsman, in look and apparel the apothecary of Romeo; and of him, not without misgivings of heart, we inquired where aught eatable could be had for love or money. He apologized, though there was scarce need of that, for not having

DEATH ON THE DESERT.

any such article at his disposal; 'but,' added he, 'in such and such a house there will certainly be something good,' and thitherward he preceded us in our search. We found indeed a large dwelling, but the door was shut; we knocked to no purpose: nobody at home.

"Our man now set us a bolder example, and we altogether scrambled through a breach in the mud wall, and found ourselves amid empty rooms and a desolate court-yard. 'Everybody is out in the fields, women only excepted,' said our guide, and we separated, no better off than before. Despairing of the village commissariat, we climbed a turret on the outer walls, and looked round. Now we saw at some distance a beautiful palm-grove, where we concluded that dates could not be wanting, and off we set for it across the stubble fields. But on arriving we found our paradise surrounded by high walls, and no gate discoverable. While thus we stood without, like Milton's fiend at Eden, but unable, like him, 'by one high bound to overleap all bound,' up came a handsome Solibah lad, all in rags, half-walking, half-dancing, in the devil-may-care way of his tribe. 'Can you tell us which is the way in?' was our first question, pointing to the garden before us; and, 'Shall I sing you a song?' was his first answer. 'We don't want your songs, but dates; how are we to get at them?' we replied. 'Or shall I perform you a dance?' answered the grinning young scoundrel, and forthwith began an Arabian polka-step, laughing all the while at our undisguised impatience. At last he condescended to show us the way, but no other than what befitted an orchard-robbing boy, like himself, for it lay a little farther off, right over the wall, which he scaled with practised ingenuity, and helped us to follow. So we did, though perhaps with honester intentions, and, once within, stood amid trees, shade, and water. The 'tender juvenile' then set up a shout, and soon a man appeared, 'old Adam's likeness set to dress this garden,' save that he was not old but young, as Adam might himself have been while yet in Eden. We were somewhat afraid of a surly reception, too well merited by our very equivocal introduction; but the gardener was better-tempered than many of his caste, and after saluting us very politely, offered his services at our disposal. We then proposed to purchase a stock of dates for our onward way, whereon the gardener conducted us to an outhouse where heaps of three or four kinds of this fruit, red and yellow, round or long, lay piled up, and bade us choose. At his recommendation we filled a large cloth, which we had brought with us for the purpose, with excellent ruddy dates, and gave in return a small piece of money, welcome here as elsewhere. We then took leave and returned, but this time through the garden gate, to the stubble fields, and passing under the broken walls of the village, reached our companions, who had become anxious at our absence."

For three days longer the travellers journeyed southward, through the valleys branching out from Djebel Toweyk, encamping for the night near some of the small towns. "In the early gray of the fourth morning," says Palgrave, "we passed close under the plantations of Rowdah down the valley, now dry and still, once overflowed with the best blood of Arabia, and through the narrow and high-walled pass which gives entrance to the great strongholds of the land. The sun rose and lighted up to our view wild precipices on either side, with a tangled mass of broken rock and brushwood below, while coveys of partridges started up at our feet, and deer scampered away by the gorges to right or left, or a cloud of dust announced the approach of peasant bands or horsemen going to and fro, and gardens or hamlets gleamed through side openings or stood niched in the bulging passes of the Wady itself, till before noon we arrived at the little hamlet of Malka, or 'the junction.'

"Its name is derived from its position. Here the valley divides in form of a Y, sending off two branches—one southerly to Derey'eeyah, the other southeast-by-east through the centre of the province, and communicating with the actual capital, Ri'ad.

"Aboo-'Eysa had meditated bringing us on that very evening to Ri'ad. But eight good leagues remained from Malka to the capital; and when the Na'ib had terminated his cosmetic operations, the easterly turning shadows left us no hope of attaining Ri'ad before nightfall. However, we resumed our march, and took the arm of the valley leading to Derey'eeyah; but before reaching it we once more quitted the Wady, and followed a shorter path by the highlands to the left. Our way was next crossed by a long range of towers, built by Ibraheem Pasha, as outposts for the defence of this important position. Within their line stood the lonely walls of a large, square barrack; the towers were what we sometimes call Martello—short, large, and round.

"The level rays of the setting sun now streamed across the plain, and we came on the ruins of Derey'eeyah, filling up the whole breadth of the valley beneath. The palace walls, of unbaked brick, like the rest, rose close under the left or northern edge, but unroofed and tenantless; a little lower down a wide extent of fragments showed where the immense mosque had been, and hard by, the market-place; a tower on an isolated height was, I suppose, the original dwelling-place of the Sa'ood family, while yet mere local chieftains, before growing greatness transferred them to their imperial palace. The outer fortifications remained almost uninjured for much of their extent, with turrets and bastions reddening in the western light; in other places the Egyptian artillery, or the process of years, had levelled them with the earth; within the town many houses were yet standing, but uninhabited, and the lines of the streets from gate to gate were distinct as in a ground plan. From the great size of the town (for it is full half a mile in length, and not much less in breadth), and from the close packing of the houses, I should estimate its capacity at above forty thousand indwellers. The gardens lie without, and still 'living waved where man had ceased to live,' in full beauty and luxuriance, a deep green ring around the gray ruins. For although the Nedjeans, holding it for an ill omen to rebuild and reinhabit a town so fatally overthrown, have transplanted the seat of government, and with it the bulk of the city population, to Ri'ad, they have not deemed it equally necessary to abandon the rich plantations and well-watered fields belonging to the old capital; and thus a small colony of gardeners in scattered huts and village dwellings close under the walls protract the blighted existence of Derey'eeyah.

"While from our commanding elevation we gazed thoughtfully on this scene, so full of remembrances, the sun set, and darkness grew on. We naturally proposed a halt, but Aboo-'Eysa turned a deaf ear, and affirmed that a garden belonging to 'Abd-er-Rahman, already mentioned as grandson of the first Wahabee, was but a little farther before us, and better adapted to our night's rest than the ruins. In truth, three hours of brisk travelling yet intervened between Derey'eeyah and the place in question; but our guide was unwilling to enter Derey'eeyah in company of Persians and Syrians, Shiya'ees and Christians; and this he afterward confessed to me. For, whether from one of those curious local influences which outlast even the change of races, and give one abiding color to the successive tenants of the same spot, or whether it be occasioned by the constant view of their fallen greatness and the triumph of their enemies, the scanty population of Derey'eeyah comprises some of the bitterest and most bigoted fanatics that even 'Aared can offer. Accordingly we moved on, still keeping to the heights, and late at night descended a little hollow, where, amid an extensive garden, stood the country villa of 'Abd-er-Rahman.

"We did not attempt to enter the house; indeed, at such an hour no one was stirring to receive us. But a shed in the garden close by sufficed for travellers who were all too weary to desire aught but sleep; and this we soon found in spite of dogs and jackals, numerous here and throughout Nedjed.

"From this locality to the capital was about four miles' distance. Our party divided next morning; the Na'ib and his associates remaining behind, while Barakat and myself, with Aboo-'Eysa, set off straight for the town, where our guide was to give notice at the palace of the approach of the Persian dignitary, that the honors due to his reception might meet him half-way. At our request the Meccans stayed also in the rear; we did not desire the equivocal effect of their company on a first appearance.

"For about an hour we proceeded southward, through barren and undulating ground, unable to see over the country to any distance. At last we attained a rising eminence, and crossing it, came at once in full view of Ri'ad, the main object of our long journey—the capital of Nedjed and half Arabia, its very heart of hearts.

"Before us stretched a wild open valley, and in its foreground, immediately below the pebbly slope on whose summit we stood, lay the capital, large and square, crowned by high towers and strong walls of defence, a mass of roofs and terraces, where overtopping all frowned the huge but irregular pile of Feysul's royal castle, and hard by it rose the scarce less conspicuous palace, built and inhabited by his eldest son, 'Abdallah. Other edifices, too, of remarkable appearance broke here and there through the maze of gray roof-tops, but of their object and indwellers we were yet to learn. All around for full three miles over the surrounding plain, but more especially to the west and south, waved a sea of palm-trees above green fields and well-watered gardens; while the singing, droning sound of the water-wheels reached us even where we had halted, at a quarter of a mile or more from the nearest town-walls. On the opposite side southward, the valley opened out into the great and even more fertile plains of Yemamah, thickly dotted with groves and villages, among which the large town of Manfoohah, hardly inferior in size to Ri'ad itself, might be clearly distinguished. Farther in the background ranged the blue hills, the ragged Sierra of Yemamah, compared some thirteen hundred years since, by 'Amroo-ebn-Kelthoom, the Shomerite, to drawn swords in battle array; and behind them was concealed the immeasurable Desert of the South, or Dahna. On the west the valley closes in and narrows in its upward windings toward Derey'eeyah, while to the southwest the low mounds of Aflaj are the division between it and Wady Dowasir. Due east in the distance a long blue line marks the farthest heights of Toweyk, and shuts out from view the low ground of Hasa and the shores of the Persian Gulf. In all the countries which I have visited, and they are many, seldom has it been mine to survey a landscape equal to this in beauty and in historical meaning, rich and full alike to eye and mind. But should any of my readers have ever approached Damascus from the side of the Anti-Lebanon, and surveyed the Ghootah from the heights above Mazzeh, they may thence form an approximate idea of the valley of Ri'ad when viewed from the north. Only this is wider and more varied, and the circle of vision here embraces vaster plains and bolder mountains; while the mixture of tropical aridity and luxuriant verdure, of crowded population and desert tracks, is one that Arabia alone can present, and in comparison with which Syria seems tame, and Italy monotonous."

CHAPTER XIV.

PALGRAVE'S TRAVELS—ADVENTURES IN RI'AD

"BARAKAT and myself stopped our dromedaries a few minutes on the height to study and enjoy this noble prospect, and to forget the anxiety inseparable from a first approach to the lion's own den. Aboo-'Eysa, too, though not unacquainted with the scene, willingly paused with us to point out and name the main features of the view, and show us where lay the onward road to his home in Hasa. We then descended the slope and skirted the walls of the first outlying plantations which gird the town.

"At last we reached a great open square: its right side, the northern, consists of shops and warehouses; while the left is entirely absorbed by the huge abode of Nedjean royalty; in front of us, and consequently to the west, a long covered passage, upborne high on a clumsy colonnade, crossed the breadth of the square, and reached from the palace to the great mosque, which it thus joins directly with the interior of the castle and affords old Feysul a private and unseen passage at will from his own apartments to his official post at the Friday prayers, without exposing him on his way to vulgar curiosity, or perhaps to the dangers of treachery. For the fate of his father and of his great-uncle, his predecessors on the throne, and each of them pierced by the dagger of an assassin during public worship, has rendered Feysul very timid on this score, though not at prayer-time only. Behind this colonnade, other shops and warehouses make up the end of the square, or, more properly, parallelogram; its total length is about two hundred paces, by rather more than half the same width. In the midst of this space, and under the far-reaching shadow of the castle walls, are seated some fifty or sixty women, each with a stock of bread, dates, milk, vegetables, or firewood before her for sale.

"But we did not now stop to gaze, nor indeed did we pay much attention to all this; our first introduction to the monarch and the critical position before us took up all our thoughts. So we paced on alongside of the long blind wall running out from the central keep, and looking more like the outside of a fortress than of a peaceful residence, till we came near a low and narrow gate, the only entry to the palace. Deep-sunk between the bastions, with massive folding-doors iron bound, though thrown open at this hour of the day, and giving entrance into a dark passage, one might easily have taken it for the vestibule of a prison; while the number of guards, some black, some white, but all sword-girt, who almost choked the way, did not seem very inviting to those without, especially to foreigners. Long earth seats lined the adjoining walls, and afforded a convenient waiting-place for visitors; and here we took up our rest at a little distance from the palace gate; but Aboo-'Eysa entered at once to announce our arrival, and the approach of the Na'ib.

"The first who drew near and saluted us was a

tall, meagre figure, of a sallow complexion, and an intelligent but slightly ill-natured and underhand cast of features. He was very well dressed, though of course without a vestige of unlawful silk in his apparel, and a certain air of conscious importance tempered the affability of his politeness. This was 'Abd-el-'Azeez, whom, for want of a better title, I shall call the minister of foreign affairs, such being the approximate translation of his official style.

"Accompanied by some attendants from the palace, he came stately up, and seated himself by our side. He next began the customary interrogations of whence and what, with much smiling courtesy and show of welcome. After hearing our replies, the same of course as those given elsewhere, he invited us to enter the precincts, and partake of his Majesty's coffee and hospitality, while he promised us more immediate communications from the king himself in the course of the day.

"If my readers have seen, as most of them undoubtedly will, the Paris Tuileries, they may hereby know that the whole extent of Feysul's palace equals about two-thirds of that construction, and is little inferior to it in height; if indeed we except the angular pyramidal roofs or extinguishers peculiar to the French edifice. But in ornament the Parisian pile has the better of it, for there is small pretensions to architectural embellishment in this Wahabee Louvre. Without, within, every other consideration has been sacrificed to strength and security; and the outer view of Newgate, at any rate, bears a very strong resemblance to the general effect of Feysul's palace.

"Aboo-'Eysa meanwhile, in company with the outriders sent from the palace, had gone to meet the Na'ib and introduce him to the lodgings prepared for his reception. Very much was the Persian astounded to find none of the royal family among those who thus came, no one even of high name or office; but yet more was his surprise when, instead of immediate admittance to Feysul's presence and eager embrace, he was quietly led aside to the very guest-room whither we had been conducted, and a dinner not a whit more sumptuous than ours was set before him, after which he was very coolly told that he might pray for Feysul and retire to his quarters, while the king settled the day and hour whereon he would vouchsafe him the honor of an audience.

"Afterward, the minister of foreign affairs condescended to come in person, and, sweetly smiling, informed us that our temporary habitation was ready, and that Aboo-'Eysa would conduct us thither without delay. We then begged to know, if possible, the king's good-will and pleasure regarding our stay and our business in the town. For on our first introduction we had duly stated, in the most correct Wahabee phraseology, that we had come to Ri'ad 'desiring the favor of God, and secondly of Feysul; and that we begged of God, and secondly of Feysul, permission to exercise in the town our medical profession, under the protection of God, and in the next place of Feysul.' For Dogberry's advice to 'set God first, for God defend but God should go before such villains,' is here observed to the letter; whatever is desired, purported, or asked, the Deity must take the lead. Nor this only, but even the subsequent mention of the creature must nowise be coupled with that of the Creator by the ordinary conjunction ' w',' that is, 'and,' since that would imply equality between the two—flat blasphemy in word or thought. Hence the disjunctive ' thumma,' or 'next after,' 'at a distance,' must take the place of ' w',' under penalty of prosecution under the statute. ' Unlucky the man who visits Nedjed without being previously well versed in the niceties of grammar,' said Barakat; 'under these schoolmasters a mistake might cost the scholar his head.' But of this more anon; to return to our subject, 'Abd-el-'Azeez, a true politician, answered our second interrogation with a vague assurance of good-will and unmeaning patronage. Meantime the Na'ib and his train marched off in high dudgeon to their quarters, and Aboo-'Eysa gave our dromedaries a kick, made them rise, and drove them before us to our new abode."

In the course of a day or two the travellers discovered what a sensation the arrival of their caravan had produced at court. The old king, Feysul, now in the thirty-third year of his reign, possessed all the superstition and bigotry of the old Wahabees, and the sudden presence of Syrians, suspected of being Christians, Persians, and Meccans, in his capital, was too much for him. He at once left the palace, took up his temporary residence in a house outside the city, and a strong guard was posted around him until the court officials should have time to examine the strangers, discover, if possible, their secret designs, and report them to the king. The first spy was a shrewd and intelligent Affghan, a pretended convert to the Wahabee doctrine, who discovered nothing, and consequently made an unfavorable report. The second was a "man of zeal," one of a committee of twenty-two inquisitors, appointed by the king to exercise constant espionage upon the inhabitants, with the power of punishing them at will for any infraction or neglect of the Wahabee discipline. Palgrave gives the following account of his visit:

"Abbood, for such was his name, though I never met the like before or after in Arabia proper, however common it may be in Syria and Lebanon, took a different and more efficacious mode of espionage than 'Abd-el-Hameed had done before him. Affecting to consider us Mahometans, and learned ones too, he entered at once on religious topics, on the true character of Islam, its purity or corruptions, and inquired much after the present teaching and usages of Damascus and the North, evidently in the view of catching us in our words. But he had luckily encountered his match; for every citation of the Koran we replied with two, and proved ourselves intimately acquainted with the 'greater' and the 'lesser' polytheism of foreign nations and heterodox Mahometans, with the commentaries of Beydowee and the tales of the Hadeeth, till our visitor, now won over to confidence, launched out full sail on the sea of discussion, and thereby rendered himself equally instructive and interesting to men who had nothing more at heart than to learn the tenets of the sect from one of its most zealous professors, nay, a Zelator in person. In short, he ended by becoming half a friend, and his regrets at our being, like other Damascenes, yet in the outer porch of darkness, were tempered by a hope, which he did not disguise, of at least putting a window in our porch for its better enlightenment."

Next day, in the forenoon, while the travellers were sauntering about the market-place, they met the minister 'Abd-el-'Azeez, who had that morning returned to the capital. With a smiling face and an air of great benignity he took them aside, and informed them the king did not consider Ri'ad a proper field for their medical skill; that they had better at once continue their journey to Hofhoof, whither Aboo-'Eysa should conduct them straightway; and that the king would furnish each of them with a camel, a new suit of clothes, and some money. To these arguments Palgrave could only answer that he greatly desired the profit to be expected from a few weeks of medical practice in Ri'ad, since his success there would give him an immediate reputation in Hofhoof, while his departure might deprive him of all reputation at the latter place. The minister promised to present his plea to Feysul, but gave him no hope of a favorable answer. The order to leave was repeated, and then, as a last experiment, Palgrave sent to two of the ministers a pound of the fragrant wood, which is burned as pastilles in Arabia, and is highly prized by the upper classes. The next day he received permission to remain longer in Ri'ad and exercise his profession. He thereupon took another residence, not so near the palace, and within convenient reach of one of the city gates.

Before describing the place he gives the following account of the famous Arabian coffee:

"Be it then known, by way of prelude, that coffee, though one in name, is manifold in fact; nor is every kind of berry entitled to the high qualifications too indiscriminately bestowed on the comprehensive genus. The best coffee, let cavillers say what they will, is that of the Yemen, commonly entitled 'Mokha,' from the main place of exportation. Now, I should be sorry to incur a lawsuit for libel or defamation from our wholesale or retail salesmen; but were the particle NOT prefixed to the countless labels in London shop windows that bear the name of the Red Sea haven, they would have a more truthy import than what at present they convey. Very little, so little indeed as to be quite inappreciable, of the Mocha or Yemen berry ever finds its way westward of Constantinople. Arabia itself, Syria, and Egypt consume fully two-thirds, and the remainder is almost exclusively absorbed by Turkish and Armenian œsophagi. Nor do these last get for their limited share the best or the purest. Before reaching the harbors of Alexandria, Jaffa, Beyrout, etc., for further exportation, the Mokhan bales have been, while yet on their way, sifted and resifted, grain by grain, and whatever they may have contained of the hard, rounded, half-transparent, greenish-brown berry, the only one really worth roasting and pounding, has been carefully picked out by experienced fingers; and it is the less generous residue of flattened, opaque, and whitish grains which alone, or almost alone, goes on board the shipping. So constant is this selecting process, that a gradation regular as the degrees on a map may be observed in the quality of Mokha, that is, Yemen, coffee even within the limits of Arabia itself, in proportion as one approaches to or recedes from Wadi Nejran and the neighborhood of Mecca, the first stages of the radiating mart. I have myself been times out of number an eye-witness of this sifting; the operation is performed with the utmost seriousness and scrupulous exactness, reminding me of the diligence ascribed to American diamond-searchers when scrutinizing the torrent sands for their minute but precious treasure.

"The berry, thus qualified for foreign use, quits its native land on three main lines of export—that of the Red Sea, that of the inner Hedjaz, and that of Kaseem. The terminus of the first line is Egypt, of the second Syria, of the third Nedjed and Shomer. Hence Egypt and Syria are, of all countries without the frontiers of Arabia, the best supplied with its specific produce, though under the restrictions already stated; and through Alexandria or the Syrian seaports, Constantinople and the North obtain their diminished share. But this last stage of transport seldom conveys the genuine article, except by the intervention of private arrangements and personal friendship or interest. Where mere sale and traffic are concerned, substitution of an inferior quality, or an adulteration almost equivalent to substitution, frequently takes place in the different storehouses of the coast, till whatever Mokha-marked coffee leaves them for Europe and the West, is often no more like the real offspring of the Yemen plant than the logwood preparations of a London fourth-rate retail wine-seller resemble the pure libations of an Oporto vineyard.

"The second species of coffee, by some preferred to that of Yemen, but in my poor opinion inferior to it, is the growth of Abyssinia; its berry is larger, and of a somewhat different and a less heating flavor. It is, however, an excellent species; and whenever the rich land that bears it shall be permitted by man to enjoy the benefits of her natural fertility, it will probably become an object of extensive cultivation and commerce. With this stops, at least in European opinion and taste, the list of coffee, and begins the list of beans.

"While we were yet in the Djowf I described with sufficient minuteness how the berry is prepared for actual use; nor is the process any way varied in Nedjed or other Arab lands. But in Nedjed an additional spicing of saffron, cloves, and the like, is still more common; a fact which is easily explained by the want of what stimulus tobacco affords elsewhere. A second consequence of non-smoking among the Arabs is the increased strength of their coffee decoctions in Nedjed, and the prodigious frequency of their use; to which we must add the larger 'finjans,' or coffee-cups, here in fashion. So sure are men, when debarred of one pleasure or excitement, to make it up by another."

Palgrave gives the following picturesque description of the Wahabee capital: "We wrap our headgear, like true Arabs, round our chins, put on our grave-looking black cloaks, take each a long stick in hand, and thread the narrow streets intermediate between our house and the market-place at a funeral pace, and speaking in an undertone. Those whom we meet salute us, or we salute them; be it known that the lesser number should always be the first to salute the greater, he who rides him who walks, he who walks him who stands, the stander the sitter, and so forth; but never should a man salute a woman; difference of age or even of rank between men does not enter into the general rules touching the priority of salutation. If those whom we have accosted happen to be acquaintances or patients, or should they belong to the latitudinarian school, our salutation is duly returned. But if, by ill fortune, they appertain to the strict and high orthodox party, an under-look with a half scowl in silence is their only answer to our greeting. Whereat we smile, Malvolio-like, and pass on.

"At last we reach the market-place; it is full of women and peasants, selling exactly what we want to buy, besides meat, firewood, milk, etc.; around are customers, come on errands like our own. We single out a tempting basket of dates, and begin haggling with the unbeautiful Phyllis, seated beside her rural store. We find the price too high. 'By Him who protects Feysul,' answers she, 'I am the loser at that price.' We insist. 'By Him who shall grant Feysul a long life, I cannot bate it,' she replies. We have nothing to oppose to such tremendous asseverations, and accede or pass on, as the case may be.

"Half of the shops, namely, those containing grocery, household articles of use, shoemakers' stalls and smithies, are already open and busily thronged. For the capital of a strongly centralized empire is always full of strangers, come will they nill they on their several affairs. But around the butchers' shops awaits the greatest human and canine crowd. My readers, I doubt not, know that the only licensed scavengers throughout the East are the dogs. Nedjeans are great flesh-eaters, and no wonder, considering the cheapness of meat (a fine fat sheep costs at most five shillings, often less) and the keenness of mountaineer appetites. I wish that the police regulations of the city would enforce a little more cleanliness about these numerous shambles; every refuse is left to cumber the ground at scarce two yards' distance. But dogs and dry air much alleviate the nuisance—a remark I made before at Ha'yel and Bereydah; it holds true for all Central Arabia.

"Barakat and I resolve on continuing our walk through the town. Ri'ad is divided into four quarters: one, the northeastern, to which the palaces of the royal family, the houses of the state officers, and the richer class of proprietors and government men belong. Here the dwellings are in general high, and the streets tolerably straight and not over-narrow; but the ground level is low, and it is perhaps the least healthy locality of all. Next the northwestern, where we are lodged; a large irregular mass of houses, varying in size and keeping from the best to the worst; here strangers, and often certain equivocal characters, never wanting in large towns, however strictly regulated, chiefly abide; here too are many noted for disaffection, and harboring other tenets than those of the son of 'Abdel-Wahab, men prone to old Arab ways and customs in 'Church and State,' to borrow our own analogous phrase; here are country chiefs, here Bedouins and natives of Zulphah and the outskirts find a lodging; here, if anywhere, is tobacco smoked or sold, and the Koran neglected in proportion. However, I would not have my readers to think our entire neighborhood so absolutely disreputable.

"But we gladly turn away our eyes from so dreary a view to refresh them by a survey of the southwestern quarter, the chosen abode of formalism and orthodoxy. In this section of Ri'ad inhabit the most energetic Zelators, here are the most irreproachable five-prayers-a-day Nedjeans, and all the flower of Wahabee purity. Above all, here dwell the principal survivors of the family of the great religious Founder, the posterity of 'Abd-el-Wahab escaped from the Egyptian sword, and free from every stain of foreign contamination. Mosques of primitive simplicity and ample space, where the great dogma, not however confined to Ri'ad, that ' we are exactly in the right, and everyone else is in the wrong,' is daily inculcated to crowds of auditors, overjoyed to find Paradise all theirs and none's but theirs; smaller oratories of Musallas, wells for ablution, and Kaabah-directed niches adorn every corner, and fill up every interval of house or orchard. The streets of this quarter are open, and the air healthy, so that the invisible blessing is seconded by sensible and visible privileges of Providence. Think not, gentle reader, that I am indulging in gratuitous or self-invented irony ; I am only rendering expression for expression, and almost word for word, the talk of true Wahabees, when describing the model quarter of their model city. This section of the town is spacious and well-peopled, and flourishes, the citadel of national and religious intolerance, pious pride, and genuine Wahabeeism.

"Round the whole town run the walls, varying from twenty to thirty feet in height; they are strong, in good repair, and defended by a deep trench and embankment. Beyond them are the gardens, much similar to those of Kaseem, both in arrangement and produce, despite the difference of latitude, here compensated by a higher ground level. But immediately to the south, in Yemamah, the eye remarks a change in the vegetation to a more tropical aspect; of this, however, I will not say more for the present.

"According to promise, Aboo-'Eysa played his part to bring us in patients and customers, and the very second morning that dawned on us in our new house ushered in an invalid who proved a very godsend. This was no other than Djowhar, treasurer of Feysul, and of the Wahabee empire. My readers may be startled to learn that this great functionary was jet black, a negro in fact, though not a slave, having obtained his freedom from Turkee, the father of the present king. He was tall, and, for a negro, handsome; about forty-five years of age, splendidly dressed, a point never neglected by wealthy Africans, whatever be their theoretical creed, and girt with a golden-hilted sword. 'But,' said he, 'gold, though unlawful if forming a part of apparel or mere ornament, may be employed with a safe conscience in decorating weapons.'

"After ceremonies and coffee, I took my dusky patient into the consulting-room, where, by dint of questioning and surmise, for negroes in general are much less clear and less to the point than Arabs in their statements, I obtained the requisite elucidation of his case. The malady, though painful, was fortunately one admitting of simple and efficacious treatment, so that I was able on the spot to promise him a sensible amendment of condition within a fortnight, and that in three weeks' time he should be in plight to undertake his journey to Bahreyn. I added that with so distinguished a personage I could not think of exacting a bargain and fixing the amount of fees; the requital of my care should be left to his generosity. He then took leave, and was re-conducted to his rooms in the palace by his fellow blacks of less degree."

The next visitor was Abd el-Kereem, of the oldest nobility of Nedjed, related to the ruling family; a bitter Wahabee, a strong, intelligent, bad, and dangerous man, who was both hated and feared by the people. His visit was a distinction for Palgrave, yet an additional danger. The latter, however, determined to draw as much information from him concerning Wahabee doctrine as he might be inclined to give; and, in reality, found him quite communicative. One day Palgrave asked him to define the difference between the *great* sins and the *little* ones —that is, those to be punished in the next world, or at least deserving of it, and those whose penalty is remissible in this life.

"Abd-el-Kereem doubted not that he had a sincere scholar before him, nor would refuse his hand to a drowning man. So, putting on a profound air, and with a voice of first-class solemnity, he uttered his oracle, that 'the first of the great sins is the giving divine honors to a creature.' A hit, I may observe, at ordinary Mahometans, whose whole doctrine of intercession, whether vested in Mahomet or in 'Alee, is classed by Wahabees along with direct and downright idolatry. A Damascene Shekh would have avoided the equivocation by answering, 'infidelity.'

"'Of course,' I replied, 'the enormity of such a sin is beyond all doubt. But if this be the first, there must be a second; what is it?'

"'Drinking the shameful,' in English, 'smoking tobacco,' was the unhesitating answer.

"'And murder, and adultery, and false witness?' I suggested.

"'God is merciful and forgiving,' rejoined my friend; that is, these are merely little sins.

"'Hence two sins alone are great, polytheism and smoking,' I continued, though hardly able to keep countenance any longer. And Abd-el-Kereem, with the most serious asseveration, replied that such was really the case. On hearing this, I proceeded humbly to entreat my friend to explain to me the especial wickedness inherent in tobacco leaves, that I might the more detest and eschew them hereafter.

"Accordingly he proceeded to instruct me, saying that, Firstly, all intoxicating substances are prohibited by the Koran; but tobacco is an intoxicating substance—ergo, tobacco is prohibited.

"I insinuated that it was not intoxicating, and appealed to experience. But, to my surprise, my friend had experience too on his side, and had ready at hand the most appalling tales of men falling down dead drunk after a single whiff of smoke, and of others in a state of bestial and habitual ebriety from its use. Nor were his stories so purely gratuitous as many might at first imagine. The only tobacco known, when known, in Southern Nedjed, is that of Oman, a very powerful species. I was myself astonished, and almost 'taken in,' more than once, by its extraordinary narcotic effects, when I experienced them, in the coffee-houses of Bahreyn."

Palgrave furnishes a tolerably complete account of the provinces of Nedjed and the tribes which inhabit them. His concluding statement, however, embodies all which will interest the reader.

"To sum up, we may say that the Wahabee empire is a compact and well-organized government, where centralization is fully understood and effectually carried out, and whose main-springs and connecting links are force and fanaticism. There exist no constitutional checks either on the king or on his subordinates, save what the necessity of circumstance imposes or the Koran prescribes. Its atmosphere, to speak metaphorically, is sheer despotism—moral, intellectual, religious, and physical. This empire is capable of frontier extension, and hence is dangerous to its neighbors, some of whom it is even now swallowing up, and will certainly swallow more if not otherwise prevented. Incapable of true internal progress, hostile to commerce, unfavorable to arts and even to agriculture, and in the highest degree intolerant and aggressive, it can neither better itself nor benefit others; while the order and calm which it sometimes spreads over the lands of its conquest are described in the oft-cited *Ubi solitudinem faciunt pacem appellant* of the Roman annalist.

"In conclusion, I here subjoin a numerical list, taken partly from the government registers of Ri'ad, partly from local information, and containing the provinces, the number of the principal towns or villages, the population, and the military contingent, throughout the Wahabee empire.

Provinces.	Towns or villages.	Population.	Military muster.
I.—'Aared	15	110,000	6,000
II.—Yemamah	32	140,000	4,500
III.—Hareek	16	45,000	3,000
IV.—Aflaj	12	14,000	1,200
V.—Wady Dowasir.	50	100,000	4,000
VI.—Seley'yel	14	30,000	1,400
VII.—Woshem	20	80,000	4,000
VIII.—Sedeyr	25	140,000	5,200
IX.—Kaseem	60	300,000	11,000
X.—Hasa	50	160,000	7,000
XI.—Kateef	22	100,000	—
	316	1,219,000	47,300 "

After a time, Palgrave was sent for by Abdallah, the eldest son of King Feysul, who pretended that he wished to learn something of the medical art. This led to a regular intercourse, which at least enabled the traveller to learn many things concerning the Wahabee government. Another important result was an opportunity of visiting the royal stables, where the finest specimens of the famous Nedjed breed of horses are kept. Of these he gives the following interesting description :

"The stables are situated some way out of the town, to the northeast, a little to the left of the road which we had followed at our first arrival, and not far from the gardens of 'Abd-er-Rahman the Wahabee. They cover a large square space, about 150 yards each way, and are open in the centre, with a long shed running round the inner walls; under this covering the horses, about three hundred in number when I saw them, are picketed during the night; in the daytime they may stretch their legs at pleasure within the central court-yard. The greater number were accordingly loose; a few, however, were tied up at their stalls; some, but not many, had horse-cloths over them. The heavy dews which fall in Wady Haneefah do not permit their remaining with impunity in the open night air; I was told also that a northerly wind will occasionally injure the animals here, no less than the land wind does now and then their brethren in India. About half the royal stud was present before me, the rest were out at grass; Feysul's entire muster is reckoned at six hundred, or rather more.

"No Arab dreams of tying up a horse by the neck; a tether replaces the halter, and one of the animal's hind legs is encircled about the pastern by a light iron ring, furnished with a padlock, and connected with an iron chain of two feet or thereabouts in length, ending in a rope, which is fastened to the ground at some distance by an iron peg; such is the customary method. But should the animal be restless and troublesome, a foreleg is put under similar restraint. It is well known that in Arabia horses are much less frequently vicious or refractory than in Europe, and this is the reason why geldings are here so rare, though not unknown. No particular prejudice, that I could discover, exists against the operation itself; only it is seldom performed, because not otherwise necessary, and tending, of course, to diminish the value of the animal.

"But to return to the horses now before us; never had I seen or imagined so lovely a collection. Their stature was indeed somewhat low; I do not think that any came fully up to fifteen hands; fourteen appeared to me about their average, but they were so exquisitely well shaped that want of greater size seemed hardly, if at all, a defect. Remarkably full in the haunches, with a shoulder of a slope so elegant as to make one, in the words of an Arab poet, 'go raving mad about it;' a little, a very little, saddle-backed, just the curve which indicates springiness without any weakness; a head broad above, and tapering down to a nose fine enough to verify the phrase of 'drinking from a pint pot,' did pint pots exist in Nedjed; a most intelligent and yet a singularly gentle look, full eye, sharp thorn-like little ear, legs fore and hind that seemed as if made of hammered iron, so clean and yet so well twisted with sinew; a neat, round hoof, just the requisite for hard ground; the tail set on, or rather thrown out at a perfect arch; coats smooth, shining, and light, the mane long, but not overgrown nor heavy, and an air and step that seemed to say, 'Look at me, am I not pretty?' their appearance justified all reputation, all value, all poetry. The prevailing color was chestnut or gray; a light bay, an iron color, white or black, were less common; full bay, flea-bitten or piebald, none. But if asked what are, after all, the specially distinctive points of the Nedjee horse, I should reply, the slope of the shoulder, the extreme cleanness of the shank, and the full, rounded haunch, though every other part, too, has a perfection and a harmony unwitnessed (at least by my eyes) anywhere else.

"Nedjee horses are especially esteemed for great speed and endurance of fatigue; indeed, in this latter quality, none come up to them. To pass twenty-four hours on the road without drink and without flagging is certainly something; but to keep up the same abstinence and labor conjoined under the burning Arabian sky for forty-eight hours at a stretch, is, I believe, peculiar to the animals of the breed. Besides, they have a delicacy, I cannot say of mouth, for it is common to ride them without bit or bridle, but of feeling and obedience to the knee and thigh, to the slightest check of the halter and the voice of the rider, far surpassing whatever the most elaborate manége gives a European horse, though furnished with snaffle, curb, and all. I often mounted them at the invitation of their owners, and without saddle, rein, or stirrup, set them off at full gallop, wheeled them round, brought them up in mid career at a dead halt, and that without the least difficulty or the smallest want of correspondence between the horse's movements and my own will; the rider on their back really feels himself the man-half of a centaur, not a distinct being."

During the last week in November the Persian Na'ib, who had been little edified by his experiences in Nedjed, set off for Bagdad. In the meantime, Feysul had made great preparations toward collecting an army for the reduction of the city of Oneyzah (near Bereydah), which still held out gallantly. Troops were summoned from the eastern coast and the adjoining provinces, and Sa'ood, the second son of Feysul, was ordered to bring them together at the capital, when the command was to be given to Abdallah, the eldest son. Palgrave had then his only opportunity of seeing the old King of the Wahabees.

"Sa'ood speedily arrived, and with him about two hundred horsemen; the rest of his men, more than two thousand, were mounted on camels. When they entered Ri'ad, Feysul, for the first and last time during our stay, gave a public audience at the palace gate. It was a scene for a painter. There sat the blind old tyrant, corpulent, decrepit, yet imposing, with his large, broad forehead, white beard, and thoughtful air, clad in all the simplicity of a Wahabee; the gold-hafted sword at his side his only ornament or distinction. Beside him the ministers, the officers of his court, and a crowd of the nobler and wealthier citizens. Abdallah, the heir to the throne, was alone absent. Up came Sa'ood with the bearing of a hussar officer, richly clad in cashmere shawls and a gold-wrought mantle, while man by man followed his red-dressed cavaliers, their spears over their shoulders, and their swords hanging down; a musket, too, was slung behind the saddle of each warrior; and the sharp dagger of Hareek glittered in every girdle. Next came the common soldiers on camels or dromedaries, some with spears only, some with spears and guns, till the wide square was filled with armed men and gazing spectators, as the whole troop drew up before the great autocrat, and Sa'ood alighted to bend and kiss his father's hand. 'God save Feysul! God give the victory to the armies of the Muslims!' was shouted out on every side, and all faces kindled into the fierce smile of concentrated enthusiasm and conscious strength. Feysul arose from his seat and placed his son at his side; another moment, and they entered the castle together."

CHAPTER XV.

PALGRAVE'S TRAVELS—HIS ESCAPE TO THE EASTERN COAST

"FOR a foreigner to enter Ri'ad is not always easy, but to get away from it is harder still; Reynard himself would have been justly shy of venturing on this royal cave. There exists in the capital of Nedjed two approved means of barring the exit against those on whom mistrust may have fallen. The first and readiest is that of which it has been emphatically said, *Stone-dead hath no fellow*. But should circumstances render the bonds of death inexpedient, the bonds of Hymen and a Ri'ad establishment may and occasionally do supply their office. By this latter proceeding, the more amiable of the two, Abdallah resolved to enchain us.

"Accordingly, one morning arrived at our dwelling an attendant of the palace, with a smiling face, presage of some good in reserve, and many fair speeches. After inquiries about our health, comfort, well-being, etc., he added that Abdallah thought we might be desirous of purchasing this or that, and begged us to accept of a small present. It was a fair sum of money, just twice so much as the ordinary token of good-will, namely, four rials in place of two. After which the messenger took his leave.

Aboo-'Eysa had been present at the interview: 'Be on the look-out,' said he, 'there is something wrong.'

"That very afternoon Abdallah sent for me, and with abundance of encomiums and of promises, declared that he could not think of letting Ri'ad lose so valuable a physician, that I must accordingly take up a permanent abode in the capital, where I might rely on his patronage, and on all good things; that he had already resolved on giving me a house and a garden, specifying them, with a suitable household, and a fair face to keep me company; he concluded by inviting me to go without delay and see whether the new abode fitted me, and take possession.

"Much and long did I fight off; talked about a winter visit to the coast, and coming back in the spring; tried first one pretext and then another; but none would avail, and Abdallah continued to insist. To quiet him, I consented to go and see the house. For the intended Calypso, I had ready an argument derived from Mahometan law, which put her out of the question, but its explanation would require more space than these pages can afford.

"The winter season was now setting in; it was the third week in November; and a thunder-storm, the first we had witnessed in Central Arabia, ushered in a marked change for cold in the temperature of Wady Haneefah. Rain fell abundantly, and sent torrents down the dry watercourses of the valley, changing its large hollows into temporary tanks. None of the streams showed, however, any disposition to reach the sea, nor indeed could they, for this part of Nedjed is entirely hemmed in to the east by the Toweyk range. The inhabitants welcomed the copious showers, pledges of fertility for the coming year, while at 'Oneyzah the same rains produced at least one excellent effect, but which I may well defy my readers to guess. The hostile armies, commanded by Zamil and Mohammed-ebn-Sa'ood, were drawn up in face of each other, and on the point of fierce conflict, when the storm burst on them, and by putting out the lighted matchlocks of either party, prevented the discharge of bullets and the effusion of blood."

Abdallah, who hated his second brother, Sa'ood, and had many other fierce enmities in the capital, then accidentally learned that Palgrave had employed a deadly poison (strychnine) in making a remarkable cure. Thenceforth all his powers of persuasion were employed in endeavoring to procure some of the drug; but Palgrave, suspecting his real design, positively refused to let him have any. His rage was suddenly and strongly expressed on his countenance, foreboding no good to the traveller, who took the first opportunity of returning to his house.

"There Aboo-'Eysa, Barakat, and myself," he says, "immediately held council to consider what was now to be done. That an outbreak must shortly take place seemed certain; to await it was dangerous, yet we could not safely leave the town in an overprecipitate manner, nor without some kind of permission. We resolved together to go on in quiet and caution a few days more, to sound the court, make our adieus at Feysul's palace, get a good word from Mahboob (no difficult matter), and then slip off without attracting too much notice. But our destiny was not to run so smoothly."

Late in the evening of November 21st, Palgrave was summoned to Abdallah's palace. The messenger refused to allow Barakat or Aboo-'Eysa to accompany him. The occasion seemed portentous, but disobedience was out of the question. Palgrave followed the messenger. On entering the reception-room, he found Abdallah, Abd-el-Lateef, the successor of the Wahabee, Mahboob, and a few others. All were silent, and none returned his first salutation. "I saluted Abdallah," says Palgrave, "who replied in an undertone, and gave me a signal to sit down at a little distance from him, but on the same side of the divan. My readers may suppose that I was not at the moment ambitious of too intimate a vicinity.

"After an interval of silence, Abdallah turned half round toward me, and with his blackest look and a deep voice said, 'I now know perfectly well what you are; you are no doctors, you are Christians, spies, and revolutionists, come hither to ruin our religion and state in behalf of those who sent you. The penalty for such as you is death, that you know, and I am determined to inflict it without delay.'

"'Threatened folks live long,' thought I, and had no difficulty in showing the calm which I really felt. So looking him coolly in the face, I replied, '*Istaghfir Allah*,' literally, 'Ask pardon of God.' This is the phrase commonly addressed to one who has said something extremely out of place.

"The answer was unexpected: he started, and said, 'Why so?'

"'Because,' I rejoined, 'you have just now uttered a sheer absurdity. "Christians," be it so; but "spies," "revolutionists"—as if we were not known by everybody in your town for quiet doctors, neither more nor less! And then to talk about putting me to death! You cannot, and you dare not.'

"'But I can and dare,' answered Abdallah, 'and who shall prevent me? You shall soon learn that to your cost.'

"'Neither can nor dare,' repeated I. 'We are here your father's guests, and yours for a month and more, known as such, received as such. What have we done to justify a breach of the laws of hospitality in Nedjed? It is impossible for you to do what you say,' continued I, thinking the while that it was a great deal too possible, after all; 'the obloquy of the deed would be too much for you.'

"He remained a moment thoughtful, then said, 'As if anyone need know who did it. I have the means, and can dispose of you without talk or rumor. Those who are at my bidding can take a suitable time and place for that, without my name being ever mentioned in the affair.'

"The advantage was now evidently on my side; I followed it up, and said with a quiet laugh, 'Neither is that within your power. Am I not known to your father, to all in his palace? to your own brother Sa'ood among the rest? Is not the fact of this my actual visit to you known without your gates? Or is there no one here?' added I, with a glance at Mahboob, 'who can report elsewhere what you have just now said? Better for you to leave off this nonsense; do you take me for a child of four days old?'

"He muttered a repetition of his threat. 'Bear witness, all here present,' said I, raising my voice so as to be heard from one end of the room to the other, 'that if any mishap befalls my companion or myself from Ri'ad to the shores of the Persian Gulf, it is all Abdallah's doing. And the consequences shall be on his head, worse consequences than he expects or dreams.'

"The prince made no reply. All were silent; Mahboob kept his eyes steadily fixed on the fireplace; 'Abd-el-Lateef looked much and said nothing.

"'Bring coffee,' called out Abdallah to the servants. Before a minute had elapsed, a black slave approached with one, and only one, coffee-cup in his hand. At a second sign from his master he came before me and presented it.

"Of course the worst might be conjectured of so unusual and solitary a draught. But I thought it highly improbable that matters should have been so accurately prepared; besides, his main cause of anger was precisely the refusal of poisons, a fact which implied that he had none by him ready for use. So I said '*Bismillah*,' took the cup, looked very hard at Abdallah, drank it off, and then said to the slave, 'Pour me out a second.' This he did; I swallowed it, and said, 'Now you may take the cup away.'

"The desired effect was fully attained. Abdallah's face announced defeat, while the rest of the assembly whispered together. The prince turned to 'Abd-el-Lateef and began talking about the dangers to which the land was exposed from spies, and the wicked designs of infidels for ruining the kingdom of the Muslims. The Kadee and his companions chimed in, and the story of a pseudo-Darweesh traveller killed at Derey'eeyah, and of another (but who he was I cannot fancy ; perhaps a Persian, who had, said Abdallah, been also recognized for an intriguer, but had escaped to Muscat, and thus baffled the penalty due to his crimes), were now brought forward and commented on. Mahboob now at last spoke, but it was to ridicule such apprehensions. 'The thing is in itself unlikely,' said he, 'and were it so, what harm could they do?' alluding to my companion and myself.

"On this I took up the word, and a general conversation ensued, in which I did my best to explode the idea of spies and spymanship, appealed to our own quiet and inoffensive conduct, got into a virtuous indignation against such a requital of evil for good after all the services which we had rendered court and town, and quoted verses of the Koran regarding the wickedness of ungrounded suspicion, and the obligation of not judging ill without clear evidence. Abdallah made no direct answer, and the others, whatever they may have thought, could not support a charge abandoned by their master.

"What amused me not a little was that the Wahabee prince had after all very nearly hit the right nail on the head, and that I was snubbing him only for having guessed too well. But there was no help for it, and I had the pleasure of seeing that, though at heart unchanged in his opinion about us, he was yet sufficienty cowed to render a respite certain, and our escape thereby practicable.

"This kind of talk continued a while, and I purposely kept my seat, to show the unconcern of innocence, till Mahboob made me a sign that I might safely retire. On this I took leave of Abdallah and quitted the palace unaccompanied. It was now near midnight, not a light to be seen in the houses, not a sound to be heard in the streets; the sky too was dark and overcast, till, for the first time, a feeling of lonely dread came over me, and I confess that more than once I turned my head to look and see if no one was following with 'evil,' as Arabs say, in his hand. But there was none, and I reached the quiet alley and low door where a gleam through the chinks announced the anxious watch of my companions, who now opened the entrance, overjoyed at seeing me back sound and safe from so critical a parley.

"Our plan for the future was soon formed. A day or two we were yet to remain in Ri'ad, lest haste should seem to imply fear, and thereby encourage pursuit. But during that period we would avoid the palace, out-walks in gardens or after nightfall, and keep at home as much as possible. Meanwhile Aboo-'Eysa was to get his dromedaries ready, and put them in a courtyard immediately adjoining the house, to be laden at a moment's notice.

"A band of travellers was to leave Ri'ad for Hasa a few days later. Aboo-'Eysa gave out publicly that he would accompany them to Hofhoof, while we were supposed to intend following the northern or Sedeyr track, by which the Na'ib, after many reciprocal farewells and assurances of lasting friendship, should we ever meet again, had lately departed. Mobeyreek, a black servant in Aboo-'Eysa's pay, occupied himself diligently in feeding up the camels for their long march with clover and vetches, both abundant here; and we continued our medical avocations, but quietly, and without much leaving the house.

"During the afternoon of the 24th we brought three of Aboo-'Eysa's camels into our courtyard, shut the outer door, packed, and laded. We then awaited the moment of evening prayer; it came, and the voice of the Mu'eddineen summoned all good Wahabees, the men of the town-guard not excepted, to the different mosques. When about ten minutes had gone by, and all might be supposed at their prayers, we opened our door. Mobeyreek gave a glance up and down the street to ascertain that no one was in sight, and we led out the camels. Aboo-'Eysa accompanied us. Avoiding the larger thoroughfares, we took our way by by-lanes and side-passages toward a small town-gate, the nearest to our house, and opening on the north. A late comer fell in with us on his way to the Mesjid, and as he passed summoned us also to the public service. But Aboo-'Eysa unhesitatingly replied, 'We have this moment come from prayers,' and our interlocutor, fearing to be himself too late and thus to fall under reprehension and punishment, rushed off to the nearest oratory, leaving the road clear. Nobody was in watch at the gate. We crossed its threshold, turned southeast, and under the rapid twilight reached a range of small hillocks, behind which we sheltered ourselves till the stars came out, and the 'wing of night,' to quote Arab poets, spread black over town and country.

"So far so good. But further difficulties remained before us. It was now more than ever absolutely essential to get clear of Nedjed unobserved, to put the desert between us and the Wahabee court and capital; and no less necessary was it that Aboo-'Eysa, so closely connected as he was with Ri'ad and its government, should seem nohow implicated in our unceremonious departure, nor any way concerned with our onward movements. In a word, an apparent separation of paths between him and us was necessary before we could again come together and complete the remainder of our explorations.

"In order to manage this, and while ensuring our own safety to throw a little dust in Wahabee eyes, it was agreed that before next morning's sunrise Aboo-'Eysa should return to the town, and to his dwelling, as though nothing had occurred, and should there await the departure of the great merchant caravan, mentioned previously, and composed mainly of men from Hasa and Kateef, now bound for Hofhoof. This assemblage was expected to start within three days at latest. Meanwhile our friend should take care to show himself openly in the palaces of Feysul and Abdallah, and if asked about us should answer vaguely, with the off-hand air of one who had no further care regarding us. We ourselves should in the interim make the best of our way, with Mobeyreek for guide, to Wady Soley', and there remain concealed in a given spot, till Aboo-'Eysa should come and pick us up.

"All this was arranged; at break of dawn, Aboo-'Eysa took his leave, and Barakat, Mobeyreek, and myself were once more high-perched on our dromedaries, their heads turned to the southeast, keeping the hillock range between us and Ri'ad, which we saw no more. Our path led us over low undulating ground, a continuation of Wady Haneefah, till after about four hours' march we were before the gates of Manfoohah, a considerable town, surrounded by gardens nothing inferior in extent and fertility to those of Ri'ad; but its fortifications, once strong, have long since been dismantled and broken down by the jealousy of the neighboring capital.

After winding here and there, we reached the spot assigned by Aboo-'Eysa for our hiding-place. It was a small sandy depth, lying some way off the beaten track, amid hillocks and brushwood, and without water; of this latter article we had taken enough in the goat-skins to last us for three days. Here we halted, and made up our minds to patience and expectation.

"Two days passed drearily enough. We could not but long for our guide's arrival, nor be wholly without fear on more than one score. Once or twice a stray peasant stumbled on us, and was much surprised at our encampment in so droughty a locality. So the hours went by, till the third day brought closer expectation and anxiety, still increasing while the sun declined, and at last went down; yet nobody appeared. But just as darkness closed in, and we were sitting in a dispirited group beside our little fire, for the night air blew chill, Aboo-'Eysa came suddenly up, and all was changed for question and answer, for cheerfulness and laughter.

"Early on November 28th we resumed our march through a light valley-mist, and soon fell in with our companions of the road.

"Next morning the whole country, hill and dale, trees and bushes, was wrapped in a thick blanket of mist, fitter for Surrey than for Arabia. So dense was the milky fog, that we fairly lost our way, and went on at random, shouting and hallooing, driving our beasts now here, now there, over broken ground and amid tangling shrubs, till the sun gained strength and the vapor cleared off, showing us the path at some distance on our right. Before we had followed it far, we saw a black mass advancing from the east to meet us. It was the first division of the Hasa troops on their way to Ri'ad; they were not less than four or five hundred in number. Like true Arabs, they marched with a noble contempt of order and discipline — walking, galloping, ambling, singing, shouting, alone or in bands, as fancy led. We interchanged a few words of greeting with these brisk boys, who avowed, without hesitation or shame, that they should much have preferred to stay at home, and that enforced necessity, not any military or religious ardor, was taking them to the field. We laughed, and wished them Zamil's head, or him theirs, whereon they laughed also, shouted, and passed on.

"On we went, but through a country of much more varied scenery than what we had traversed the day before, enjoying the 'pleasure situate in hill and dale,' till we arrived at the foot of a high white cliff, almost like that of Dover; but these crags, instead of having the sea at their foot, overlooked a wide valley full of trees, and bearing traces of many violent winter torrents from east to west; none were now flowing. Here we halted, and passed an indifferent night, much annoyed by 'chill November's surly blast,' hardly less ungenial here than on the banks of Ayr, though sweeping over a latitude of 25°, not 56°.

"Before the starlight had faded from the cold morning sky, we were up and in movement, for a long march was before us. At sunrise we stood on the last, and here the highest, ledge of Toweyk, that long chalky wall which bounds and backs up Nedjed on the east; beyond is the desert, and then the coast.

"After about three hours of level route we began to descend, not rapidly, but by degrees, and at noon we reached a singular depression, a huge natural basin, hollowed out in the limestone rock, with tracks resembling deep trenches leading to it from every side. At the bottom of this crater-like valley were a dozen or more wells, so abundant in their supply that they not unfrequently overflow the whole space, and form a small lake; the water is clear and good, but no other is to be met with on the entire line hence to Hasa.

"For the rest of the day we continued steadily to descend the broad even slope, whose extreme barrenness and inanimate monotony reminded me of the pebbly uplands near Ma'an on the opposite side of the peninsula, traversed by us exactly seven months before. The sun set, night came on, and many of the travellers would gladly have halted, but Aboo-'Eysa insisted on continuing the march. We were now many hundred feet lower than the crest behind us, and the air felt warm and heavy, when we noticed that the ground, hitherto hard beneath our feet, was changing step by step into a light sand, that seemed to encroach on the rocky soil. It was at first a shallow ripple, then deepened, and before long presented the well-known ridges and undulations characteristic of the land ocean when several fathoms in depth. Our beasts ploughed laboriously on through the yielding surface; the night was dark, but starry, and we could just discern amid the shade a white glimmer of spectral sand-hills, rising around us on every side, but no track or indication of a route.

"It was the great Dahna, or 'Red Desert,' the bugbear of even the wandering Bedouin, and never traversed by ordinary wayfarers without an apprehension which has too often been justified by fatal incidents. So light are the sands, so capricious the breezes that shape and reshape them daily into unstable hills and valleys, that no traces of preceding travellers remain to those who follow; while intense heat and glaring light reflected on all sides combine with drought and weariness to confuse and bewilder the adventurer, till he loses his compass and wanders up and down at random amid a waste solitude which soon becomes his grave. Many have thus perished; even whole caravans have been known to disappear in the Dahna without a vestige, till the wild Arab tales of demons carrying off wanderers, or ghouls devouring them, obtain a half credit among many accustomed elsewhere to laugh at such fictions.

"For, after about three hours of night travelling, or rather wading, among the sand-waves, till men and beasts alike were ready to sink for weariness, a sharp altercation arose between Aboo-'Eysa and El-Ghannam, each proposing a different direction of march. We all halted a moment, and raised our eyes, heavy with drowsiness and fatigue, as if to see which of the contending parties was in the right. It will be long before I forget the impression of that moment. Above us was the deep black sky, spangled with huge stars of a brilliancy denied to all but an Arab gaze, while what is elsewhere a ray of the third magnitude becomes here of the first amid the pure vacuum of a mistless, vaporless air; around us loomed high ridges, shutting us in before and behind with their white, ghost-like outlines; below our feet the lifeless sand, and everywhere a silence that seemed to belong to some strange and dreamy world where man might not venture.

"When not far from the midmost of the Dahna, we fell in with a few Bedouins, belonging to the Aal-Morrah clan, sole tenants of this desert. They were leading their goats to little spots of scattered herbage and shrubs which here and there fix a precarious existence in the hollows of the sands.

"Theirs is the great desert from Nedjed to Hadramaut. Not that they actually cover this immense space, a good fourth of the peninsula, but that they have the free and undisputed range of the oases which it occasionally offers, where herbs, shrubs, and dwarf-palms cluster round some well of scant and briny water. These oases are sufficiently numerous to preserve a stray Bedouin or two from perishing, though not enough so to become landmarks for any regular route across the central Dahna, from the main body of which runs out the long and broad arm which we were now traversing.

"Another night's bivouac, and then again over the white down-sloping plain.

"It was now three days and a half since our last supply of water, and Aboo-'Eysa was anxious to reach the journey's end without delay. As darkness closed around we reached the farthermost heights of the coast-range of Hasa. Hence we overlooked the plains of Hasa, but could distinguish nothing through the deceptive rays of the rising moon; we seemed to gaze into a vast milky ocean. After an hour's halt for supper we wandered on, now up, now down, over pass and crag, till a long, corkscrew descent down the precipitous sea-side of the mountain, for a thousand feet or near it, placed us fairly upon the low level of Hasa, and within the warm, damp air of the sea-coast.

"The ground glimmered white to the moon, and gave a firm footing to our dromedaries, who, by their renewed agility, seemed to partake in the joy of their riders, and to understand that rest was near. We were, in fact, all so eager to find ourselves at home and homestead, that although the town of Hofhoof, our destined goal, was yet full fifteen miles to the northeast, we pressed on for the capital. And there, in fact, we should have all arrived in a body before day-dawn, had not a singular occurrence retarded by far the greater number of our companions.

"Soon after, the crags in our rear had shut out, perhaps for years, perhaps forever, the desert and Central Arabia from our view, while before and around us lay the indistinct undulations and uncertain breaks of the great Hasa plain, when on a sloping bank at a short distance in front we discerned certain large black patches, in strong contrast with the white glister of the soil around, and at the same time our attention was attracted by a strange whizzing like that of a flight of hornets, close along the ground, while our dromedaries capered and started as though struck with sudden insanity. The cause of all this was a vast swarm of locusts, here alighted in their northerly wanderings from their birthplace in the Dahna; their camp extended far and wide, and we had already disturbed their outposts. These insects are wont to settle on the ground after sunset, and there, half stupefied by the night chill, to await the morning rays, which warm them once more into life and movement. This time our dromedaries did the work of the sun, and it would be hard to say which of the two were the most frightened, they or the locusts. It was truly laughable to see so huge a beast lose his wits for fear at the flight of a harmless, stingless insect; of all timid creatures none equals the 'ship of the desert' for cowardice.

"The swarm now before us was a thorough godsend for our Arabs, on no account to be neglected.

Thirst, weariness, all was forgotten, and down the riders leapt from their starting camels; this one spread out a cloak, that one a saddle-bag, a third his shirt, over the unlucky creatures destined for the morrow's meal. Some flew away whirring across our feet, others were caught and tied up in cloths and sacks. Cornish wreckers at work about a shattered East Indiaman would be beaten by Ghannam and his companions with the locusts. However, Barakat and myself felt no special interest in the chase, nor had we much desire to turn our dress and accoutrements into receptacles for living game. Luckily Aboo-'Eysa still retained enough of his North Syrian education to be of our mind also. Accordingly we left our associates hard at work, turned our startled and still unruly dromedaries in the direction of Hofhoof, and set off full speed over the plain.

"It was not till near morning that we saw before us in indistinct row the long black lines of the immense date-groves that surround Hofhoof. Then, winding on amid rice-grounds and cornfields, we left on our right an isolated fort (to be described by daylight), passed some scattered villas, with their gardens, approached the ruined town walls, and entered the southern gate, now open and unguarded. Farther on a few streets brought us before the door of Aboo-'Eysa's house, our desired resting-place.

"It was still night. All was silent in the street and house, at the entrance of which we now stood; indeed, none but the master of a domicile could think of knocking at such an hour, nor was Aboo-

'Eysa expected at that precise moment. With much difficulty he contrived to awake the tenants; next the shrill voice of the lady was heard within in accents of joy and welcome; the door at last opened, and Aboo-'Eysa invited us into a dark passage, where a gas-light would have been a remarkable improvement, and by this ushered us into the k'hawah. Here we lighted a fire, and after a hasty refreshment all lay down to sleep, nor awoke till the following forenoon."

CHAPTER XVI.

PALGRAVE'S TRAVELS—EASTERN ARABIA

"OUR stay at Hofhoof was very pleasant and interesting, not indeed through personal incidents and hairbreadth escapes—of which we had our fair portion at Ri'ad and elsewhere—but in the information here acquired, and in the novel character of everything around us, whether nature, art, or man. Aboo-'Eysa was very anxious that we should see as much as possible of the country, and procured us all means requisite for so doing, while the shelter of his roof, and the precautions which he adopted or suggested, obviated whatever dangers and inconveniences we had experienced in former stages of the journey. Besides, the general disposition of the inhabitants of Hasa is very different from that met with in Nedjed, and even in Shomer or Djowf, and much better adapted to make a stranger feel himself at home. A sea-coast people, looking mainly to foreign lands and the ocean for livelihood and commerce, accustomed to see among them not unfrequently men of dress, manners, and religion different from their own, many of them themselves travellers or voyagers to Basrah, Bagdad, Bahreyn, Oman, and some even farther, they are commonly free from that half-wondering, half-suspicious feeling which the sight of a stranger occasions in the isolated, desert-girded centre. In short, experience, that best of masters, has gone far to unteach the lessons of ignorance, intolerance, and national aversion.

Hofhoof, whose ample circuit contained during the last generation about thirty thousand inhabitants, now dwindled to twenty-three or twenty-four thousand, is divided into three quarters or districts. The general form of the town is that of a large oval. The public square, an oblong space of about three hundred yards in length by a fourth of the same in width, occupies the meeting point of these quarters; the Kôt lies on its northeast, the Rifey'eeyah on the northwest and west, and the Na'athar on the east and south. In this last quarter was our present home; moreover, it stood in the part farthest removed from the Kôt and its sinister influences, while it was also sufficiently distant from the overturbulent neighborhood of the Rifey'eeyah, the centre of anti-Wahabee movements, and the name of which alone excited distrust and uneasiness in Nedjean minds.

"The Kôt itself is a vast citadel, surrounded by a deep trench, with walls and towers of unusual height and thickness, earth-built, with an occasional intermixture of stone, the work of the old Carmathian rulers; it is nearly square, being about one-third of a mile in length by one-quarter in breadth.

"On the opposite side of the square, and consequently belonging to the Rifey'eeyah, is the vaulted market-place, or 'Keysareeyah,' a name by which constructions of this nature must henceforth be called up to Mascat itself, though how this Latinism found its way across the peninsula to lands which seem to have had so little commerce with the Roman or Byzantine empires, I cannot readily conjecture. This Keysareeyah is in form a long barrel-vaulted arcade, with a portal at either end; the folding doors that should protect the entrances have here in Hofhoof been taken away, elsewhere they are always to be found. The sides are composed of shops, set apart in general for wares of cost, or at least what is here esteemed costly; thus, weapons, cloth embroidery, gold and silver ornament, and analogous articles, are the ordinary stock-in-hand in the Keysareeyah. Around it cluster several alleys, roofed with palm-leaves against the heat, and tolerably symmetrical; in the shops we may see the merchandise of Bahreyn, Oman, Persia, and India exposed for sale, mixed with the manufactured produce of the country; workshops, smithies, carpenters' and shoemakers' stalls, and the like, are here also. In the open square itself stand countless booths for the sale of dates, vegetables, wood, salted locusts, and small ware of many kinds.

"The Rifey'eeyah, or noble quarter, covers a considerable extent, and is chiefly composed of tolerable, in some places of even handsome, dwellings. The comparative elegance of domestic architecture in Hofhoof is due to the use of the arch, which, after the long interval from Ma'an to Hasa, now at last reappears, and gives to the constructions of this province a lightness and a variety unknown in the monotonous and heavy piles of Nedjed and Shomer. Another improvement is that the walls, whether of earth or stone, or of both mixed, as is often the case, are here very generally coated with fine white plaster, much resembling the 'chunam' of Southern India; ornament, too, is aimed at about the doorways and the ogee-headed windows, and is sometimes attained.

"The Na'athar is the largest quarter; it forms, indeed, a good half of the town, and completes its oval. In it every description of dwelling is to be seen—for rich and poor, for high and low, palace or hovel. Here, too, but near the Kôt, has the pious policy of Feysul constructed the great mosque.

"But perhaps my reader, after accompanying me thus far, may feel thirsty, for the heat, even in December, is almost oppressive, and the sky cloudless as though it were June or July. So let us turn aside into that grassy plantation, where half a dozen buffaloes are cooling their ugly hides in a pool, and drink a little from the source that supplies it. When behold! the water is warm, almost hot. Do not be surprised; all the fountain sources and wells of Hasa are so, more or less; in some one can hardly bear to plunge one's hand; others are less above the average temperature, while a decidedly sulphurous taste is now and then perceptible. In fact, from the extreme north of this province down to its southernmost frontier, this same sign of subterranean fire is everywhere to be found. The rocks, too, are here very frequently of tufa and basalt, another mark of igneous agency.

"The products of Hasa are many and various; the monotony of Arab vegetation, its eternal palm and ithel, ithel and palm, are here varied by new foliage, and growths unknown to Nedjed and Shomer. True, the date-palm still predominates, nay, here attains its greatest perfection. But the nabak, with its rounded leaves and little crab-apple fruit, a mere bush in Central Arabia, becomes in Hasa a stately tree; the papay, too, so well known in the more easterly peninsula, appears, though seluom, and stunted in growth, along with some other trees, common on the coast from Cutch to Bombay. Indigo is here cultivated, though not sufficiently for the demands of commerce; cotton is much more widely grown than in Yemamah; rice fields abound, and the sugar-cane is often planted, though not, I believe, for the extraction of the sugar. The peasants of Hasa sell the reed by retail bundles in the market-place, and the purchasers take it home to gnaw at leisure in their houses. Corn, maize, millet, vetches of every kind, radishes, onions, garlic, beans, in short, almost all legumina and cerealia, barley excepted (at least I neither saw nor heard of any), cover the plain, and under a better administration might be multiplied tenfold.

"The climate of Hasa, as I have already implied, is very different from that of the uplands, and not equally favorable to health and physical activity. Hence, a doctor, like myself, if my readers will allow me the title, has here more work and better fees; this latter circumstance is also owing to the greater amount of ready money in circulation, and the higher value set on medical science by men whose intellects are much more cultivated than those of their Nedjean neighbors. In appearance, the inhabitants of Hasa are generally good-sized and well-proportioned, but somewhat sallow in the face, and of a less muscular development than is usual inland; their features, though regular, are less marked than those of the Nedjeans, and do not exhibit the same half-Jewish type. On the contrary, there is something in them that reminds a beholder of the Rajpoot or the Guzeratee. They are passionately fond of literature and poetry.

"I have already said that our great endeavor in Hasa was to observe unobserved, and thus to render our time as barren as might be in incidents and catastrophes. Not that we went into the opposite extreme of leading an absolutely retired and therefore uneventful life. Aboo-'Eysa took care from the first to bring us into contact with the best and the most cultivated families of the town, nor had my medical profession anywhere a wider range for its exercise, or better success than in Hofhoof. Friendly invitations, now to dinner, now to supper, were of daily occurrence; and we sat at tables where fish, no longer mere salted shrimps, announced our vicinity to the coast; vermicelli, too, and other kinds of pastry, denoted the influence of Persian art on the kitchen. Smoking within doors was general; but the nargheelah often replaced, and that advantageously, the short Arab pipe; perfumes are no less here in use than in Nedjed.

"We had passed about a week in the town when Aboo-'Eysa entered the side room where Barakat and I were enjoying a moment of quiet, and copying out 'Nabtee' poetry, and shut the door behind him. He then announced to us, with a face and tone of serious anxiety, that two of the principal Nedjean agents belonging to the Kôt had just come into the k'hawah, under pretext of medical consultation, but in reality, said he, to identify the strangers. We put on our cloaks—a preliminary measure of decorum equivalent to face- and hand-washing in Europe—and presented ourselves before our inquisitors with an air of conscious innocence and scientific solemnity. Conversation ensued, and we talked so learnedly about bilious and sanguine complexions, cephalic veins, and Indian drugs, with such apposite citations from the Koran, and such loyal phrases for Feysul, that Aboo-'Eysa was beside himself for joy; and the spies, after receiving some prescriptions of the breadpill and aromatic-water formula, left the house no wiser than before. Our friends, too, and they were now many, well guessing what we might really be, partly from our own appearance and partly from the known character of our host (according to old Homer's true saying, *Heaven always leads like to like*), did each and all their best to throw sand into Wahabee eyes, and everything went on sociably and smoothly. A blessing on the medical profession! None other gives such excellent opportunities for securing everywhere confidence and friendship.

"Before we leave Hasa I must add a few remarks to complete the sketch given of the province and of its inhabitants. Want of a suitable opportunity for inserting them before has thrown them together at this point of my narrative.

"My fair readers will be pleased to learn that the veil and other restraints inflicted on the gentle sex by Islamitic rigorism, not to say worse, are much less universal, and more easily dispensed with in Hasa; while in addition, the ladies of the land enjoy a remarkable share of those natural gifts which no institutions, and even no cosmetics, can confer; namely, beauty of face and elegance of form. Might I venture on the delicate and somewhat invidious task of constructing a 'beauty-scale' for Arabia, and for Arabia alone, the Bedouin women would, on this kalometer, be represented by zero, or at most 1°; a degree higher would represent the female sex of Nedjed; above them rank the women of Shomer, who are in their turn surmounted by those of Djowf. The fifth or sixth degree symbolizes the fair ones of Hasa; the seventh those of Katar; and lastly, by a sudden rise of ten degrees at least, the seventeenth or eighteenth would denote the pre-eminent beauties of Oman. Arab poets occasionally languish after the charmers of Hedjaz; I never saw anyone to charm me, but then I only skirted the province. All bear witness to the absence of female loveliness in Yemen; and I should much doubt whether the mulatto races and dusky complexions of Hadramaut have much to vaunt of. But in Hasa a decided improvement on this important point is agreeably evident to the traveller arriving from Nedjed, and he will be yet further delighted on finding his Calypsos much more conversible, and having much more, too, in their conversation than those he left behind him in Sedeyr and 'Aared.

"During our stay at Hofhoof, Aboo-'Eysa left untried no arts of Arab rhetoric and persuasion to determine me to visit Oman, assuring me again and again that whatever we had yet seen, even in his favorite Hasa, was nothing compared to what remained to see in that more remote country. My companion, tired of our long journey, and thinking the long distance already laid between him and his Syrian home quite sufficient in itself without further leagues tacked on to it, was very little disposed for a supplementary expedition. Englishmen, on the contrary, are rovers by descent and habit; my own mind was now fully made up to visit Oman at all risks, whether Barakat came with me or not. Meanwhile, we formed our plan for the next immediate stage of our route. My companion and I were to quit Hofhoof together, leaving Aboo-'Eysa behind us for a week or two at Hasa, while we journeyed northward to Kateef, and thence took ship for the town of Menamah in Bahreyn. In this latter place Aboo-'Eysa was to rejoin us. Our main reason for thus separating our movements in time and in direction, was to avoid the too glaring appearance of acting in concert while yet in a land under Wahabee government and full of Wahabee spies and reporters, especially after the suspicions thrown on us at Ri'ad. The Oman arangements were to be deferred till we should all meet again.

"Barakat and myself prepared for our departure; we purchased a few objects of local curiosity, got in our dues of medical attendance, paid and received the customary P. P. C. visits, and even tendered our respects to the negro governor Belal, where he sat at his palace door in the Kôt, holding a public audience, and looking much like any other well-dressed black. No passport was required for setting out on the road to Kateef, which in the eyes of government forms only one and the same province with Hasa, though in many respects very different from it. The road is perfectly secure; plundering Bedouins or highway robbers are here out of the question. However, we stood in need of companions, not for escort, but as guides. Aboo-'Eysa made inquiries in the town, and found three men who chanced to be just then setting out on their way for Kateef, who readily consented to join band with us for the road. Our Abyssinian hostess supplied us with a whole sack of provisions, and our Hofhoof associates found us in camels. Thus equipped and mounted, we took an almost touching leave of Aboo-'Eysa's good-natured wife, kissed the baby, exchanged an *au revoir* with its father, and set out on the afternoon of December 19th, leaving behind us many pleasant acquaintances, from some of whom I received messages and letters while at Bahreyn. So far as inhabitants are concerned, to no town in Arabia should I return with equal confidence of finding a hearty greeting and a welcome reception, than to Hofhoof and its amiable and intelligent merchants.

"We quitted the town by the northeastern gate of the Rifey-'eeyah, where the friends, who, according to Arab custom, had accompanied us thus far in a sort of procession, wished us a prosperous journey, took a last adieu, and returned home. After some hours we bivouacked on a little hillock of clean sand, with the dark line of the Hofhoof woods on our left, while at some distance in front a copious fountain poured out its rushing waters with a noise distinctly audible in the stillness of the night, and irrigated a garden worthy of Damascus or Antioch. The night air was temperate, neither cold like that of Nedjed, nor stifling like that of Southern India; the sky clear and starry. From our commanding position on the hill I could distinguish Soheyl or Canopus, now setting; and following him, not far above the horizon, the three upper stars of the Southern Cross, an old Indian acquaintance; two months later in Oman I had the view of the entire constellation.

"Next morning we traversed a large plain of light and sandy soil, intersected by occasional ridges of basalt and sandstone.

"We journeyed on all day, meeting no Bedouins and few travellers. At evening we encamped in a shallow valley, near a cluster of brimming wells, some sweet, some brackish, where the traces of half-obliterated watercourses and the vestiges of crumbling house-walls indicated the former existence of a village, now also deserted. We passed a comfortable night under the shelter of palms and high brushwood, mixed with gigantic aloes and yuccas, and rose next morning early to our way. Our direction lay northeast. In the afternoon we caught our first glimpse of Djebel Mushahhar, a pyramidical peak some seven hundred feet high and about ten miles south of Kateef. But the sea, though I looked toward it and for it with an eagerness somewhat resembling that of the Ten Thousand on their approach to the Euxine, remained shut out from view by a further continuation of the heights.

"Next day we rose at dawn, and crossed the hills of Kateef by a long winding path, till after some hours of labyrinthine track we came in sight of the dark plantation-line that girdles Kateef itself landward. The sea lies immediately beyond; this we knew, but we could not obtain a glimpse of its waters through the verdant curtain stretched between.

"About midday we descended the last slope, a steep sandstone cliff, which looks as though it had been the sea-limit of a former period. We now stood on the coast itself. Its level is as nearly as possible that of the Gulf beyond; a few feet of a higher tide than usual would cover it up to the cliffs. Hence it is a decidedly unhealthy land, though fertile and even populous; but the inhabitants are mostly weak in frame and sallow in complexion. The atmosphere was thick and oppressive, the heat intense, and the vegetation hung rich and heavy around; my companions talked about suffocation, and I remembered once more the Indian coast. Another hour of afternoon march brought us to Kateef itself, at its western portal; a high stone arch of elegant form, and flanked by walls and towers, but all dismantled and ruinous. Close by the two burial-grounds, one for the people of the land, the other for the Nedjean rulers and colony—divided even after death by mutual hatred and anathema. Folly, if you will, but folly not peculiar to the East.

"The town itself is crowded, damp, and dirty, and has altogether a gloomy, what for want of a better epithet I would call a *mouldy*, look; much business was going on in the market and streets, but the ill-favored and very un-Arab look of the shopkeepers and workmen confirms what history tells of the Persian colonization of this city. Indeed, the inhabitants of the entire district, but more especially of the capital, are a mongrel race, in which Persian blood predominates, mixed with that of Bassora, Bagdad, and the 'Irak.

"We urged our starting dromedaries across the open square in front of the market-place, traversed the town in its width, which is scarce a quarter of its length (like other coast towns), till we emerged from the opposite gate, and then looked out with greedy eyes for the sea, now scarce ten minutes distant. In vain as yet, so low lies the land, and so thick cluster the trees. But after a turn or two we came alongside of the outer walls, belonging to the huge fortress of Karmoot, and immediately afterward the valley opening out showed us almost at our feet the dead shallow flats of the bay. How different from the bright waters of the Mediterranean, all glitter and life, where we had bidden them farewell eight months before at Gaza! Like a leaden sheet, half ooze, half sedge, the muddy sea lay in view, waveless, motionless; to our left the massive walls of the castle went down almost to the water's edge, and then turned to leave a narrow esplanade between its circuit and the Gulf. On this ledge were ranged a few rusty guns of large calibre, to show how the place was once guarded; and just in front of the main gate a crumbling outwork, which a single cannon-shot would level with the ground, displayed six pieces of honey-combed artillery, their mouths pointing seaward. Long stone benches without invited us to leave our camels crouching on the esplanade, while we seated ourselves and rested a little before requesting the governor to grant us a day's hospitality, and permission to embark for Bahreyn.

"Barakat and I sat still to gaze, speculating on the difference between the two sides of Arabia. But our companions, like true Arabs, thought it high time for 'refreshment,' and accordingly began their inquiries at the castle-gate where the governor might be, and whether he was to be spoken to. When, behold! the majesty of Feysul's vicegerent issuing in person from his palace to visit the new man-of-war. My abolitionist friends will be gratified to learn that this exalted dignitary is, no less than he of Hofhoof, a negro, brought up from a curly-headed imp to a woolly-headed black in Feysul's own palace, and now governor of the most important harbor owned by Nedjed on the Persian Gulf, and of the town once capital of that fierce dynasty which levelled the Kaabah with the dust, and filled Kateef with the plunder of Yemen and Syria. Farhat, to give him his proper name, common among those of his complexion, was a fine tall negro of about fifty years old, good-natured, chatty, hospitable, and furnished with perhaps a trifle more than the average amount of negro intellect.

"Aboo-'Eysa, who had friends and acquaintances everywhere, and whose kindly manner made him always a special favorite with negroes high or low, had furnished us with an introductory letter to Farhat, intended to make matters smooth for our future route. But as matters went there was little need of caution. The fortunate coincidence of a strong north wind, just then blowing down the Gulf, gave a satisfactory reason for not embarking on board of a Bassora cruiser, while it rendered a voyage to Bahreyn, our real object, equally specious and easy. Besides, Farhat himself, who was a good, easy-going sort of man, had hardly opened Aboo-'Eysa's note, than without more ado he bade us a hearty welcome, ordered our luggage to be brought within the castle precincts, and requested us to step in ourselves and take a cup of coffee, awaiting his return for further conversation after his daily visit of inspection to Feysul's abridged fleet.

"The next day passed, partly in Farhat's k'hawah, partly in strolling about the castle, town, gardens, and beach, making, meanwhile, random inquiries after boats and boatmen.

"It was noon when we fell in with a ship captain, ready to sail that very night, wind and tide permitting. Farhat's men had spoken with him, and he readily offered to take us on board. We then paid a visit to the custom-house officer to settle the embarkation dues for men and goods. This foreman of the Ma'asher, whether in accordance with orders from Farhat, or of his own free will and inclination, I know not, proved wonderfully gracious, and declared that to take a farthing of duty from such useful servants of the public as doctors, would be 'sheyn w' khata',' 'shame and sin.' Alas, that European custom house officials should be far removed from such generous and patriotic sentiments! Lastly, of his own accord he furnished us with men to carry our baggage through knee-deep water and thigh-deep mud to the little cutter, where she lay some fifty yards from shore. Evening now came on, and Farhat sent for us to congratulate us, but with a polite regret on having found so speedy conveyance for our voyage. Meanwhile he let us understand how he was himself invited for the evening to supper with a rich merchant of the town, and that we were expected to join the party; nor need that make us anxious about our passage, since our ship captain was also invited, nor could the vessel possibly sail before the full tide at midnight.

"From our town supper we returned by torchlight to the castle; our baggage, no great burden, had been already taken down to the sea gate, where stood two of the captain's men waiting for us. In their company we descended to the beach, and then with garments tucked up to the waist waded to the vessel, not without difficulty, for the tide was rapidly coming in, and we had almost to swim for it. At last we reached the ship and scrambled up her side; most heartily glad was I to find myself at sea once more on the other side of Arabia."

After a slow voyage of three days Palgrave reached Bahreyn, the headquarters of the pearl fisheries, and established himself in the little town of Moharrek, to wait for the arrival of Aboo-'Eysa before undertaking his projected exploration of Oman. He and his companion enjoyed a grateful feeling of rest and security in this seaport among the sailors, to whom all varieties of foreigners were well known, and who, having no prejudices, felt no suspicion.

On January 9, 1863, Aboo-'Eysa arrived, and after much earnest consultation the following plan was adopted: Aboo-'Eysa was to send twenty loads of the best Hasa dates, and a handsome mantle, as presents to the Sultan of Oman, with three additional mantles for the three chiefs whose territories intervened between Bahreyn and Muscat. Palgrave was to accompany these gifts, under his character of a skilled physician in quest of certain rare and mysterious herbs of Oman. Meanwhile, Aboo-'Eysa and Barakat would take passage for Aboo-Shahr (Busheer), in Persia, where the former would be employed for three months in making up his next caravan of Mecca pilgrims. Here Palgrave was to rejoin them after his journey.

In place of Barakat his companion was a curious individual named Yoosef, whom Aboo-'Eysa had rescued from misery and maintained in a decent condition. He was a native of Hasa, half a jester and half a knave; witty, reckless, hare brained to the last degree, full of jocose or pathetic stories, of poetry, traditions, and fun of every description. When everything had been arranged the four parted company, Palgrave and his new companion sailing for the port of Bedaa', on the Arabian coast, where resided the first of the three chiefs whose protection it was necessary to secure. They reached there after a cruise of five or six days, finding the place very barren and desolate, with scarcely a tree or a garden; but, as the chief said to Palgrave, "We are all, from the highest to the lowest, the slaves of one master—Pearl." The bay contains the best pearl-fishery on the coast, and the town depends for its existence on the trade in these gems.

The chief was intelligent and friendly, and appears to have interposed no obstacle to the proposed journey into the interior, but Palgrave decided to go on by sea to the town of Sharjah, on the northern side of the peninsula of Oman. Embarking again on February 6th, the vessel was driven by violent winds across to the Persian shore, and ten days elapsed before it was possible to reach Sharjah. Here, again, although their reception was hospitable, the travellers gave up their land journey and re-embarked in another vessel to pass around the peninsula, through the Straits of Ormuz, and land on the southern shore, in the territory of Muscat.

In three days they reached the island of Ormuz, of which Palgrave says: "I was not at all sorry to have an opportunity of visiting an island once so renowned for its commerce, and of which its Portuguese occupants used to say, 'that, were the world a golden ring Ormuz would be the diamond signet.' The general appearance of Ormuz indicates an extinguished volcano, and such I believe it really is; the circumference consists of a wide oval wall, formed by steep crags, fire-worn and ragged; these enclose a central basin, where grow shrubs and grass; the basaltic slopes of the outer barrier run in many places clean down into the sea, amid splinter-like pinnacles and fantastic crags of many colors, like those which lava often assumes on cooling. Between the west and north a long triangular promontory, low and level, advances to a considerable distance, and narrows into a neck of land, which is terminated by a few rocks and a strong fortress, the work of Portuguese builders, but worthy of taking rank among Roman ruins—so solid are the walls, so compact the masonry and well-selected brickwork, against which three long centuries of sea-storm have broken themselves in vain. The greater part of the promontory itself is covered with ruins. Here stood the once thriving town, now a confused extent of desolate heaps, amid which the vestiges of several fine dwellings, of baths, and of a large church may yet be clearly made out. Close by the fort cluster a hundred or more wretched earth-hovels, the abode of fishermen or shepherds, whose flocks pasture within the crater; one single shed, where dried dates, raisins, and tobacco are exposed for sale, is all that now remains of the trade of Ormuz."

After being detained three days at Ormuz by a storm, the vessel passed through the Strait, skirted the southern coast of the peninsula, and reached the harbor of Sohar on March 3d. Palgrave determined to set off with Yoosef the same evening on the land-journey of eight or nine days to Muscat; but he had already lost so much time by delays since leaving Bahreyn that he yielded to the persuasions of the captain of another vessel, who promised to take him to Muscat by sea in two days. He sailed on the 6th, weighed down with a vague presentiment of coming evil, which was soon to be justified. His wanderings in Arabia, and also in this world, very nearly came to an end. The vessel slowly glided on for two days, and Muscat was almost in sight when a dead, ominous calm befell them near the Sowadah Islands—some low reefs of barren rocks, about three leagues from shore. It proved to be a calm, ominous indeed for Palgrave, as well as for the captain of the vessel and all on board. It was followed by a furious storm that ended in the wreck of the dhow, and the loss of several lives, together with the entire outfit of the expedition. Palgrave and the survivors of the crew and passengers, nine in number, barely escaped with their lives, and reached the shore utterly exhausted, with nothing but the shirts they wore.

In sorry plight the traveller made his way along the coast to Muscat. He was obliged to give up the idea of exploring the interior of Oman, partly on account of the loss of the stores but chiefly because his identity as a European had been disclosed; and so in this disastrous manner ended the most important and interesting journey that had yet been made by any traveller in Arabia.

CHAPTER XVII.

LADY BLUNT'S PILGRIMAGE TO NEJD

IN 1878–79, sixteen years after Palgrave's journey, Lady Anne Blunt, with her husband and several native servants, accomplished a journey, which, in many respects was more remarkable than the exploits of any of their predecessors. Whereas Palgrave and others had travelled in disguise, believing it impossible to penetrate into the interior otherwise than as mussulmans, the Blunts made no pretences of the kind, but went as European travellers, desirous of seeing the country, and visiting its rulers. They traversed the whole breadth of the peninsula, from Beyrout on the Mediterranean coast, to Bagdad on the Tigris, crossing the Great Nefood, or central desert, and visiting Hail, Jebel Shammer, and other places in Nejd.*

On their return Lady Blunt published the remarkably interesting story of their adventures, under the title of "A Pilgrimage to Nejd," a book which added greatly to our knowledge of the Arabian in-

---

* It is well to point out here that Palgrave and Lady Blunt spell the names of places quite differently, which makes it rather difficult at times to identify them as referring to places mutually visited. Thus, Blunt's "Hail" and Palgrave's "Ha'yel" are one; as are also "Jôf" and "Djowf." Other differences are "Nejd," "Nejed," "Djebel Shomer," "Jebel Shammer," etc.

terior, and to which the compiler of this chapter is largely indebted.

The travellers entered upon their adventurous undertaking with the advantage of experiences gained on a previous journey among the Arab tribes of the Euphrates Valley, and a knowledge of the Arab tongue. Their native servants, who had accompanied them on their previous expedition, eagerly joined their service for the new venture; camels, horses, and all necessary supplies for the journey were purchased at Damascus, and on December 12th, 1879, the start was made.

Though unwilling to travel under false colors as to race or nationality, the English travellers found it convenient to adopt the Bedouin costume for the desert journey, to avoid attracting more notice than was necessary. Their first objective point was Jôf, an important oasis in the desert, four hundred miles away. Lady Blunt, describing the start from Damascus, says:

"At first we skirted the city, passing the gate where St. Paul is said to have entered, and the place where he got over the wall, and then along the suburb of Maïdan, which is the quarter occupied by Bedouins when they come to town, and where we had found the Tudmuri and our camels. Here we were to have met the Jerdeh, and we waited some time outside the Bawâbat Allah, or 'Gates of God,' while Mohammed went in to make inquiries and take leave of his Tudmuri friends.

"It is in front of this gate that the pilgrims assemble on the day of their start for Mecca, and from it the Haj road leads away in a nearly straight line southward. The Haj road is to be our route as far as Mezárib, and is a broad, well-worn track, though of course not a road at all according to English ideas. It has, nevertheless, a sort of romantic interest, one cannot help feeling, going as it does so far and through such desolate lands, a track so many thousand travellers have followed never to return. I suppose in its long history a grave may have been dug for every yard of its course from Damascus to Medina, for, especially on the return journey, there are constantly deaths among the pilgrims from weariness and insufficient food."

A leisurely journey of a week brought the party to Salkhad, a Druse community at the edge of the desert, where Huseyn, the Sheykh of the Druses provided them with guides to the Kâf oasis, a five days' journey into the desert. On the way to Kâf they passed areas of sand, white as snow, and encountered violent sand-storms, in one of which they lost a camel who seized his opportunity to escape back to Mezárib. Beyond Kâf they met with rather a thrilling adventure, which is thus graphically described:

"Friday, January 3d.—We have had an adventure at last, and rather a disagreeable one; a severe lesson as to the danger of encamping near wells. We started early, but were delayed a whole hour at Jerawi taking water, and did not leave the wells till nearly eight o'clock. Then we turned back nearly due east across the wady. The soil of pure white sand was heavy going, and we went slowly, crossing low undulations without other landmark than the tells we had left behind us. Here and there rose little mounds, tufted with ghada. To one of these Wilfrid and I cantered on, leaving the camels behind us, and dismounting, tied our mares to the bushes, that we might enjoy a few minutes' rest and eat our midday mouthful; the greyhounds meanwhile played about and chased each other in the sand.

"We had finished, and were talking of I know not what, when the camels passed us. They were hardly a couple of hundred yards in front, when suddenly we heard a thud, thud, thud, on the sand, a sound of galloping. Wilfrid jumped to his feet, looked round, and called out: 'Get on your mare. This is a ghazú!'

"As I scrambled round the bush to my mare, I saw a troop of horsemen charging down at full gallop with their lances, not two hundred yards off. Wilfrid was up as he spoke, and so should I have been but for my sprained knee and the deep sand, both of which gave way as I was rising. I fell back. There was no time to think, and I had hardly struggled to my feet when the enemy was upon us, and I was knocked down by a spear. Then they all turned on Wilfrid, who had waited for me, some of them jumping down on foot to get hold of his mare's halter. He had my gun with him, which I had just before handed to him, but unloaded, his own gun and his sword being on his delúl (riding camel). He fortunately had on very thick clothes, two abbas one over the other, and English clothes underneath, so the lances did him no harm. At last his assailants managed to get his gun from him and broke it over his head, hitting him three times and smashing the stock.

"Resistance seemed to me useless, and I shouted to the nearest horseman, '*Ana dahílak*' (I am under your protection), the usual form of surrender. Wilfrid hearing this, and thinking he had had enough of this unequal contest, one against twelve, threw himself off his mare. The *Khayal* (horsemen) having seized both the mares, paused, and as soon as they had gathered breath, began to ask us who we were and where we came from.

"'English, and we have come from Damascus,' we replied, 'and our camels are close by. Come with us and you shall hear about it.'

"Our caravan, while all this had happened, and it only lasted about five minutes, had formed itself into a square, and the camels were kneeling down, as we could plainly see from where we were. I hardly expected the horsemen to do as we asked, but the man who seemed to be their leader at once let us walk on (a process causing me acute pain), and followed with the others to the caravan. We found Mohammed and the rest of our party entrenched behind the camels with their guns pointed, and as we approached, Mohammed stepped out and came forward.

"'Min entum?' (Who are you?) was the first question.

"'Roala min Ibn Debaa.' 'Wallah?' (Will you swear by God?) 'Wallah!' (We swear).

"'And you?' 'Mohammed ibn Arûk of Tudmur.'

"'Wallah?' 'Wallah!' 'And these are Franjis

travelling with you?' 'Wallah! Franjis, friends of Ibn Shaalan.'

"It was all right; we had fallen into the hands of friends. Ibn Shaalan, our host of last year, was bound to protect us, even so far away in the desert, and none of his people dared meddle with us, knowing this. Besides, Mohammed was a Tudmuri, and as such could not be molested by Roala, for Tudmur pays tribute to Ibn Shaalan, and the Tudmuris have a right to his protection. So as soon as the circumstances were made clear orders were given by the chief of the party to his followers to bring back our mares, and the gun, and everything which had been dropped in the scuffle. Even to Wilfrid's tobacco-bag, all was restored."

The robbers and the travellers fraternized after the affair was over, and the former were very much ashamed of themselves for having used their spears against a woman. Lady Blunt apologizes for them, however, as the Bedouin dress she wore for riding prevented them distinguishing her sex in the confusion of the sudden attack.

Two days after the encounter in the desert the party arrived at Jôf, where they spent three days, and found the people very hospitable. Their chief servant and camel-driver, Mohammed, was an Arab, who had distant connections in this part of Arabia; and as tribal kinship, no matter how remote, is regarded as a matter of great importance, this relationship was of material aid in securing them the good-will of the inhabitants. The Blunts were less favorably impressed with Jôf than was Palgrave, who, however, uses the term "Djowf" in a broader sense, as including a number of oases situated in "a large oval depression of sixty or seventy miles long by ten or twelve broad, lying between the northern desert that separates it from Syria and the Euphrates, and the southern Nefood, or sandy waste, and interposed between it and the nearest mountains of the Central Arabian plateau."

Lady Blunt writes of it: "Jôf is not at all what we expected. We thought we should find it a large cultivated district, and it turns out to be merely a small town. There is nothing at all outside the walls except a few square patches, half an acre or so each, green with young corn," etc.

How true is it that no two travellers see things with the same eyes. Doubtless both these distinguished travellers are reasonably correct in their descriptions, but summed up their impressions from opposite stand-points in a topographical sense; a common enough mistake in Asia, where the name of a place often indicates, equally accurately, a large scope of country and the central spot in it. In Central Asia, for example, there is Merv, which is the name of a city, and also of the large fertile oasis in which it is situated; also Herat, meaning a broad area of oases, with a population of probably half a million people, in which the fortress-city Herat stands, no less than the city itself.

Important political changes had taken place since Palgrave's visit. The rule of the Wahabees had been overthrown in Jôf, and the only representatives of staple authority found there were a Sheykh and six soldiers, who represented the authority of Mohammed ibn Rashid, Emir of Jebel Shammar, with his seat of government at Hail.

From Jôf the travellers proceeded toward Hail, crossing the dreaded Nefood, of which they give a very interesting, and far less gloomy, account than did Palgrave. They, however, crossed it in January, while Palgrave crossed it in midsummer; so that, in the case of the Nefood, as with Jôf, the apparently conflicting accounts are doubtless both fairly accurate, the one describing the desert in winter, the other in summer. On January 12th, the travellers found themselves on the edge of the desert.

"At half-past three o'clock we saw a red streak on the horizon before us, which rose and gathered as we approached it, stretching out east and west in an unbroken line. It might at first have been taken for an effect of mirage, but on coming nearer we found it broken into billows, and but for its red color not unlike a stormy sea seen from the shore, for it rose up, as the sea seems to rise, when the waves are high, above the level of the land. Somebody called out 'Nefûd,' and though for a while we were incredulous, we were soon convinced. What surprised us was its color, that of rhubarb and magnesia, nothing at all like what we had expected. Yet the Nefûd it was, the great red desert of Central Arabia. In a few minutes we had cantered up to it, and our mares were standing with their feet in its first waves.

"January 13th.—We have been all day in the Nefûd, which is interesting beyond our hopes, and charming into the bargain." After taking issue with

Mr. Palgrave, who, Lady Blunt thinks, overlooked its brighter side, the narrator continues her own observations thus:

"The thing that strikes one first about the Nefûd is its color. It is not white like the sand dunes we passed yesterday, nor yellow as the sand is in parts of the Egyptian desert, but a really bright red, almost crimson in the morning, when it is wet with dew. The sand is rather coarse, but absolutely pure, without admixture of any foreign substance, pebble, grit, or earth, and exactly the same in tint and texture everywhere. It is, however, a great mistake to suppose it barren. The Nefûd, on the contrary, is better wooded and richer in pasture than any part of the desert we have passed since leaving Damascus. It is tufted all over with ghada bushes, and bushes of another kind called *yerta*, which at this time of the year, when there are no leaves, is exactly like a thickly matted vine.

"There are, besides, several kinds of camel pasture, especially one new to us, called *adr*, on which they say sheep can feed for a month without wanting water, and more than one kind of grass. Both camels and mares are therefore pleased with the place, and we are delighted with the abundance of firewood for our camps. Wilfrid says that the Nefûd has solved for him at last the mystery of horse-breeding in Central Arabia. In the hard desert there is nothing a horse can eat, but here there is plenty. The Nefûd accounts for everything. Instead of being the terrible place it has been described by the few travellers who have seen it, it is in reality the home of the

Bedouins during a great part of the year. Its only want is water, for it contains but few wells; all along the edge it is thickly inhabited, and Radi tells us that in the spring, when the grass is green after rain, the Bedouins care nothing for water, as their camels are in milk, and they go for weeks without it, wandering far into the interior of the sand desert."

In the desert of sand the travellers found many curious hollows, which the native guide called fulj. Some of these holes were a quarter of a mile in diameter, and as much as 230 feet deep. They were chiefly of horse-hoof shape. They took observations, and at one point on the desert found the elevation to be 3,300 feet above sea-level. After seven days in the Nefûd, the last two of which tried the endurance of men and beasts, the party reached the oasis of Jobba, which is described as being one of the most curious, as also most beautiful, places in the world.

"Its name Jobba, meaning a well, explains its position, for it lies in a hole or well in the Nefûd; not indeed in a fulj, for the basin of Jobba is quite on another scale, and has nothing in common with the horse-hoof depressions I have hitherto described. It is, all the same, extremely singular, and quite as difficult to account for geologically as the fuljes. It is a great bare space in the ocean of sand, from four to five hundred feet below its average level, and about three miles wide; a hollow, in fact, not unlike that of Jôf, but with the Nefûd round it instead of sandstone cliffs. That it has once been a lake is pretty evident, for there are distinct water marks on the rocks, which crop up out of the bed just above the town; and, strange to say, there is a tradition still extant of there having been formerly water there. The wonder is how this space is kept clear of sand. What force is it that walls out the Nefûd and prevents encroachments? As you look across the subbkha, or dry bed of the lake, the Nefûd seems like a wall of water which must overwhelm it; and yet no sand shifts down into the hollow, and its limits are accurately maintained."

At length the Nefûd was overcome and the travellers approached Hail, not without apprehensions as to the reception that might await them. Their guide from Jôf enlightened them in regard to many changes that had occurred since Palgrave's visit, changes that will be equally interesting to readers who have followed Palgrave's narrative in preceding chapters.

Telal, then despotic ruler at Hail (Ha'yel), had gone insane and committed suicide by stabbing himself with his own dagger four years after Palgrave's visit. He was succeeded by his brother Metaab, who, however, died suddenly after reigning three years; when a dispute arose between his brother Mohammed and Telal's oldest son, Bender, about the succession. Mohammed being away at the time, Bender, a youth of twenty, was proclaimed Emir. Mohammed returned, and in a violent quarrel with his nephew drew his dagger and stabbed him to death.

"Then Mohammed galloped back to the castle, and finding Hamúd (son of Obeyd, uncle of Telal) there, got his help and took possession of the palace. He then seized the younger sons of Tellál (Palgrave's

Telal), Bender's brothers, all but one child, Naïf, and Bedr, who was away from Hail, and had their heads cut off by his slaves in the court-yard of the castle. They say, however, that Hamúd protested against this. But Mohammed was reckless, or wished to strike terror, and not satisfied with what he had already done, went on destroying his relations.

"He had some cousins, sons of Jabar, a younger brother of Abdallah and Obeyd; and these he sent for. They came in some alarm to the castle, each with his slave. They were all young men, beautiful to look at, and of the highest distinction; and their slaves had been brought up with them, as the custom is, more like brothers than servants. They were shown into the kahwah of the castle, and received with great formality, Mohammed's servants coming forward to invite them in. It is the custom at Hail, whenever a person pays a visit, that before sitting down he should hang up his sword on one of the wooden pegs fixed into the wall, and this the sons of Jabar did, and their slaves likewise. Then they sat down and waited and waited, but still no coffee was served to them. At last Mohammed appeared, surrounded by his guard, but there was no 'salaam aleykum,' and instantly he gave orders that his cousins should be seized and bound. They made a rush for their swords, but were intercepted by the slaves of the castle and made prisoners. Mohammed then, with horrible barbarity, ordered their hands and their feet to be cut off, and the hands and feet of their slaves, and had them, still living, dragged out into the court-yard of the palace, where they lay till they died.

"These ghastly crimes, more ghastly than ever in a country where wilful bloodshed is so unusual, seem to have struck terror far and wide, and no one has since dared to raise a hand against Mohammed."

The knowledge of these terrible doings naturally made the travellers feel that they were venturing into dangerous quarters as they rode up to the gates of Hail. The Emir, whose title was Mohammed-ibn-Rashid (Mohammed, son of Rashid), however, received them kindly; and it was discovered that, apart from the bloody work of the succession, he had turned out to be not a bad ruler. In any part of his dominions, it was understood that a person might travel unarmed, and with any amount of gold on him, without fear of molestation. Moreover, he seemed to have been deeply stricken with remorse for his past misdeeds, lived in constant fear of assassination, and was endeavoring to make what amends he could by lavishing honors and kindness on the youth Naïf, the only one of his nephews he had spared—for Bedr, too, had been executed.

It all reads much like a tale from the "Arabian Nights;" and that Arabia is still the land of romance and poetry is confirmed by a curious bit of news learned of Obeyd, about whom it will be remembered Mr. Palgrave had also a good deal to say.

"He (Obeyd) lived to a great age, and died only nine years ago (*i.e.*, 1869). It is related of him that he left no property behind him, having given away everything during his lifetime—no property but his sword, his mare, and his young wife. These he left to his nephew Mohammed-ibn-Rashid, the reigning

Emir, with the request that his sword should remain undrawn, his mare unridden, and his wife unmarried forever after."

The travellers give an interesting account of the Emir's horses, the most famous stud in Nejd.

Though interested, they were, on the whole, disappointed with the horses of Nejd as compared with those of Northern Arabia. "In comparing what we see here with what we saw last year in the north, the first thing that strikes us is that these are ponies, the others horses. It is not so much the actual difference in height, though there must be quite three inches on an average, as the shape, which produces this impression."

The average height was found to be under fourteen hands; and though great care was taken to obtain and preserve pure strains of blood, in the matter of feeding and grooming, gross negligence seemed to be the rule, even in the royal stud. The stables were mere open yards, in which the animals stood, each tethered to a manger. No shelter was provided, but each horse was protected by a heavy rug. They wore no headstalls, being fastened solely with ropes or chains about the fetlocks. No regular exercise was given them, their food was almost exclusively dry barley, and their appearance generally was far different from what Europeans would naturally expect of the finest stable of horses in the "horse peninsula."

The travellers also enlighten us, on the subject of horses, in other directions. Except in the north, horses were found to be exceedingly rare. It is possible to travel vast distances without meeting a single horse, or even crossing a horse-track; on the whole journey across the Nefûd, and on to the Euphrates, they scarcely saw a horse, apart from the stables of the rich and great in the cities. The horse is a luxury to be afforded only by people of wealth or position. Journeys and raids and wars are all made on camels; the Sheykhs who have horses, when going to war save them to mount at the moment of actual engagement with the enemy. It was considered a great boast by a Nejd tribe of Bedouins that they could mount one hundred horsemen; while the Muteyr tribe, reputed to be the greatest breeders of thoroughbred stock in Central Arabia, would be expected to muster not more than four hundred mares.

Mohammed-ibn-Rashid recruited his stables by compelling the Sheykhs of tributary tribes to sell him their best animals, an improvement on some of his predecessors, who kept their studs up to the proper mark becoming Arab royalty by making raids against the tribes for the purpose of bringing in celebrated mares, waiving the matter of payment.

In the spring the horses of the Emir's stables are distributed among the neighboring Bedouins to be pastured on the Nefûd, which at that period affords excellent grazing. Had the visitors seen the herd after a month on the Nefûd, they would likely have carried away a much more favorable impression. During the winter quartering the colts seemed to fare even worse than their dams and sires, from the following:

"Besides the full-grown animals, Ibn Rashid's

yards contain thirty or forty foals and yearlings, beautiful little creatures, but terribly starved and miserable. Foals bred in the desert are poor enough, but those in town have a positively sickly appearance. Tied all day long by the foot, they seem to have quite lost heart, and show none of the playfulness of their age. Their tameness, like that of the 'fowl and the brute,' is shocking to see."

The contrast between the actual treatment of these royal animals and the following Arab recipe for rearing a colt is sufficiently striking:

"During the first month of his life let him be content with his mother's milk; it will be sufficient for him. Then, during five months, add to this natural supply goats' milk, as much as he will drink. For six months more give him the milk of camels, and besides a measure of wheat steeped in water for a quarter of an hour and served in a nose-bag. At a year old the colt will have done with milk; he must be fed on wheat and grass, the wheat dry from a nose-bag, the grass green, if there is any.

"At two years old he must work or he will be worthless. Feed him now, like a full-grown horse, on barley; but in summer let him also have gruel daily at mid-day. Make the gruel thus: Take a double-handful of flour and mix it in water well with your hands till the water seems like milk, then strain it, leaving the dregs of the flour, and give what is liquid to the colt to drink.

"Be careful, from the hour he is born, to let him stand in the sun; shade hurts horses; but let him have water in plenty when the day is hot. The colt must now be mounted and taken by his owner everywhere with him, so that he shall see everything and learn courage. He must be kept constantly in exercise, and never remain long at his manger. He should be taken on a journey, for the work will fortify his limbs. At three years old he should be trained to gallop; then, if he be true blood, he will not be left behind. Yalla!"

Lady Blunt thinks this represents a traditional practice of rearing colts in Arabia since the days of the Prophet Mohammet.

From Hail, the party joined the Haj, or caravan of Persian pilgrims, returning home from Mecca and Medina; and after eighty-four days' travel from Damascus their Arabian journey came to an end at Bagdad. Their route from Hail took them far north of Palgrave's route, so that they did not visit Ri'ad, the headquarters, in Palgrave's time, of the Wahabee ruler Feysul. Lady Blunt, however, in an appendix to her narrative enlightens us in regard to the end of Feysul, and the continued decline of the Wahabee regime after the visit of Palgrave.

Three years after Palgrave's visit Feysul died, and the Wahabee state, which under him had regained much of its power and influence (which had been all but crushed by the Turks after the Crimean war) was again weakened by internal dissensions. Feysul left two sons, Abdallah and Saoud, who quarrelled and put themselves at the head of their respective adherents. Saoud proved himself the stronger party, and in 1871 Abdallah fled to Jebel Shammar and sought the aid of Midhat Pasha, Turkish governor at Bagdad.

The result was that a Turkish expedition of 5,000 regular troops occupied the seaboard territory of Hasa, and took possession of Hofhoof (mentioned by Palgrave); whilst Abdallah and his adherents, and a third rival, Abdallah-ibn-Turki, attacked Saoud at Ri'ad. Saoud was defeated, and Abdallah essayed to govern at Ri'ad; but in the following year he was again ejected by Saoud who reigned till 1874, when he died, not without suspicion of poison.

Lady Blunt's account of affairs at the Wahabee capital ends with the information that Abdallah and a half-brother, Abderrahman, were in joint and amicable control, Abdallah as Emir, the latter as his chief minister. Hasa and the seaboard was held by the Turks, whose policy was the stirring up of strife and feudal enmity among the Arabs, with a view to weakening the power and authority of the Emir at Ri'ad, and so making the country easy prey whenever opportunity arrives for its incorporation in the Ottoman dominions. The power and fanaticism of the once powerful Wahabee Empire, has become but little more than a name and a remembrance among the Bedouin tribes, who once paid tribute to its Emirs; and whatever was national in thought and respectable in inspiration in Central Arabia seemed to be grouping itself around the new dynasty of the Emir of Jebel Shammar, Mohammed-ibn-Rashid of Hail.

THE END.

www.ingramcontent.com/pod-product-compliance
Lightning Source LLC
Chambersburg PA
CBHW021353290426